Fortiter et Fideliter

The Armorial Bearings of

The Family of

Bryant

BRYANT FAMILY HISTORY

ANCESTRY AND
DESCENDANTS OF

DAVID BRYANT
(1756)

OF SPRINGFIELD, N. J.;
WASHINGTON CO., PA.; KNOX CO., OHIO;
AND WOLF LAKE, NOBLE CO., IND.

COMPILED BY

CLARA VAILE BRAIDEN

———

Fair is our lot—O goodly is our heritage.
—KIPLING.

———

1913
PRIVATELY PRINTED
CHICAGO, ILL.

Originally published
Chicago
1913

Reprinted by:

Janaway Publishing, Inc.
732 Kelsey Ct.
Santa Maria, California 93454
(805) 925-1038
www.JanawayGenealogy.com

2012

ISBN: 978-1-59641-277-4

Made in the United States of America

TO THE MEMORY OF OUR PIONEER FATHERS AND MOTHERS, WHO BY PERSONAL SACRIFICE AND THE GIFT OF THEIR NOBLEST ENERGIES, BLAZED THE WAY AND FOUGHT THE BATTLES TO ESTABLISH THIS NATION OF AMERICA.

"Good blood — descent from the great and good — is a high honor and privilege. He that lives worthily of it is deserving of the highest esteem; he that does not, of the deeper disgrace."—COLTON.

FOREWORD

"History should be painted as a stern goddess, with truth on her right hand and memory on her left. While in the background should appear tradition, like a wandering light glimmering along the quicksands of oblivion, and in the foreground should stand an angel pointing to the future."— *Sorrows of Nancy.*

The history of this family discloses a long line of patriots, and many pioneers worthy of permanent record. The history of the first four generations is as complete as it could be made by a diligent research of the records in the Congressional Library of Washington and the public libraries of Chicago, of Boston, New York, and other cities. Much data of the early Bryants was obtained from records of the Holland Society of New York, and from tombstone inscriptions at Springfield, N. J., Connecticut Farms, N. J., Westfield, N. J., Mt. Freedom, N. J.; from church records of early New York City and New Jersey; from histories of Bergen, Morris, Hudson and Essex counties, N. J., and from marriage records of Essex county. Modern records have been obtained from family bibles and other family records. More time could have been spent searching records for early history of the family, but it was thought best to publish at this time the material collected. We trust that some interested descendant may carry on the work. All persons having further data on the ancestors or descendants of David Bryant or his wife are requested to send a copy of the same to the undersigned for preservation. As soon as enough additional data is received supplementary pages will be issued. Delineations of character have but rarely been attempted, since it would have been impossible to render justice to all. The virtues ascribed by their kindred are a gratifying testimony that many individuals of the later generations have been worthy descendants of an honored ancestry. We learn from those yet living some of the characteristics of the pioneer forefathers. The mothers stood side by side with their pioneer husbands in the dignity and resolution required to subdue and build up a new country. They truly possessed great fortitude which enabled them to withstand the dangers and privations encountered. They had refinement of character, the outgrowth of strong religious sentiment, and loyalty of principles which gave Statehood as the outcome of the lives of these generations of pioneers, first in the East, then ever Westward.

An interest in the Bryant family led the compiler for more than thirty years to collect data. A desire to become a charter member of the Daughters of the American Revolution in 1890 was the motive to inquire into the military record of David Bryant. An increasing interest in the research came in meeting the Bryant family in the annual reunions. These reunions have afforded valuable aid in collecting history and traditions held in remembrance by the older members. However, traditions have not been used in the book except when so stated or verified by records.

We thank the descendants who have assisted in any way. We wish to mention especially Miss Ida E. Fisher, of Hebron, Ind., and Mr. John M. Lindly, of Winfield, Iowa. We ask the indulgence of the Bryant family for any inaccuracies, omissions, or errors which may have occurred.

(Mrs.) CLARA VAILE BRAIDEN,

June, 1913 ROCHELLE, ILLINOIS.

BRYANT FAMILY ASSOCIATION

A gathering of the Bryant relatives was proposed by Miss Ida E. Fisher, of Hebron, Ind. After consultation with Mr. Elias W. Bryant, of Lafayette, Ind., and Miss Eva Bryant, of Hebron, Ind., invitations were sent out to all the known relatives. The result was the presence of one hundred and twenty-four Bryant descendants at a meeting held in August, 1902, at Hebron, Ind. Of those present a score were the grandchildren of the revolutionary ancestor, David Bryant (No. 37, p. 31). Some of these were octogenarians. Acquaintances and friendships were formed among the relatives, who had been strangers, and a desire to meet again. The second meeting was held August 22, 1903, at Hebron, Ind. The Bryant Association was then organized with the following officers:

President — Elias W. Bryant, Lafayette, Ind.
Vice-President — Clara V. Braiden, Rochelle, Ill.
Recording Secretary — Eva Bryant, Hebron, Ind.
Corresponding Secretary — Ida E. Fisher, Hebron, Ind.
Treasurer — M. C. Bryant, Hebron, Ind.

Historical Committee — Clara V. Braiden, Ida E. Fisher, Eva Bryant. The following year J. M. Lindly, of Winfield, Ia., who is a well-informed historian, was added to this committee; also Dora L. Bryant, of Clifton Forge, Va., and Adelaide Post, of Carthage, Mo.

Committee on Badges — Mr. Oscar Dinwiddie, Hebron; Mrs. Orah Doddridge, Mentone; Nettie Bryant and Laura Bryant of Hebron, Ind.

The badge selected was the Bryant coat of arms. A recognition card to be worn by those present at the reunions indicating ancestral line, from David Bryant (37), was also adopted. Ten of these family reunions have been held; nine of them at

Hebron, Ind., and the tenth, in 1912, was held in Rochelle, Ill., at the home of Mrs. C. V. Braiden. Fifteen states have been represented. Reminiscences from older members formed an interesting part of the programs. When the society decided to publish a family history, the corresponding secretary sent out the Claypool genealogical blanks to addresses of all known Bryant descendants, and the information obtained from these blanks and other correspondence was compiled by Mrs. Clara V. Braiden.

TABLE OF CONTENTS

LIST OF ILLUSTRATIONS

xi

WALICH VAN WINKLE

ORIGIN OF THE NAME

Henry Barber, in his book on "British Family Names," says: "The name Bryant is from Breaunt, a locality in Normandy; French, Briand, Briant." In "A Dictionary of Names," by Mark Antony Lower, we find that Bryan (Bryant) is a Celtic personal name of great antiquity, implying originally Regulus, or Chieftain. H. A. Long, in "The Names We Bear," says: "Briant, Bryan (whence Bryant) means strong. Mr. Versteeg, of Holland Society, New York City, gives the Dutch spelling Breyandt, meaning broad hand. In the early New Amsterdam records the name is also spelled Breijandt."

The name is found on English records as early as the 13th century. A coat of arms was granted to Guy de Brian at this period of time. The name is found in Dorsetshire, Gloucestershire, Somersetshire, Suffolk and Wiltshire.

THE COAT OF ARMS

Tradition gives the Bryants an English origin, they having gone from England to Holland on account of religious persecution.

The Bryant coat of arms, in frontispiece, is that granted in 1634 to Thomas Bryant of Bampton, in Devonshire, age 28. Description: Azure, a cross, or (gold) charged with a cinquefoil (five leaves) between four lozenges, gules (red).

Crest: A flag azure (blue), charged with a saltier argent (silver).

Motto: Fortiter et Fidelity; i. e., Boldly and Faithfully.

Cinquefoil (five leaf) signifies hope and joy, lozenges represent honesty and constancy, also held to be a token of noble birth. Azure signifies loyalty and truth. Red donates military fortitude and magnaminity, or (gold) denotes generosity and elevation of mind. Argent (silver) signifies peace and sincerity.

A saltier is a St. Andrew's cross, or a cross in the form of an X. It is one of the nine greater or honorable ordinaries.

EXPLANATIONS

The system employed in compiling this genealogy is believed to be the most approved in use at the present time. The aim has been to simplify so that it may be readily understood. Each descendant has his own number, placed at the left of his name. When the name is followed by a + mark on the right, it occurs again in capital letters as the head of a family in the succeeding generation with the same number. When descendants do not have issue, their full biography, with a few exceptions, will be found with their names first mentioned.

Small superior figures at the end of the names denote the generation.

When tardy data was sent in, after numbering had been completed, it was necessary to give the child the parents' number with a letter of the alphabet added. Conflicting dates have been sent in, and dates given from memory are often erroneous. Some of the writing has been almost illegible, but many letters have been sent out in the endeavor to secure correct information. If a name or date has been omitted, then it has not been given. If notification of errors shall be given to the secretary of the Bryant Association, corrections will be printed and furnished to purchasers of the Bryant Genealogy.

ABBREVIATIONS

Abt., about; bap., baptized; b., born; Ch., church; dau., daughter; deft., defendant; d., died; m., married; pltf., plaintiff; R. D., Reformed Dutch; rec., record; unm., unmarried.

Usually genealogies follow only the line bearing the name of the male ancestor. In the Bryant Genealogy a record has been given, as far as obtainable, of all of the descendants of DAVID BRYANT and CATHERINE WOOLLEY BRYANT of whatever name, thus including the female lines of descent.

DUTCH RECORDS

PIETER CORNELISSE & ANCESTOR

Bergen Reformed Dutch Church Record

BAPTISMS

Child & Date	Parents	Witnesses
Cornelis	Pieter Cornelise	None
bap. Apr. 18, 1676	Hendrickje Aerts	
	[See for bap. p. 2 of these notes]	
Arent	Pieter Cornelisse	Willem *Hoppe*, young man
bap. Oct. 7, 1678	Hendrickje Aerts	Merritje Ariaense
Andries	Pieter Cornelise	Matys *Hoppe*
bap. Aug. 21, 1681	Hendrickje Aerts	Minouw Pouluse
Andries	Pieter Cornelise	Matys *Hoppe*
bap. June 30, 1684	Hendrickje Aertse	Mynouw Pouluse
Willem	Hendrick *Hoppe*	Willem *Hoppe*
bap. Apr. 2, 1684	Mareytje Jans	Hendrickje *Aerts*

Accepted as a Member of Bergen Reformed Dutch Church
May 29, 1672 Hendrickje *Aerts*, by Rev. Wilhelmus Nieuwenhuysen

BERGEN BAPTISMS

Dierck	Fredrick Thomassen	Gerrit Van Dien
bap. Apr. 4, 1692	Catryna *Hoppe*	Hendrickje *Aert*, widow of *Pieter Cornelise Van Steenwyck*

(This shows that *Pieter Cornelisse* had *died* in *1692*)

NEW YORK REFORMED DUTCH CHURCH BAPTISMS

Tryntie	Andries Willemszen	*Jan Van de Bildt*
Sept. 10, 1651	Soppe (Hoppe)	*Wyntie Elberts*
		Arentje Gerrits
Willem	Andries Hop	Joris Stephenszen
Mar. 29, 1654		Stoffel Andrieszen
		Cornelis Arentszen
		Beelitie Hendricks

1

Mattheus Albertus   Andries Hoppe   Lambert *Huybertszen Mol.*

Mar. 3, 1658   Geertie Hendricks   *Arie Corneliszen*
Christina Harmens
Engeltje Wouters

Hendrick   Andries Hop   *Cornelis Aertszen*
Jan. 9, 1656   Geertie Hendricks   *Belitje Hendricks*
Abraham   Jan Corneliszen   Cornelis Aertszen
Oct. 24, 1649   Engel Egberts
Engel Borgers
Grietie Joosten

Lambert   Gerrit Hendrickszen   Cornelis Aertszen
Sept. 7, 1653   Hendrick Lambertszen (Mol?)
Lysbeth Dircks

Beletje   Arie Corneliszen   *Cornelis Aertszens*
Oct. 1, 1663   Rebecca Yrens   Guiliam d'honneur
Christina Steentiens

Isaac   Jan Theuniszen   *Cornelis Aertszen*
July 2, 1670   Tryntie Pieters   Jan *Aertszen*
Adriaentie

Sara   Caspar Corneliszen   Cornelis Arentszen
Sept. 3, 1681   Neeltje Jans   [This is another family]
* Hendrickje   Cornelis *Aertszen*   Jacob Steoffelszen
July 7, 1641   Tryntie Simons
* She may have died young, or more probably *m. Lambert H. Moll.*
Arie   Cornelis *Aertszen*   Huyck Aertszen
July 9, 1642   Marie Hans
Anneken Loockermans

Hendrick   Cornelis *Aertszen*   Capt. Jan De Vries
Sept. 23, 1646   Evert Corn. Van der Wel
Sara & Tryntie Roelofs

Lysbeth   Cornelis *Aertszen*   Willem Beeckman & wife
Oct. 1, 1651   Jacob Claeszen
Annetje   Pieter Corneliszen   Dirck Gerritsen
Sept. 10, 1671   Hendrickje Aerts   Catharina *Foppe*
[This Foppe should be *Hoppe*]

Geertruyd   *Pieter Corneliszen*   *Hendrick Corneliszen*
[V. Schaick?]

Nov. 8, 1673   Hendrickje Aerts   *Geertie Hoppe*
Thomas   Thomas *Fredrickszen**   *Pieter Cornelissen*
Jan. 4, 1672   Marritie Ariaens   *Hendrickje Aerts*
* His mother was *Catharina Hopper*

Cornelis   Pieter *Corneliszen*   Hendrick *Hoppen*
  May 3, 1676   Hendrickje Hoppen (sic) Neeltje Cornelis
      [See for this the first Bergen entry]

NEW YORK REFORMED DUTCH MARRIAGES

July 10, 1662   Cornelis Aertszen, widower of Belitje Hendricks
                     and
      Weyntje Elberts, wid. of Aert Willemszen

NEW YORK BAPTISM RECORD

Andries   Fredrick Thomas   *Adriaen* [Arie] *Corneliszen*
                          [*Van Schaick?*]
  Aug. 23, 1673   Catharina *Hoppe*   Sophia Jans
Andries   Hendrick *Hoppen*   *Adriaen Corneliszen*
                          [*Van Schaick?*]
  Jan. 12, 1681   Marie Jans   Geertis *Hoppen*
NOTE.— The daughters of the above family *adopted* the name of Van Schaick.

ANCESTORS OF PIETER CORNELISZ BRYANT

Minutes of the Orphanmasters of New Amsterdam

p. 5.

Nov. 9, 1655. Cornelis Clasen Swits & Tobias Teunissen perished in the Indian massacre of September 15. Egbert Woutersen, Tomas Hall and *Cornelis Aertsen* appointed managers of their estate (especially cattle) left by them.

p. 58.

Geertje *Hendrick* widow of Andries *Hoppe*, deceased, appearing states that her deceased husband has appointed as guardians of the children *Cornelis Aarsen* and *Lambert Huybersen* Mol, but has not made a testament. It is ordered that said guardians shall inform the Orphanmasters by inventory of the estate of Andries *Hoppe*, dec'd, real and personal, debts and credits (1658).

p. 59.

Whereas Andries *Hoppe* has died and has left here besides the widow & children some property and whereas he has named, before he died, as guardians of his infant children, Cornelis *Aarsen*, and Lambert Huybersen Mol, Therefore deeming it necessary that a proper inventory of the property may be taken to prevent loss and injury to the widow and the children in their rights and possessions, the orphanmasters herewith order said guardians to take as soon as possible an inventory of the estate, including furniture, property, real and personal, debts and credits here in the country and to report to the Orphanmasters who will then advise what disposition of it shall be made. Dec. 18, 1658.

p. 61.

Jan. 8, 1659. The wife of Ryck Hendricksen had died in 1658. Besides her husband she left Hendrick Rycken in his 10th year and dau. Gosewyn Rycken in her 9th year. Guardians Cornelis *Aarsen* & Pieter Stoutenburgh.

p. 75.

Whereas Cornelis *Aarsen* & Lambert Huybertsen Mol have been appointed by Andrees *Hoppe* before his death as guardians of his children, Therefore having learned that an inventory has been made of the property of deceased, the Orphanmasters hereby direct said guardians to appear before this Board at the City Hall next Wednesday, Feb. 26 & to show by inventory the condition of the estate of Andrees *Hoppe*, dec'd, when such disposition shall be made of it as shall be found proper. Feb. 19, 1658.

p. 79.
Feb. 26, 1659.

Geertje Hendricks comes with *Cornelis Aarsen* & Lambert Huyberzen Mol, the guardians of the children of *Andrees Hoppe*, dec'd, and said guardians report that they have agreed with the widow Geertje Hendricks about a settlement on the children of their paternal inheritance and 1000 guilders that is 200 for each child have been allowed, but the agreement has not yet been written out. So ordered.

Ryck Hendrickzen coming with Pieter Stoutenburgh and *Cornelis Aarsen*, guardians of the children left by Ryck's deceased wife, the guardians report that they have agreed with the widower & that Ryck is to pay to each child on coming of age 50 guilders. Write it out.

p. 101.

July 7, 1659. Pieter Lauwerens produces an account, according to which Jacob Coppe [dec'd] still owes him a balance of 110 guilders. The Orphanmasters order their Secretary to write to *Cornelis Aarsen* & Jan Van der *Bilt* directing them not to take to themselves any goods of Jacob Coppe dec'd before they have proved to the Board their rights.

p. 104.
Aug. 2, 1659.

Before the Board appeared *Cornelis Aarsen* who was informed of some declarations, made before the Board, that the testament made by Jacob Coppe had been destroyed. He says, that may be reported by some people, because they would like it to be so; he requests a copy of the declarations, which was allowed to him.

p. 110.

Sep. 27, 1659. Having seen that the Burgomasters & Schepens of this City, after reading the statements of Willem Pietersen, Master Paulus Van der Beecq, Pieter Lauwerensen & wife, do not consider them sufficient to invalidate the last will and testament, made by *Jacob Coppe*, dec'd, the orphanmasters have decided that, for the best of the heirs, guardians and administrators must be appointed, electing thereto Timotheus De Gabry & Isaac Kip.

Commission.

Whereas Jacob *Coppe* has died and there has been found among his papers and property here a testament made December 14, 1653, before Notary D. Van Schelluyne & witnesses in favor of Lysbeth *Cornelis, daughter* of *Cornelis Aarsen* & Merritje Jans, dau. of Jan Van der Bilt, naming both heiresses of his estate, Therefore the Orphanmasters have resolved to appoint administrators of said estate, so that the heiresses may come to their own & they have elected & authorized, as they hereby do, Timotheus De Gabry & Isaac Kip, who are directed to make as soon as possible a complete inventory of all the goods & property, etc.

p. 117.

Nov. 13, 1659. *Cornelis Aarzen* & Jan Van der Bilt request that they with some other persons may be authorized by the Worshipful

Orphanmasters to administer upon the estate left by Jacob *Coppe*, dec'd, as their children are heirs of his property.   Granted.

p. 134.

Apr. 29, 1660.   Before the Board appeared *Cornelis Aarzen* who requested that the settlement of the estate of Jacob *Coppe*, dec'd, may go on, whereupon Jacobus Vis & Isaacq Kip were called in. Jan Van der Bilt directed to appear before the Board a week from date, showing inventory of cattle, lands etc. left by Coppe.

p. 136.

May 7, 1660.   Before the Board appeared Jan Van der Bilt & *Cornelis Aarzen*, parents of the children named as his heirs by Jacob Coppe, dec'd, in the testament executed before Notary Dirck Van Schelluyne & witnesses.   Said *Jan* Van der Bilt declares, that he undertakes to pay for his child Merritje *Jans*, & for the child of *Cornelis* Aarsen, called *Lysbet Cornelis*, the sum of 700 guilders in wampum, or for each 350 gldrs, out of the property left by Jacob *Coppe* in goods, lands and otherwise, including the charges on his farm, viz. 30 guilders still due to Tousein Bryeel for the land; he binds as security for the payment of said 700 guilders to the Orphans Court here said farm & cattle & generally his person & property, real & personal, present & future, nothing excepted, subject to all Courts & laws.

May 23, 1660.   Before us the underwritten Orphanmasters of the City of Amsterdam in New Netherland, appeared Geertje *Hendricks*, widow of Andrees *Hoppe*, dec'd, who stated she would give to her children Catrina, Wilhelmus, Hendrick, Matthys & Adolf Hoppe, as their share of their father's estate, the sum of 1000 guilders, or 200 gldrs to each child at once & not more when they came of age or married, according to the agreement, made with the chosen guardians *Cornelis Aarssen* & Lambert Huybersen *Mol* and executed before Notary Mattheus De Vos & witnesses March 6, 1659.

p. 142.
Aug. 6, 1660.

[Geertje Hoppe] was asked what had become of the 13 bearskins, 6 elkhides & 170 deerskins sent to Holland.   She answers she had not sent any deerskins to Holland, only the bearskins & elkhides, but in partnership with *Cornelis Aarsen* . . . The Orphan-masters direct that *Cornelis Aarzen* & wife, Geertje Hendricks, Jacobus Vis & Isaack Kip shall be summoned for next Monday.

p. 143.

Aug. 9, 1660. Jacobus Vis & Isaack Kip, administrators of the estate of Jacob *Coppe*, dec'd, came with *Cornelis Aarsen* & wife, Jan Vander Bilt & Geertje Hendricks . . . *Cornelis Aarsen* & Jan Van der Bilt asked whether they knew anything about it [some items in the inventory], said no.

p. 157.

Nov. 17, 1660. *Cornelis Aarzen* is asked, what shall be done to collect from *his wife's sister** the money due to the estate of Jacob *Coppe* & whether execution shall be ordered. He asks for delay until the next session, so that he may speak with Jan Van der Bilt.

*This wife's sister was Geertje Hendrick's widow [wife] of Andries Hoppe, deceased.

p. 207.

March 2, 1662. Weyntje Elberts, wid. of Aart Willemsen de-livers an inventory of her property & requests, that Burgomaster Paulus Leendersen Van der Grift & Symon Jansen Romeyn be appointed guardians of her children, which is allowed & they are to make an agreement with her according to the following order:

Whereas Weyntje Elberts, widow of Aart Willemsen intends to marry again & take *Cornelis Aarssen*, widower of *Beletje Hendrickn*, as husband and whereas said Weyntje has four minor children by said Aart Willemsen upon whom before the solemnization of her marriage she is willing to settle their paternal inheritance, so that when they come of age or marry they may have their own, therefore the Orphanmasters of this City herewith after communication with and approbation of the widow, appoint the Hon. Paulus Leendersen Van der Grift, at present burgomaster of this City & Simon Jansen Romeyn, burgher & inhabitant here, as guardians, who are author-ized to make as guardians & administrators with the widow such an agreement on behalf of the children concerning what comes to them from their father's estate by a complete inventory & appraisal, statement of debts & credits, as justice may require & to report the same to this Board for approval.

p. 209.

March 9, 1662.

Before us the Orphanmasters of the City of Amsterdam in New Netherland appeared Weyntje Elberts widow of Aart Willemsen who declared that according to the agreement made with Burgomaster Paulus Leendersen Van der Grift & Symon Jansen Romeyn, Burgher residing here, guardians of said Weyntje's children she truly owes to her children *Willem,** *Annetje, Elbert &* *Evert Arents** the sum of 2200 guilders for their paternal inheritance, that is to each child 550 gldrs, for which she gives as security to the orphans chamber a mortgage on her house, mill & lot on the Eastside of the Heere Straat.   (Broadway)

* As there was no child *Hendrickje* Arents or *Aerts* among these children it is plain that Hendrickje *Aerts* could not have been the stepsister of *Pieter Cornelissen Van Steenwyck Breyant.*

p. 212.

Mrch. 23, 1662.   The son [*Aart Cornelissen*] of *Cornelis Aarsen,* appearing says that Willem the orphaned son of Margriet Samuel has lived for some time at his parents' house & his father *after the death of his mother* has turned the farm over to him, he requests the Orphanmasters to leave said Willem in his service.   He is told, first to speak with Willem & then to come with him to the next session of the Board.

Year Book Holland Society for 1900.

p. 128.

Dec. 10, 1666.

Fietske Gerrits, late wife of Jan Jacobsz De Vries, died, leaving 4 minors: Gerrit, Oewe, Mynske and Grietie Janske (De Vries). Jan Jacobsz informs orphanmasters that he intends to marry Briete Olofs, widow of dec'd. Pieter Cornelissen *Sweet.*   Foeke Jansz & *Cornelis Aerts* appointed guardians of above 4 children.

p. 127.

Dec. 10, 1666.   Pieter Cornelissen, alias the Swede, had died leaving daughter Margrieta Pietersz, and widow Brieta Oloffs. Her farm situate opposite Stuyvesant's farm.

From this and above entry it will be shown that Pieter Cornelisz

Sweet and *Pieter Cornelisz Van Steenwyck* or *Bryant* were two distinct persons, having no relationship. As guardians of Margrieta Pietersz were appointed Pieter Stoutenburgh & Jan Jansz Langestraet (Longstreet). Nor was this Pieter Cornelisz Sweet any relation of *Cornelis Aerts*.

p. 113.

Sep. 19, 1657. Tryntie Hendricks, widow of Cors Pietersz. Children Cornelis Corssen Cornelissen, 12 years, Pieter 6 years and Hendrick Corssen Cornelissen 3 years old. She intends to marry Fredrick Lubberts.

[Year Book Holland Soc. for N. Y. as above.]
Court Minutes of New Amsterdam.
Vol. II, p. 373.

This day 10 April, 1658, Claas Teunisen, farm servant, living on *Cornelis Aarsen's* bouwery, appears before me Joannes Nevius, Secretary on the part of the Burgomasters & Schepens of the City of Amsterdam in N. Netherland, and declares to appeal to the Director General & Council of N. Netherland from the judgment pronounced by the Court of this City in date of 8th April, between him & Pieter Van de Linde.

p. 380.

May 6, 1658. *Cornelis Aarsen* v. s. Pieter Jansen & Gerrit his partner, defts. Defts. in default.

Vol. III, p. 12.

Sep. 17, 1658. *Cornelis Aarsen* demands from Cristiaan Barenzen's widow 100 guilders in beavers arising from the sale of a horse. Deft. says she has no objection to it, but has no beavers, offers to pay in seawant at beavers price. The Court orders deft. to pay pltf. the sum demanded within 14 days in beavers.

p. 33. Sep. 2, 1659.

Raghel Van Tienhoven demands from *Cornelis Aarsen* according to obligation 401 gldrs, saying thereon is paid 2 skepels winterwheat, 1 skepel of white & 1 skepel of gray pease, 99 gldrs. 4 stivers. Deft. says he offered an ox to which pltf. answers she does not know what to do with it. Referred to arbitrators.

Vol. III, p. 146.

Mrch 16, 1660.

Raghel Van Tienhoven demands from *Cornelis Aarzen* 401 gldrs according to obligation whereon she declares she has received 99 gldrs 4 stivers in zeawant & 1 skepel of white pease at 3 gldrs. & 1 skepel of gray peas at 4 gldrs & 2 skepels of wheat at 5 gldrs the skepel, amounting together to 117 guilders. Deft. denies owing so much producing an offset a/cc but without date. Pltf. demands costs of suit. The Court orders deft. to pay pltf. according to obligation, deducting the 117 gldrs pltf. acknowledges to have received, & if any further payment has been made on the obligation he shall have duly to prove it.

p. 251.

Jan. 25, 1661. The Court refer the matter in dispute between J. J. Van de Langh Straat (Longstreet) and Simon De Sweedt to *Cornelis Aarsen* & Pieter Stoutenburgh as arbitrators.

p. 376.   Oct. 4, 1661.

François De Bruyn demands from *Cornelis Aarzen* 5 beavers for ½ aam of French wine, drawn in his name at the funeral of *Jacob Coppe*, dec'd. Deft. admits the wine was drawn in his name, but says he cannot obtain any proceeds from the estate. The Court orders deft. to pay pltf.

p. 424.   Dec. 13, 1661.

Cornelis Aarsen pltf. vs. Lodowyck Pos, deft.   Deft. in default.

Vol. IV, p. 2.

Jan. 3, 1662.

Cornelis Aarsen as curator of the residuary estate of Jacob *Coppe*, dec'd, demands from Lodvwyck Pos 24 gldrs. in bvrs, according to obligation. The Court order deft. to deposit the money with the Secretary of this City.

p. 267.   June 26, 1663.

Freryck Flipzen, pltf. vs. *Cornelis Aarzen* deft.   Deft. in default.

Vol. V, p. 31.   Feb. 24, 1664.

Among the 94 subscribers towards a City loan of 27500 guilders towards repairing New Amsterdam's fortifications *Cornelis Aarzen* was one among 48 subscribing 100 guilders each.

p. 41.   Mrch 25, 1664.

Thomas Hall, pltf. vs. *Cornelis Aarenzen* & wife, defts.   Both in default.

p. 52.   May 6, 1664.

Jan Vigne, Eghbert Wouterzen, *Cornelis Aarzen, Aart Corneliszen,* Severy Lauwerens & Cornelis Jacobsen Stil appearing with the R^t. Hon. D^r. General [Stuyvesant], Jan Vigne states that the General has enclosed the Highway heretofore made use of & made another road, which is not passable in winter.   Whereunto the Hon. General answered he shall attend to it.

p. 225.   Apr. 19, 1665.

Among those ordered taxed to pay for the *maintenance* of the *English* soldiery on Manhattan, *Cornelis Aarsen,* living outside the land gate (Broadway), was assessed 2 guilders weekly.

Vol. VI, p. 13.

June 6, 1666.

In the case in dispute between Thomas Hal att of Willem Beeckman & Jan Vinge & *Cornelis Aertzen* on the one side pltfs., against Wolfert Webber on the other side, deft. the U. Court at deft's request orders that the land in question shall be again surveyed at his own expense by the surveyor Cortelyou in presence of Alderman Cornelis Van Ruyven, Pieter Stoutenburgh & Jan Langestraat [Longstreet], and — on behalf of deft.— Mr. Jacob Kip.   Which done, said persons are requested to settle the question between parties, if possible & reconcile them; if not to report their verdict to the W. Court.

p. 17.   June 12, 1666.

Dirck Gerrits Van Tright demands from *Cornelis Aertsen* delivery of 2 horses & a foal bought by him from deft. for 925 in seawant. Deft. demands that pltf. shall give security for the promised money, as he is given a long time to pay.   The U. Court having heard parties order pltf. to enter security within 8 days on pain of the trade being declared null.

N.B.   This June 12 pltf. gave as his security Casper Steinmets.

p. 67.   Apr. 2, 1667.

Jacob Van Couwenhoven, Egbert Woutersen, *Cornelis Aartsen*, Albert Leendertsen & 3 Commissioners from the Bench to be present at the surveying of land in dispute between

Wolfert Webber [a Minton ancestor]
&
Willem Beeckman

p. 69.
April 16, 1667.

In the matter in question between the Rev. D°. Johannes Mega-polensis, Dom^e; Samuel Drisius & M^r. Cornelis Van Ruyven on the one side and *Cornelis Aertsen*, Huygh Barentsen & Cornelis Jacobsen Stille on the other side, regarding the tilling of the land & the pastur-ing of cattle in the common, the U. Mayor's Court appointed the newly elected & old retiring Overseers of Roads & Fences, who are requested to examine the matter, to hear arguments & if possible to decide the case; if not to report to the U. Court.

p. 118.   Mrch 10, 1668.

Thomas Breden sued John Garland for payment of debt in Boston.

p. 118.   Mrch 10, 1668.

M^r. Paulus Leendersen Van de Grift & M^r. Allard Anthony, pltfs, against Jan Bastiaensen, deft.   The U. Court having heard parties order (with free consent of parties) that the case shall be referred to impartial arbitrators and to this end the U. Court elects Thomas Hal, Egbert Woutersen, Jan Langestraet (Long-street) and *Cornelis Aertsen*, who are hereby authorized to hear the matter in question argued by parties after examination, to decide this if possible, to reconcile them, & to report their conclusion to the U. Court on the next day.

Vol. I, p. 316.
May 31, 1655.

Thomas Hall & *Cornelis Aertsen* pltfs. contra Dirck d'Pottebacker, Pieter Linde, Hendrick Van Dyck, Paulus Leednertsen, Jan

Geraerdy, Pieter Stoutenburgh & Egbert Woutersen, defts.   Pltfs.
& all the defts. (except Pieter Linde) in default.

p. 320.   June 7, 1655.

Thomas Hall & *Cornelis Aertsen*, in quality of *overseers*, appointed
by the Hon. Director General & Council, of the Common Fences on
the Island of Manhattan Pltfs vs. Pieter Van de Linde, Hendrick
Van Dyck, the wife of Paulus Leend[n] Van die Grift and Egbert
Woutersen, defts.

Defts. accused of not attending to their share in the repairing of
the fence of the common pasture land on Manhattan Island.

Vol. II, p. 91.   May 1, 1656.

Cornelis Jansen, Woodsawyer, says that in the last trouble with
the Indians *Cornelis Aertsen* requested and engaged him to remain
with him on the General's (Stuyvesant's) Bouwery, and that he
would pay him therefor as much as the others, being Frenchmen.
And as each of the Frenchmen received for his part 25 gldrs, he
requests that deft. be condemned to pay him likewise 25 gldrs. Deft.
acknowledges that during the late troubles (in September, 1655) with
the Indians he requested & engaged pltf. on the Hon. General's
Bouwery on aforesaid conditions; but that he did so in the absence
of the Hon. General, by the order of Fiscal Tienhoven. Maintains
he must look to the Fiscal, but offers to pay pltf., if he may deduct it
from the rent of the Bouwery. Parties being heard, the Court
decide as *Corn[s] Aertsen* engaged & hired pltf. Cornelis Jansen as
aforesaid he is bound to pay him as well as the others, who were
then there. Therefore deft. is condemned to satisfy pltf., saving his
guarantee against whomsoever gave him orders & directions to
hire pltf.

p. 92.   May 1, 1656.

Thomas Hall & *Cornelis Aersen* in their quality as *Overseers of
Fences* on the Island of Manhattan commissioned by the Director
General & Council, pltfs. contra Ide Van Vorst, Hendrick Pietersen,
Claes Pietersen Cos, Jan Vinje, Leendert Aerden, Cornelis Jacobsen
Stille, Wolfert Webber, Gerrit Hendricksen & Jacob Schellinger,
defts.

Demanded to bear their equal share in the cost of repairing the
fence for the common pasturage.

p. 117.   June 19, 1656.

Cornelis Jansen, Woodsawyer, states whereas *Cornelis Aertsen* fails to pay him according to judgment dated 1st May last, he requests the Court to give orders that he may be paid.   So ordered.

p. 125.   June 26, 1656.

Andries Lourensen, Sergeant, demands payment of a balance of 24 guilders for wages earned & agreed upon, by Thomas Hall & *Cornelis Aertsen*.   Deft. Thomas Hall acknowledges the debt; says it was incurred for the Common Fence; requests as those who have cattle fail to pay their quota, that they be constrained thereto. Pay in 3 days.

p. 127.   July 3, 1656.   [See p. 141.   July 10, 1656.]

W[m]. Beeckman, Tomas Hall & Wolfert Webber, pltfs., contra Leendert Aerden & Cornelis Jacobs Stille, defts.   Pltfs. complain about damage done to their tilled land by cattle of defts.   *Cornelis Aertsen* & Dirck Clasen to value the damage & act as arbitrators.

p. 131.   July 3, 1656.

Nicasius De Sille in quality as Schout (prosecutor) of this City vs. Dirck Clasen Braeck, deft.   For that deft. on last Sunday afternoon during the sermon tapped for & gave drink to 3 or 4 different persons against the placard & ordinance.   Deft. denies the same; says he only treated Nicolaes Verleth, *Corn[s] Aertsen* & Ide Van Vorst & their wives to a drink of beer, through friendship and good neighborhood, without taking a penny therefor, as they did him many favors heretofore when after his cattle.   Parties being heard, deft. is excused with a warning, this being his first offence, & pltf's. demand herein dismissed.

p. 131.

Nicasius de Sille in his quality as Schout pltf. vs. *Cornelis Aersen*, Ide Van Vorst & their servants, defts.   For that their servantmen raced last Sunday evening after the sermon, within the City, with horses & wagons & much noise & singing, from which great damage & disaster might have arisen.   Concludes, therefore, that defts. or their servants be condemned each in a fine of £4—Flemish. *Cornelis Aersen* & Ide Van Vorst, as masters of their servants, for their committed fault, condemned each in a fine and penalty of three guilders.

p. 141. July 10, 1656.

Whereas Dirck Clasen is frequently absent on business, the Court has, at the request of W^m. Beeckman, appointed in his place Ide Van Vorst, who is authorized with *Cornelis Aertsen* to value the damage (as noted on p. 10 of these notes, July 3, 1656, p. 127 of New Amst. records).

Pieter Cornelissen, carpenter & millwright, had died prior to Jan. 22, 1660. Vol. 3, p. 108.

Documents relating to the Colonial History of New York. Vol. I, p. 195:

Before me Cornelis Van Tienhoven, Sec^y. of New Netherland, appeared *Cornelis Arissen*, aged about 36 years, who at the request of Cornelis Leendersen, deposes,— that it is true that he accompanied Jacob Stoffelsen & Gerrit Dyrksen into the fort on the day after the attack on the Indians & there heard the Director [kieft] say: "'Tis the fault of the freemen that the Indians were attacked— but your neighbor, Abraham Planck, was well aware of it, who might have warned you." All which deponent declares to be fact & truth. Done in Fort Amsterdam, 28 March, 1643, in New Netherland.

The mark X of *Cornelis Arissen*.

At that time Cornelis Aersen doubtless was living at Pavonia (Jersey City).

Vol. II, p. 183.

Emigrants to the Colony of the City of Amsterdam, on the Delaware River, from 1657 to 1661. *Cornelis Aertsen* of Zevenhoven, his boy & nephew.

Zevenhoven, or Sevenhoven, a village about 12 miles northeast of Leyden.

Vol. XIII, p. 419.

We who have hereunto subscribed our names are willing to take our dividends or lots, at the furthest New Dorpe or village (Marbletown) when the governor shall please to give the order for the laying them out unto us. Esopus (Kingston, N. Y.), Sep. 26, 1668. *Cornelis Arson*, and 23 others.

Documents relating to Col. Hist. of N. Y.

Vol. XIV, p. 377.

To D^r. Stuyvesant & Council of New Netherland:

Shows with due reverence Johannes Theod. Polheym, preacher, that he has some time ago bought from *Cornelis Aerssen* a parcel of land lying in the village of Midwout (Long Island), & as a payment of 100 guilders has become due, petitioner finds himself compelled to request that your Honors will please to pay for his account, debiting the same for it, so much to *Cornelis Aerssen.*

The Acting Receiver is ordered to pay for the account of the petitioner 100 gldrs to *Cornelis Aerssen.*

Dec. 21, 1656, at Fort Amsterdam in New Netherland.
Calendar of Dutch Manuscripts.

Sep. 12, 1648. Note. *Cornelis Arentsen* of Pavonia (Jersey City) to Isbrandt Dircksen Goethardt for 322 guilders in seewant.
[Calendar of Dutch Manuscripts]

This will show that before locating on Manhattan *Cornelis Aertsen* had settled at Pavonia. Thence he seems to have gone to Midwout, L. I., and from there to Manhattan Island.

There was also a very prominent merchant, *Cornelis* Jacobsen *Steenwyck*, living at New Amsterdam at the time, but there is not the least evidence to connect him with *Pieter Cornelissen Bryant Van Steenwyck.*

HACKENSACK REFORMED DUTCH CHURCH RECORDS
Baptisms

Child & Date	Parents	Witnesses
	p. 74	
Lysbeth	Pieter Cornelisse Breyandt	Gerrit Van Dien
Mrch 26, 1686	Hendriktie Arents	Angenitie Strickers
	p. 82	
Hendrickie	Roelof Bongaert	Jan Bongaert
&	Geertruy Breyandt	Lammetie Bongaert
Marretie		Cornelis Breyandt
Sep. 29, 1700		Antie Breyandt

p. 85

Annetie	Cornelis Breyandt	Simeon Jacobse Van
June 28, 1702	Margrit Simese Van Winckel	Winckel & wife Antie

p. 86

Rachel	Mattys *Hoppe*	*Cornelis Breyandt*
Feb. 20, 1703	Antie Jurckse	Hendriktie Housman

p. 88

Johannis	Cornelis *Breyandt*	Siarel Housman *
Aug. 27, 1704	Margritie Van Winckel	& wife Hendriktie
		* A *Hoppe* relation

p. 96

Hendricktie	Cornelis Breyandt	Nicases Kip
Apr. 24, 1709	Margrita Simese Van Winckel	& wife Antie

p. 96

Simon	Isack Vreeland	Cornelis Breyandt
June 5, 1709	Trintie S. Van Winckel	Margrytie Van Winckel

p. 97

Petrus	Egbert Ackerman	Cornelis ⎫ Breyandt
Dec. 7, 1709	Elysabeth Breyandt	Antie ⎭

p. 99

Simeon	Cornelis Breyandt	Isack Vreland
Apr. 22, 1710	Margrita S. Van Winckel	& wife Trintie

p. 105

Andries	Cornelis Breyandt	Jacob S. Van Winckel
Jan. 3, 1714	Margrita S. Van Winckel	& wife Jakemintie

p. 108

Hendrick	Gerrit Van Dien	Cornelis Breyandt
Jan. 23, 1715	Vrouwtie Verwey	Catr. Ackerman, wife of Jan Verwey

p. 78

Isack	Nic. Kip	Siarel *Huysman*
	Antie *Breyandt*	Geertruy *Breyandt*

p. 81

| Cornelis | Nic. Kip | Antie Jurkse |
| Jan.   1, 1700 | Antie *Breyandt* | (She was wife of *Mattys Hoppe*) |

p. 85

| Jacob | Nic. Kip | Mattys *Hoppe* |
| Dec. 14, 1702 | Antie *Breyandt* | Marg. S. Van Winkel |

p. 90

| Annatie | Nic. Kip | Roelof Bongaert |
| Jan.   3, 1706 | Antie Breyandt | Elis Breyandt |

p. 95

| Catrina | Nic. Kip | Egbert Ackerman |
| Sep. 12, 1708 | Antie Breyandt | Vrouwtie Van Dien |

p. 99

| Elisabeth | Nic Kip. | Hendrick *Hoppe* |
| Mrch 11, 1711 | Antie *Breyandt* | & wife Mary |

p. 101

| Antie | Miggiel Schors | Antie Breyandt |
| Dec. 16, 1711 | Elisabeth | |

p. 113

| Cornelia | Hendrik Van Gisse | Isack Van Gisse |
| Sep. 16, 1716 | Sara Romeyn | Antie Breyandt |

After this the number of other & later family connections increases
to such an extent that they crowd out the earlier & now more distant
Hopper relations as baptismal witnesses & vice versa.

p. 93

| Louwerens | Egbert Ackermans | Herman Bras |
| Jan. 18, 1708 | Elisabeth Breyandt | Geertie Egbers |

p. 106

Geertie	Egbert Ackerman	Isack Van Gyse
May 2, 1714	Elis. Breyandt	Vrouwtie Van Dien
Same remark as above.		

p. 82

| Cornelia | Pieter De Groot | Hendrick *Hoppe* |
| Oct. 13, 1700 | Belitie *Van Schaieck* | *Hendricktie Arens* |

It is stated that *Cornelis Aerts'* children, born in this country, took the
name *Van Schaick*.   Note the witnesses.

p. 85

| Gritie | Pieter De Groot | Matthys *Hoppe*, & |
| Nov.   1, 1702 | Belitie *Van Schaick* | A daughter of Jan DeGroot |

p. 88

| Joannes | Pieter De Groot | Gerrit *Van Dien* |
| July   5, 1704 | Belitie *Van Schaieck* | Belitie, wife of G. Jurrise |

p. 89

| Dina | Pieter De Groot | Jacob De Groot |
| Aug. 12, 1705 | Belitie *Van Schaick* | *Antie Hoppe* |

The entries on pp. 82, 85 & 89 are strong indications of the relationship between Van *Schaick* & *Hopper*.

p. 83

| Cornelis | Gerrit Van Dien | Jan Verwey |
| Dec.   8, 1700 | Vrouwtie Verwey | *Hendricktie Arense* |

p. 77

| Elisabeth | Gerrit Leydekker | *Siarel Huysman* |
| Aug.   9, 1696 | *Neeltie Cornelisse* | *Hendriktie Arentse* |

It is quite probable that a close and critical study of the *Hackensack* records and a thorough knowledge of family relations would still further disclose the relationship between *Cornelis Aertse* & *Pieter Cornelissen Bryant* & the *Van Schaicks*.

MEMBERS OF THE REFORMED DUTCH CHURCH OF NEW
AMSTERDAM BETWEEN 1649 & 1660

N. Y. Biogr. & Geneal. Record

Vol. 9, p. 45

Lambert *Moll* & *Tryn Pieters* his WIFE
        Baptisms Reformed Dutch Church of New Amsterdam:

Child & Date	Parents	Witnesses
Geertje	Lambert Huybertszen **Moll**	Pieter Wolfertszen
Sep. 6, 1648		Aeltje Pilms
Abraham	Lambert **Huybertsz**	Jan Snedeker
Mrch 23, 1642		Gerrit Wolfertszen
		Christine Hunen
		Hester Jans
Cornelis	Lambert Huybertszen	No witnesses
May 4, 1661	**Hendrickje Cornelis**	

This doubtless accounts for Lambert Huyberts' *Moll* being in the Hopper Aerts family circle.   After the death of his 1st wife he married

Hendrickje to all appearances the daughter of *Cornelis Aerts* [probably before 1658].

Pieter Cornelissen

In the absence of any absolute, primary documentary proof of the close relationship between *Pieter Cornelissen Van Steenwyck* or *Bryant* and *Cornelis* Aertsen of Manhattan Island we have to rely on secondary or circumstantial proof or evidence. And this is abundantly furnished, especially by the baptismal records.

In the first place, the name or patronymic of the subject of our investigation was *Cornelissen* which according to the well established Dutch and New Netherland usage of the time meant that he was the *son of Cornelis*. The investigator, in his extensive search, has found only one *Cornelis* among the very many bearing this name who could logically have been the parent of *Pieter Cornelissen Bryant*, and this Cornelis was *Cornelis Aertsen*.

There existed a very close relationship between the *Hopper* and *Cornelis Aertsen* families, as shown by the baptismal records, first of New Amsterdam, where [see p. 1 of the notes] *Cornelis Aertsen* & his wife *Belitje Hendricks* were constant witnesses at the baptisms of *Hoppe* or *Hopper* children. The wife of *Andries Hoppe* & the wife of *Cornelis Aertsen* were sisters. The baptismal records of Bergen show the close relationship — thro their continually acting as witnesses for each other — between the *Cornelissen* and *Hopper* families. This generation were cousins, through their mother. At the baptism [p. 1 of notes] of *Dierck* son of *Fredrick Thomassen* & Catryna *Hoppe, Hendrickje Aert*, wid. of *Pieter Cornelise* was a witness. Why? Because through her deceased husband she was a cousin by marriage of Catryna *Hoppe*. On page 1 of the notes we find Lambert Huybertszen *Mol* acting as a witness with *Arie Corneliszen* for a child of Andries *Hoppe*. Why? Doubtless because having recently married *Hendrickje Cornelis* (dau. of *Cornelis* Aertsen) he, *Mol*,— through his wife,— had become a relative of the *Hoppers*. These notes also contain several instances where *Cornelissens* acted as witnesses at *Hopper* baptisms and vice versa.

The Hackensack baptismal records again bear testimony to the close relationship between the *Breyants* & the *Hoppers*, as indicated through their continually officiating as witnesses for each other, and interrelated families. Note also at the foot of p. 13 of thcse notes that both *Hendricktie Arens* [wid. of *Pieter Cornelissen Van Steenwyck* or *Bryant*] and Hendrick *Hoppe* were witnesses, in 1700, at the *baptism* of a daughter of *Belitie Van Schaick*. On p. 53, Vol. 7, of the N. Y. Genealogical and Biographical Record it is stated that the *children* of *Cornelis Aertse* & *Belitje Hendricks* took the name *Van Schaick*. All except *Hendrickje* bap. July 7, 1641, who *probably* died unmarried. We *know* that she did not, but *married* Lambert Huybertszen *Mol*.

Therefore the *Van Schaicks* and *Bryants* were brothers and sisters, which accounts for their often acting as witnesses for or with each other under the name of *Cornelissen*, as well as once at Hackensack under the name of *Van Schaick* & *Hendricktie Arens* or Aerts as the wid. of *Pieter Cornelissen*.

The question of why *Pieter Cornelissen* then did not share in his paternal inheritance [p. 53, Vol. 7, N. Y. Gen. & Biogr. Record] remains to be considered. *Pieter* doubtless was the oldest son of *Cornelis Aertsen* and settled in New Jersey while his younger brothers and sisters were growing up, and assisting their father on his farm. As happened with so many older sons who set out for themselves, he doubtless had received advances from his father which fully covered his share in the paternal inheritance. If we could find *Cornelis Aertsen's* will, this would have been stated, as it was stated in the wills of many later testators which have come down to us. *Pieter* was busy developing his Bergen or Hackensack holdings which occupied all his time and energy, and at the time of *Pieter's* marriage to *Hendrickje Aerts* (July 10, 1670) his father had just died.

Joining the various links in the chain of secondary or circumstantial evidence, as shown in the accompanying notes, there can be no doubt that *Pieter Cornelissen Van Steenwyck* or *Bryant* was the son of *Cornelis Aertsen* of Manhattan.

It is not plain why *Cornelis Aerts'* younger children should have taken the name *Van Schaieck*. There is a Schaick, a neighborhood, section or district, 2½ miles northèast of Leerdam in the province of South Holland, besides 2 polders (drained lakes) in the same location. There are also two manors, Great and Little Schaick, 1½ miles northeast of Scherpenzeel in the province of Gelderland, and about 25 or 30 miles distant from Steenwyck in the Province of Overysel.

Aardrykskundig Woordenboek van Nederland, by S. Gille Heringa. 3d Edition, 1874.

It was nothing unusual among the Holland Dutch in those early pioneer days for children of the same parents to adopt entirely different family names. It, in reality, occurred so often that the practice almost became a custom. This custom doubtless accounts for the disappearance of many descendants of early pioneers from the records. Those descendants adopted certain names and where the records do not clearly indicate the connection or relationship between the bearer of the original name and the bearers of the later adopted name, the means of identification are lost.

N. Y., Dec. 10, 1912. DINGMAN VERSTEEG.

THE VAN WINKLE HOMESTEAD. OLDEST HOUSE IN PATERSON, N. J.
RIVER STREET

BRYANTS IN AMERICA

I

CORNELIS AERTSZEN (Bryant[1]), b. 1607, probably in Steenwick, Holland; m. (1st) Belitje Hendricks, who died before March 2, 1662. He m. (2nd) July 10, 1662, Weyntje Elberts, widow of Aert Willemszen (N. Y. R. D. ch. rec., Marriages). Cornelis Aertszen was in New Netherlands (now New York) prior to 1650.

His children by his first marriage were:

2. I. Pieter Cornelisse Breijandt (see Dutch rec., p. 16); m. Hendrickje Arentse+
3. II. Hendrickje Breijandt, b. July 7, 1641; m. Lambert Huybersen Moll (Dutch rec., p. 19).
4. III. Arie (Adriaen) Breijandt, b. July 9, 1642; m. Rebecca Yrens.
5. IV. Hendrick Breijandt, b. Sept. 23, 1646; m. Geertie Hoppe. (Dutch rec., p. 1.)
6. V. Lysbeth Breijandt, b. Oct. 1, 1651.

CORNELIS AERTSZEN, the founder of the American branch of the Dutch family of Breyant, like so many thousands of others (says Mr. Dingman Versteeg of New York, an expert on the records of early Holland Dutch in this country, and who has made extensive research on the Bryant ancestry), appears to have been known and referred to only by his patronymic. One of his sons seems to have adopted the family name of BREYANT [a customary proceeding which was regarded as both proper and legal]. Tradition states that two brothers of the family of Bryant went from England to Holland to escape religious persecution. They may have married in Holland before then, or more probably their descendants emigrated to America. The custom of taking surnames, sometimes, of a near relative makes it possible that Pieter Cornelisse adopted the name of Breyant, which may have belonged to the maternal side of the house. As in most all similar instances, the evidence

23

appears to be only circumstantial. Sufficient time has not been taken to solve this problem.

Cornelis Aertszen was worthy in every respect, enterprising and public-spirited, a pioneer entitled to recognition among the founders of this great nation. He was in New Netherlands prior to 1650 and took a prominent part in the affairs of his day, "so you certainly have reason to be proud of him."

2   SECOND GENERATION

PIETER CORNELISSE BREYANDT[2] (Cornelis Aertszen[1]), b. prior to 1650; d. 1692; m. July 31, 1670, Hendrickje Arentse. Marriage rec., Bergen R. D. ch., p. 281, Holland Society copy: "July 10, 1670, Banns Piet Cornelisse Van Steenwyck (Breyandt) young man, and Henrickje Arentse, young woman; married July 31, 1670, before the court at Bergen."

> *Children:*
>
> 7.   I.   Annatie (Annatje Anna Breyandt), bap. Sept. 10, 1671; m. Dec. 20, 1691, Nicassius Kip; m. (2nd) Oct. 10, 1713, Isaac Van Gysse+
> 8.   II.   Geertruyd Breyandt, bap. Nov. 8, 1673; witnesses, Hendrick Cornelissen and Hendrickji Aerts+
> 9.   III.   Cornelius Breyandt, b. Apr. 18, 1676; m. Dec. 7, 1700, Margrita Simese Van Winkel+
> 10.   IV.   Arent Breyandt, bap. Oct. 7, 1678; witnesses, William Hoppe and Marritje Arentse (p. 69, Holland Society rec.).
> 11.   V.   Andries Breyandt, bap. Aug. 21, 1681, at Bergen, N. J.; witnesses, Matys Hoppe+, Mynonn Paulase.
> 12.   VI.   Andries Breyandt, bap. June 30, 1684; witnesses, Matys Hoppe and Mynonn Paulase.
> 13.   VII.   Lyzabet (Elizabeth) Breyandt, bap. Mar. 26, 1686; m. Oct. 26, 1695, Roelf Bongaert+

7   THIRD GENERATION

ANNATIE BREYANT[3] (Pieter Cornelisse,[2] Cornelis Aertszen[1]), b. Sept. 10, 1671; m. Dec. 20, 1691, Nicasius Kip, b. abt. 1660,

New Anstel (New Castle) on the South or Delaware River in
Delaware; d. in latter part of 1712; son of Hendrick H. Kip
and Anna de Sill. Both Nicasius Kip and his wife Annatie
were admitted to membership in the Hackensack ch. Sept. 22,
1694. Both were witnesses to a baptism Oct. 4, 1712, soon
after which Nicasius died. Since his widow m. Isaac Van
Gysse, widower of Hildegond Kuyper. (History Preakness
Ref. Ch. by Rev. George Labaw, p. 45.) He was made a deacon
Apr. 16, 1695.

Children:

14. I. Isaak Kip, bap. 1697; witnesses, Gertruy Breyandt
and Siarel Huysman.

15. II. Cornelis Kip, bap. Jan. 1, 1700; witness, Antie Jurkse,
wife of Mattys Hoppe.

16. III. Jacob Kip, bap. Dec. 14, 1702; witnesses, Mattys
Hoppe and Marg. S. Van Winkel.

17. IV. Annatie Kip, bap. Jan. 3, 1706; witnesses, Roelof
Bongaert and Elis Breyandt.

18. V. Catrina Kip, bap. Sept. 12, 1708; witnesses, Egbert
Ackerman and Vrouwtie Van Dien.

19. VI. Elisabeth Kip, bap. Mar. 11, 1711; witnesses, Hendrick Hoppe and wife Mary.

8

GEERTRUYD BREYANDT[3] (Pieter Cornelisse,[2] Cornelis Aertszen[1]), bap. Nov. 8, 1673; m. Oct. 26, 1695, Roelf (Ralph)
Bongaert of Hackensack, N. J., son of Cornelisse Janse Boomgaert or Bongaert, Bongart; descendants known as Bogart of
Flushing. (See Bergens, Kings Co., p. 42.)

Children:

20. Hendrickie Bongaert
21. Marretie Bongaert
bap. Sept. 29, 1700; witnesses, Jan
Bongaert, Lammertie Bongaert,
Cornelis Breyandt, Antie Breyandt.

9

CORNELIUS BRYANT[3] (Pieter Cornelisse,[2] Cornelis Aertszen[1]),
b. Apr. 18, 1676, in Bergen, N. J.; d. 1729-30; m. Dec. 7, 1700,
Margrietje (Marguerite) Simese Van Winkel, who was bap.

Nov. 4, 1676; d. Dec. 1, 1730; dau. of Symon Jacobse Van
Winkel, bap. July 24, 1653, and Annatje Arianse Sip, dau. of
Claas A. Sip.   An abstract of his will is given as follows in Vol.
23, p. 68, New Jersey Archives: Cornelis (Cornelius) Breyandt
of Elizabethtown, Essex Co., yeoman, dated Oct. 2, 1720.
Wife, Margarett.   Children, Johanis, Simon, Andris, Hanne,
Stepson Peter, Winne.   House in Springfield on south side of
road, a negro boy.   Executors, the wife, John Kewman of
Newark, John Blanchard, Jr., of Elizabeth Town.   Proved
Dec. 19, 1720.   Also will of his widow, viz., Nov. 8, 1729,
Margaret Breyant, widow of Cornelius, of Elizabeth Town,
Essex Co.   Sons, Peter Wenem, Johannis, Simeon, and Andris.
Daughters, Hannah, wife of Cornelius Westerveld, Rachel
Breyant (under age), Hendrickie, wife of Jonah Carl, who has
dau. Elizabeth.   Two tracts of land, bought of John Blan-
chard, Jr., personal estate.   Executors, Johannis Knewman
and Egbert Ackerman of Bergen Co.   Proved Jan. 13, 1729–30.
Margrietje Simese Van Winkle; m. (1st) Martin Winne, Oct.
30, 1697, who d. 1698.

Children:

22.   I.   Annetie Breyant, bap. June 28, 1702, at Hackensack;
m. Cornelis Juriese Westerveld.   The record
of her marriage is as follows: "Anntie Breyant,
young dame living at New Britain and Cornelis
Juriese Westerveld, young man living at Aken-
sack, both born at Ackensack, announce their
intention of marriage Sept. 14, 1723."

23.   II.   Johannes Breyant, bap. Aug. 27, 1704.

24.   III.   Hendricktie (Henrietta) Breyant, bap. April 22, 1710;
m. Jonah Carl, had dau.

24a.   Elizabeth Carl

25.   IV.   Simeon Briant, b. 1710; bap. April 22, 1711; m. Hannah Searing+

26.   V.   Andris Briant, bap. Jan. 3, 1714; m. Elizabeth
. . . . . .+

27.   VI.   Rachel Briant, under age of 18 years in 1729.

S.P. HOMESTEAD JERSEY CITY BUILT 1660

13
LYZABET (Elizabeth) BREYANDT[3] (Bryant) (Pieter Corne-
lisse,[2] Cornelis[1]), bap. 1686 in R. D. ch., Hackensack, N. J.; m.
EGBERT ACKERMAN, who was b. at Bergen, in East N. J.
Banns published Apr. 12, 1707, at Hackensack, N. J. [New
Jersey Archives, Vol. 22, p. 470.]

Children:

27a.   I.   Lauwrens Ackerman, b. Jan. 18, 1708; witnesses,
            Herman Bras and Geertie Egbers.
27b.   II. Petrus Ackerman, b. Dec. 7, 1709; witnesses, Cor-
            nelius and Antie Breyandt.
27c.   III. Geertie Ackerman, b. Feb. 5, 1712; witnesses, Isaac
            Van Gyse, Vrouwtie Van Dien.
27d.   IV. Geertie Ackerman, b. May 2, 1714; witnesses, Isaac
            Van Gyse, Vrouwtie Van Dien.
27e.   V.   Lauwrens Ackerman, b. Aug. 5, 1716.
27f.   VI. Hendricktie Ackerman, b. Sept. 29, 1717.
27g.   VII. Annatie Ackerman, b. Aug. 14, 1720.
27h. VIII. Lauwrens Ackerman, b. Mar. 3, 1723.
27i.   IX. Cornelis Ackerman, b. Apr. 17, 1726.

25   FOURTH GENERATION
SIMEON BRYANT[4] (Briant, Breyandt) Cornelius[3] [9], Pieter
Cornelisse,[2] Cornelis[1]), b. 1710; bap. Apr. 22, 1711; d. June 25,
1784; m. HANNAH SEARING, who was b. ......, 1718; d. Apr.
7, 1785; dau. of John Searing. They lived on a farm near
Springfield, N. J.; probably inherited the farm. This farm is
still in possession of a descendant of his family. They are
both buried in the old churchyard at Springfield, N. J.

Children:

28.   I.   Phoebe Bryant, b. Oct. 6, 1736; m. Samuel Littell;
            had eight children.
29.   II. Jacob Bryant, b. Feb. 23, 1739; m. Abigail Rush-
            more+
30.   III. Hannah Bryant, b. July 7, 1741; d. Feb. 2, 1803;
            buried in Springfield, N. J.

31. IV. Sarah Bryant, b. Jan. 23, 1743; m. (1st) Daniel Ross; (2nd) Constance Cooper.

32. V. Samuel Bryant, b. Jan. 9, 1746; m. Lydia Craig of Westfield, N. J.; had nine children; lived at Mt. Freedom, N. J.+

33. VI. Elias Bryant, b. Jan. 5, 1748; d. unm.

34. VII. Rachel Bryant, b. Feb. 2, 1750; m. Nathaniel Ross+

35. VIII. Elizabeth Bryant, b. Oct. 2, 1753; m. Abraham Mulford; had children:

    35a. I. Elizabeth Mulford.
    35b. II. Sarah Mulford.

36. IX. James Bryant, b. ......, 1754 (probably the James who moved to Washington Co., Pa., and thence to Fredericktown, Ohio).

37. X. David Bryant, b. May 22, 1756; m. Catherine Woolley+

38. XI. Rhoda Bryant, b. Aug. 5, 1758; m. (1st) Isaac Marsh; had six children; m. (2nd) Jonah Cooper+

39. XII. Simeon Bryant, b. Mar. 16, 1760; m. Mary Searing+

26

ANDRIS (Andrew) BRIENT[4] (Cornelius,[3] Pieter Cornelisse[2] Cornelis[1]), bap. 1714; witnessed by Nicassius Kip and Anntie Breyandt; d. about Nov. 1750, (yeoman). Lived in Elizabethtown. His will made in 1749 names his wife Elizabeth and his sons John and Cornelius, also Samuel and Andres, both under age, and appoints his brother Simeon Brient executor.

Children:

39a. I. John Bryant (Brient), b. ......, 1739; d. Oct. 26, 1801; m. Abigail ......, who was b. Oct. 19, 1705; d. Feb. 2, 1856. Children:

    1023. I. Mary Bryant, b. ......, 17...
    1024. II. Andrew Bryant.

39b. II. Cornelius Bryant.
39c. III. Samuel Bryant.
39d. IV. Andres Bryant.

29 FIFTH GENERATION

JACOB BRIENT[5] (Bryant) (Simeon[4] [25], Cornelius,[3] Pieter
Cornelisse,[2] Cornelis[1]), b. Feb. 23, 1739; m. ABIGAIL RUSHMORE.

Children:

40. I. Abigail Brient, b. ......; m. Richard Kissam+
41. II. Samuel Brient, b. ....
42. III. Mary Brient, b. ......; m. A. M. Meeker.
43. IV. Hannah Brient, b. ......; m. A. M. Kissam.
44. V. Nancy Brient, b. ......; m. Samuel Meeker of
Philadelphia, Pa.

31

SARAH BRIENT[5] (Bryant) (Simeon[4] [25], Cornelius,[3] Pieter
Cornelisse,[2] Cornelis[1]), b. Jan. 23, 1743; m. (1st) DANIEL ROSS
m. (2nd) CONSTANCE COOPER.

Children 1st m.:

45. I. Daniel Ross, Jr., who m. Phoebe Frieson of Orange,
N. J.
46. II. Rachel Ross, who m. William Lawrence of Rahway,
N. J.
Children of 2nd m.:
47. IV. Fanny Cooper.
48. V. Sarah Cooper, m. ...... Day.

32

SAMUEL BRIENT[5] (Bryant) (Simeon[4] [25], Cornelius,[3] Pieter
Cornelisse,[2] Cornelis[1]), b. Jan. 9, 1746; m. Lydia Craig, dau. of
Andrew Craig of Westfield, N. J.; resided at Westfield, N. J.

Children:

49. I. Simeon Brient.
50. II. Jacob Brient.
51. III. James Brient.
52. IV. David Brient.
53. V. Elias Brient.
54. VI. Hannah Brient; m. Mr. Horton.
55. VII. Elizabeth Brient; m. Mr. Brown.
56. VIII. Sarah Brient; m. Mr. Young.

34
RACHEL BRIENT[5] (Bryant) (Simeon[4] [25], Cornelius,[3] Pieter Cornelisse,[2] Cornelis[1]), b. Feb. 2, 1750; d. Sept. 14, 1810; m. NATHANIEL ROSS.

>   *Children:*
>
> 57.   I. James Ross; m. Margaret Moore.
> 58.   II. Abigail Ross; m. Samuel Magie.

Rachel Bryant lived in the home of her brother David for a few years before her marriage, where she left a loving remembrance. She is buried in the old graveyard at Springfield, New Jersey.

NEW JERSEY BRANCH

No effort has been made to trace the Bryant descendants other than those of David Bryant of 1756; however, we include the following data:

38
RHODA BRIENT[5] (Bryant) (Simeon[4] [25], Cornelius,[3] Pieter Cornelisse,[2] Cornelis[1]), b. Aug. 5, 1760; m. ISAAC MARSH of Rahway, N. J.

>   *Children:*
>
> 38a.   I.   John Marsh.
> 38b.   II. Isaac Marsh.
> 38c.   III. Abram Marsh.
> 38d.   IV. Bryant Marsh.
> 38e.   V.   Susan Marsh.
> 38f.   VI. Hannah Marsh.

39
SIMEON BRYANT[5] (Simeon,[4] Cornelius,[3] Pieter Cornelisse,[2] Cornelis[1]), b. Mar. 16, 1760; m. MARY SEARING, b. Feb. 14, 1766; d. Aug. 22, 1856. Simeon d. Sept. 28, 1831. Simeon Bryant and Mary his wife and three of their children are buried in the old churchyard in Springfield, N. J.

Children:

39a.   I.   Elizabeth Bryant, b. Jan. 5, 1784.
39b.   II.   Chloe Bryant, b. Nov. 11, 1786.
39c.   III.   Fanny Bryant, b. Aug. 30, 1788.
39d.   IV.   Daniel Saering Bryant, b. Dec. 15, 1790.
39e.   V.   Hannah Bryant, b. Dec. 1, 1794.
39f.   VI.   Nancy Bryant, b. Feb. 1, 1797; d. April 15, 1798.
39g.   VII.   Jacob Bryant, b. Apr. 9, 1800; d. June 5, 1803.
39h.   VIII.   Mary Bryant, b. May 6, 1803.
39i.   IX.   Jane Bryant, b. Nov. 12, 1804; m. Mr. Keeler; lives
                in New York City.
39j.   X.   Simeon Alfred Bryant, b. Mar. 12, 1807.
39k.   XI.   Sarah Ann Bryant, b. Sept. 12, 1810.

40

ABIGAIL BRIENT[6] (Bryant) (Jacob[5] [32] Simeon,[4] Cornelius,[3]
Pieter Cornelisse,[2] Cornelis[1]), b. ......; m. RICHARD KISSAM,
who was a cousin of Mrs. William K. Vanderbilt.

Children:

40a.   I.   Daniel Kissam, who m. Mary Bryant and had chil-
                dren as follows:
40b.   II.   John Rushmore Kissam.
40c.   III.   Franklin Kissam; resided in East Orange, N. J.
40d.   IV.   Anna Kissam; resided in Newark, N. J.

37   DESCENDANTS OF DAVID BRYANT, 1656–1835

DAVID BRYANT[5] (Simeon[4] [25], Cornelius,[3] Pieter Cornelisse,[2]
Cornelis[1]), son of Simeon Briant and Hannah Searing, b. May
22, 1756, at Springfield, N. J.; d. Aug., 1835, at Wolf Lake,
Noble Co., Ind.; was m. abt. 1782, probably near Springfield,
N. J., to Catherine Woolley, b. abt. 1759; d. Aug., 1835, at
Wolf Lake, Ind., who was a dau. of Abraham Woolley and
Catherine Woodruff.

Children:

59.   I.   Sarah Bryant, b. Jan. 23, 1783; m. Ephriam Vas-
                binder+

60.   II.   Elias Bryant, b. Nov. 5, 1784; m. Ann Vance+
61.   III. Isaac Bryant, b. June 18, 1786; m. Maria Louisa
            Fisher+
62.   IV.   Joseph Bryant, b. Apr. 14, 1788; m. Dorothy Camp-
            bell+
63.   V.   Samuel Bryant, b. Jan. 25, 1790; m. Mary Ross; 2nd,
            Joanna Woodruff.
64.   VI.   Abraham Bryant, b. Nov. 5, 1791; d. Aug. 17, 1793+
65.   VII. Mary Bryant, b. Mar. 25, 1793; m. Sylvanus Cooper+
66. VIII. Simeon Bryant, b. Apr. 26, 1795; m. Elizabeth
            McCauley+
67.   IX.   David Bryant, b. May 12, 1797; m. Rachel Adams;
            m. 2nd, Margaret Steinbrook; m., 3rd, Mercy
            H. Ransom+
68.   X.   Hannah Bryant, b. Apr. 16, 1799; m. Matthew Black
            Mitchell+
69.   XI.   Elizabeth Bryant, b. Mar. 13, 1801; m. Charles
            Cracraft Post+
70.   XII. Jacob Bryant, b. Jan. 15, 1803; m. Jane Anne Welsh+
71. XIII. John Bryant, b. July 5, 1805; killed at the age of 15 by
            the falling of a tree.
72. XIV.   Nancy Bryant, b. Dec. 16, 1807; m. (1st), David
            Agnew; (2nd), John Keller+
73.   XV.   Jane Bryant, b. May 8, 1810; m. Madison Washing-
            ton Welch+

DAVID BRYANT

It is a difficult matter to pay worthy tribute to these early
pioneers of America.   We cannot even fancy what trials they met,
what hardships they endured, or with what determination they
braved the dangers of the times to provide homes for their families.
Of this sturdy stock was our ancestor, DAVID BRYANT, soldier and
pioneer, courageous to face the foe in securing liberty for the
American people, and one of the earliest pioneers to brave the
savage and blaze the way for the civilization of the West.   Born
in 1756, he spent his early childhood in New Jersey, where he
found that strength of character so essential in the higher development of our nation.   At the age of nineteen he entered the Continental Army, enlisting at Springfield, New Jersey, and remaining in

service five years. In 1790 he, with his family, moved to Washington County, Pennsylvania. He there purchased a farm in Buffalo Township, near Owl Creek. The name of David Bryant appears in the first census of the United States taken in 1790, as residing in Washington County, Pennsylvania, his family consisting then of seven members. In 1816 he again moved westward to Knox County, Ohio. Here he owned three farms near Fredericktown, Ohio. The following is a communication dated August 8, 1911, from the recorder of Knox County, Ohio: "David Bryant purchased one hundred acres from Reuben Sutton, another one hundred and ninty-eight acres from Jacob Mitchel, another about two hundred acres from Wm. Mitchell."

At an advanced age he started westward with his wife, in company with the family of his son Elias, this time for Indiana. Mrs. Bryant objected to the new venture, and as they visited friends on the way, each tried to dissuade them from going further, but David was not a man to brook opposition. They finally came to Wolf Lake, about fifteen miles northwest of Fort Wayne, Indiana, where they spent the summer of 1835. Elias bought land there from the government. The aged parents could not withstand the hardships incident to pioneer life. They both sickened and died in the month of August. They are buried on the east bank of Eel River, on ground which Elias Bryant sold to his nephew David Vasbinder.

Mr. Strain lived within three miles of the graves; there is also a wagon road not more than twenty rods east of them. The exact spot, as far as we can ascertain, is unkown. The indomitable will and progressive spirit of this ancestor led him always in the foremarch of western emigration, and he gave to this country sons and daughters who have proved to be loyal patriots and faithful citizens. There have come down to us through the older members of the family many interesting traditions of this great-grandfather David. Mrs. J. K. Blackstone, his granddaughter remembers hearing her father say that his father was a strict disciplinarian, which might have been due to his military training. He was over six feet in height, and an average weight of about one hundred and ninety pounds, his frame large and powerful with a commanding presence. In later life he fell and fractured a hip so that he was obliged to use a cane. The wife, Catherine Woolley Bryant, was a small woman. She lost her eyesight and was blind for fifteen

years before her death.   She left a memory of sweetness and loving
kindness that was a benediction to all who were privileged to
know her.   Her mother, Catherine Woodruff Woolley (widow of
Abraham Woolley) spent her last years in the home of her grandchildren, Joseph and Dorothy Campbell Bryant, who lived in
Buffalo Township, Washington County, Pennsylvania, near Claysville.   She died there in 1825 at the advanced age of one hundred
and six years and was buried near Claysville, Pennsylvania.   Mr.
Joseph Bryant of Clifton Forge, Virginia, son of the above Joseph,
is authority for this record of the good old age of our ancestress,
Catherine Woodruff Woolley.   Military record of David Bryant:
"State of New Jersey, office of Adjutant General.   It is certified
that the records of this office show that David Bryant served one
month in 1776 as private, minute man Captain Horton's Co., 1st
Regiment, Essex Co., N. J. militia; again served 8 days in same
company and regiment; served 3 months in the winter of 1778–79
as private, same company and regiment; afterwards served 7
monthly tours under Capt. Joseph Horton during Revolutionary
War."

[Signed] William S. Stryker, *Adjutant General.*

From Department of the Interior, Washington, D. C.: "David
Bryant served several short tours with the New Jersey Troops in
each year from 1776 to 1780 on alarms and guard duty under
Capt. Brookfield, Capt. Horton and Capt. Townley, Col. Thomas
and Col. Spencer.   Battles engaged, Springfield, Conn., Farms,
and Elizabethtown.   Applied for pension Oct. 5, 1833; res. at date
of application, Wayne, Knox Co., Ohio; age at date of application,
born in Springfield, N. J., May 22, 1756.   His pension was allowed.
He moved about 1791 to Washington Co., Pa., and about 1816 to
Knox Co., Ohio."

[Signed] H. Clay Evens, *Commissioner.*

There were many smaller engagements during his five years of
active service in and around Springfield.   It is probable that he
faced the enemy many times with ball and powder.   On the 17th
of September, 1776, there was a brisk skirmish at Springfield which
is described as follows by Col. Symmes, the American commander:
"On the approach of Gen. Lesley's 'British' troops towards Spring-

field they were discovered by Maj. Spencer's cadets stationed on the western road. Major Spencer instantly dispatched a light horseman at full speed four miles to Chatam to notify the Col. Commandant that the enemy in considerable force were within two miles of Springfield. The brigade 'American' was already under arms and was ordered instantly to march towards Springfield to sustain Maj. Spencer. Meantime, the Major prudently abandoned Springfield and retreated toward Chatam, westward, where he was reinforced by the American brigade at Bryant's Tavern. After Maj. Spencer had communicated to the Col. Commandant the position of the enemy then occupying Springfield, the brigade advanced to the attack. The center of the enemy occupied the ground in front of and the meadow behind the Woodruff Tavern. The Col. Commandant of the militia supported by Col. Lindly on the left and Major Spencer (who now commanded the Essex Regiment) on the right brought up the center of the brigade until they were within pistol shot of the enemy. The conflict continued about an hour, when darkness forbade a longer contest at that time and the firing seemed mutually to cease on both sides. The Brigade fell back that evening only one mile to Briant's Tavern, struck up fires and lay all night on their armes, intending to make a second attack in the morning, but in the morning the enemy was not to be found: he had withdrawn in the night with all possible speed. This was the first instance in the state of New Jersey when the British troops turned their backs and fled from those they called rebels, and this success, small as it was, taught the Jersey militia that the foe was not invincible."

There was another skirmish at Springfield on the fifth of January, 1777. Again was fought the battle at Springfield on June 23, 1780, when 5,000 British tried to enter the hill country surrounding Morristown, where General Washington had his camp, but were severely repulsed. On the occasion of the burning of Springfield by General Clinton, Chaplain Caldwell, whose wife with babe in her arms was shot by a British soldier, rushed to the church when the men were in want of wadding, came out with his arms filled with hymn books and shouted, "Put Watt's into them, boys." History states that all but three of the houses of Springfield were burned. Many family records were destroyed. The following shows that the father and mother of David Bryant received slight reimbursement for their losses (Report of Commission on Public Records of New Jersey, filed at State House, page 104): "Hannah Briant 1776–1780 16£. Simeon Briant 462£ 11 shillings. Inventory of losses by depredation of English Troops, dated Springfield, N. J., May 11, 1789."

Family tradition harbors many interesting experiences of these ancestors during the Revolutionary period. The horrors of war were nowhere greater, if as great, as in New Jersey. The winter of 1779–80 is memorable for the severity of the season and for the devastation made by the merciless foe.

The following is a fac-simile of signature of David Bryant of 1756 (37):

59   SIXTH GENERATION

SARAH BRYANT[6] (David[5] [37], Simeon,[4] Cornelius,[3] Pieter Cornelisse,[2] Cornelis[1]), b. Jan. 23, 1783, in Springfield, N. J.; d. Dec. 1, 1867; m. ......, 1804, EPHRAIM VASBINDER, b. July 17, 1779; d. Sept. 17, 1836. Soon after their marriage, which took place near Washington, Pa., they moved to Mansfield, O., where they accumulated a large property. They donated a fountain with statuary to the city of Mansfield. They are buried in the cemetery at Mansfield.

Children:

74.   I. David Vasbinder, b. Sept. 6, 1805; unm.; d. May 9, 1882.

75.   II. Jane Vasbinder, b. ......, 1803; unm.; d. Sept. 28, 1897.

60

ELIAS BRYANT[6] (David[5] [37], Simeon,[4] Cornelius,[3] Pieter Cornelisse,[2] Cornelis[1]), b. Nov. 5, 1784, in Springfield, N. J.; d. at Pleasant Grove, Sept. 10, 1850; m. March, 1821, ANN VANCE, b. July 20, 1784, in Middletown, Washington Co., Pa,; d. Feb. 10, 1847; buried at Pleasant Grove, Lake Co.,

MARIA FISHER BRYANT

ISAAC BRYANT

Ind.; dau. of Robert Vance, one of the pioneer settlers of Pennsylvania and a native of Ireland.

Children:

76.   I.   Arthur Vance Bryant, b. June 25, 1822; m. Henrietta Hill+
77.   II.   David Bryant, b. Sept. 20, 1824; m. Mary McGill+
78.   III.   Robert Bryant, b. Dec. 17, 1826; m. Mary Jane Merriss+
79.   IV.   Isaac Bryant, b. ......; d. at the age of thirteen from the bite of a rattlesnake while crossing a prairie.
80.   V.   Son, died in infancy.
81.   VI.   John Bryant, b. July 20, 1833; m. Mary Angeline Lawrence+

Elias Bryant accompanied his parents on their removal from New Jersey to Washington County, Pennsylvania, and there he was reared and educated. He afterwards removed to Knox County, Ohio, about 1820. He followed farming in the Buckeye State until the fall of 1835, when he went by wagon to Lake County, Indiana, settling at Pleasant Grove in Cedar Creek Township. Here he was one of the first settlers and purchased land from the government for which he paid one dollar and twenty-five cents an acre. On March 16, 1839, Elias Bryant entered from the United States the west half of southeast quarter of section 18. His patent is dated June 25, 1841, and is recorded in Book 87, page 102, Indiana Land Records. He transformed this raw tract into richly cultivated fields and carried on farming until his death at the age of sixty-six years. He was a zealous and active member of the Presbyterian Church, in which he served as an elder. He gave his political support to the Whig party and during his early residence in Lake County his enterprise and energy made him a valuable citizen of the frontier district.

61

Isaac Bryant,[6] (David[5] [37], Simeon,[4] Cornelius,[3] Pieter Cornelisse,[2] Cornelis[1]), b. June 18, 1786, near Springfield, N. J.; d. Feb. 16, 1859; buried at Wyandot, Ohio; m. ......, 1844, at Circleville, Ohio, Maria Louisa Fisher, who was b. Nov. 7,

1819, in Utica, N. Y. She d. Feb. 4, 1890; buried in Bucyrus, Ohio.

Children:

82.   I.   Isaac W. Bryant, b. Feb. 17, 1845; d. Mar. 16, 1845.

83.   II.   Katharine Bryant, b. Jan. 10, 1847; m. Richard Carter+

84.   III.   Frederick Bryant, b. Mar. 3, 1848; d. Aug. 3, 1849.

85.   IV.   John Quincy Bryant, b. Feb. 16, 1850; m. Emma Wheeler+

86.   V.   Maria Louisa Bryant, b. Mar. 28, 1852; d. Mar. 25, 1869.

87.   VI.   Ann Bryant, b. Oct. 5, 1854; d. Jan. 4, 1855.

88. VII.   Jeannie Bryant, b. Nov. 27, 1855; m. Frank J. Sheckler+

89. VIII.   Charles Post Bryant, b. Nov. 27, 1855+

90.   IX.   Benjamin Franklin Bryant, b. May 29, 1858; m. Mar. 17, 1880, ELLA MAY DE LANCY, who was b. Jan., 1863, at Shiloh, Ohio; dau. of Joseph De Lancy and Rebecca Deurdorff. Occupation, carpenter; Democrat. Res., Heyburn, Idaho.

Isaac Bryant served in the War of 1812. He was a very extensive stock-raiser and meat-packer in Columbus, Ohio. He sustained a heavy loss in 1844, when his extensive packing houses were washed away by a flood. In 1845 he purchased a farm near Wyandot and engaged in stock-raising and shipping, which occupied his time until his death. His children were educated by a governess in the home.

Mrs. Bryant was the daughter of Frederick Fisher, who was born in Elsasse, France. He was a ropemaker, and made the kite-cord that carried the first wire across the Niagara Falls for the first suspension bridge. The kite was made of silk and was ten feet long. Her mother was ...... Quigley, born in Ireland.

62

JOSEPH BRYANT[6] (David[5] [37], Simeon,[4] Cornelius,[3] Pieter Cornelisse,[2] Cornelis[1]), b. Apr. 14, 1788, in Springfield, N. J.; d. May 22, 1867, at Salem, Franklin Co., Tenn.; m. Jan. 13,

JOSEPH BRYANT

1813, in Bethany, Va., to DORATHY CAMPBELL, b. July 27, 1793, at Market Hill, Armaugh Co., Ireland. Dau. of Thomas Campbell and Jane Carneigle.

Children:

91.   I.   Jane Bryant, b. ......; m. Samuel Grafton+
92.   II. Thomas Campbell Bryant, b. ......, 1818; m. Eliza Chapman+
93.   III. Joseph William Cullen Bryant, b. Nov. 13, 1824; m. Elizabeth Postlewaite+
94.   IV. Alexander Campbell Bryant, b. Oct. 8, 1828; m. (1st) Jenevieve Gallager; m. (2nd) Mary Calvert Berry+

Thomas Campbell was a member of the celebrated Campbell clan of Scotland, and Duke of Argyle. He sailed from Ireland for America with his family. They were shipwrecked off the coast of Scotland, so returned and spent the winter in Glasgow, where his son Alexander attended the University. They came to United States the following spring and lived in Bethany, Burke County, Virginia, where he and his son Alexander established Bethany College and became the founders of the Christian Disciple Church. In 1832 Alexander Campbell went into Kentucky where he established the new faith. Dorathy Campbell Bryant died December 12, 1861, in Indianapolis, Indiana. She was a woman of fine intellect, and was called a better theologian than her brother Alexander, the great teacher, and bequeathed to her descendants fine intellectual and physical strength. Joseph Bryant was a very extensive farmer and stock-raiser. A strong Whig and Republican. He was a friend of John Brown, whom he met at Pleasant Hill Seminary, Washington County, Pennsylvania, and planned ways and means for aiding negroes to escape by means of the "Under ground Railroad." He was a prominent member of the Campbellite or Christian Church and was the first member baptized by the Rev. Alexander Campbell. The baptism took place in Owl Creek on the Bryant Farm in Washington County, Pennsylvania.

63
SAMUEL D. BRYANT,[6] (David[5] [37], Simeon,[4] Cornelius,[3] Pieter Cornelisse,[2] Cornelis[1]), b. Jan. 25, 1790, in Buffalo Twp.,

Washington Co., Pa.; d. Feb. 23, 1875, near Hebron, Ind.; m. (1st) MARY ROSS of Washington Co., Pa.   She was b. Aug. 14, 1799; d. Mar. 23, 1825, in Washington Co., Pa.; m. (2nd) JOANNA WOODRUFF, who was b. 1802 in Green Co., Pa.; d. Apr. 2, 1840, near Crown Point, Ind.; m. (3rd) in 1843, near Crown Point, Ind., SARAH ANN (Davis) YOUNG of Lake Co., Ind.   She d. 1874, near Lowell, Ind.

Children:

95.   I.   David E. Bryant, b. Mar. 3, 1819; d. unm. Apr. 13, 1846, at Crown Point, Ind., of typhoid fever.
96.   II.   Sarah Ann Bryant, b. Oct. 15, 1820; m. Harvey Sanger+
97.   III.   Samuel Ross Bryant, b. Nov. 27, 1822; m. Isabelle Lomax+
      Children of 2nd marriage:
98.   IV.   Mary Bryant, b. ......, 1827; d. Oct. 13, 1829, near Cresline, Ohio.
99.   V.   Jacob C. Bryant, b. Nov. 26, 1828; m. Adelia Frances Tyler+
100.   VI.   Hannah Bryant, b. Jan. 18, 1831; m. Eli Marion Robertson+
101. VII.   Harvey W. Bryant, b. Jan. 8, 1833; m. Lucretia Dowd+
102. VIII.   Isaac C. Bryant, b. Mar. 11, 1836; m. Harriet Pearce+
103.   IX.   Jane Bryant, b. Jan. 26, 1838; m. John Statler+
104.   X.   Joanna Bryant, b. Apr. 2, 1840; m. Edward Ruthven Beebe+

The boyhood days of Samuel D. Bryant were spent on a farm. He was taught the tanner's trade, but, due perhaps to his love for horses, he spent more of his early life as a teamster than tanner. As a teamster over the Allegheny Mountains he encountered dangers that might have ended disastrously had it not been for his marked skill as a horseman.   Later in life he was clerk for his uncle, Lieutenant Colonel Abram Roll Woolley, at the Arsenal near Pittsburgh.   He served well in that capacity.   He was enlisted in the War of 1812, but was never mustered into service. A few years later he was married to Mary Ross.   In 1829 Samuel Bryant, with his second wife, Joanna Woodruff, and their two

SAMUEL BRYANT

children, Mary and Jacob, left the Pennsylvania farm and moved to Ohio, where he continued his occupation of farming and stock-raising. Possessed with the spirit of change, in the spring of 1835, accompanied by his brothers, Simeon and David, and a brother-in-law named Agnew, he moved his family to Indiana. They settled in Pleasant Grove, on what was later known as the Jones' place, seven and a half miles south of Crown Point. In the fall they were joined by Elias Bryant, thus forming what was known as the "Bryant Settlement." In the fall of 1848 Samuel returned to Ohio and lived on his brother Isaac's farm, being his partner in the raising of stock and grain. Here he remained until the spring of 1857, when he again removed to Indiana and bought a farm south of South East Grove, near Hebron, where he lived until 1874 when he sold his farm, broke up housekeeping, and went to live with his stepson, John Young. Here in the fall his wife died. He then made his home with his daughter, Hannah Robertson, until his death in 1875 at the age of 85 years. Although he was a man of great physical endurance, his death was caused by exposure. Throughout life he seemed possessed of untiring industry and great resoluteness. In politics he was a Democrat until 1840, then a Whig, and later a Republican.

65
MARY BRYANT,[6] (David[5] [37], Simeon,[4] Cornelius,[3] Pieter Cornelisse,[2] Cornelis[1]), b. Mar. 25, 1793 at Van Buren, Washington Co., Pa.; d. Aug. 9, 1846; m. Oct. 17, 1812, at the home farm to SYLVANUS COOPER, who was b. Dec. 27, 1789, near Van Buren, Pa.; d. Apr. 10, 1873, in Winfield, Iowa.

Children:

105.	I.	Zebulon Cooper, b. Nov. 2, 1813; m. Sarah Nicely+
106.	II.	Catharine Cooper, b. Apr. 20, 1815; m. Harvey Gamble+
107.	III.	David Bryant Cooper, b. Apr. 17, 1817; m. Hannah Dille+
108.	IV.	Jane Cooper, b. Feb. 27, 1819; m. Thomas Hanna+
109.	V.	Mary Cooper, b. Feb. 23, 1821; m. John Atkinson+
110.	VI.	Sarah Cooper, b. Dec. 20, 1822; m. Ralph Vankirk+

111. VII.   James Monroe Cooper, b. Nov. 28, 1824; d. Dec. 14, 1826.

112. VIII. Elizabeth Cooper, b. Sept. 29, 1826; m. John Nelson Day+

113. IX.   Caroline Cooper, b. June 27, 1828; m. Edward Gallatin Vaile+

114. X.   Charles White Cooper, b. Mar. 18, 1830; m. Sarah F. Duyckink+

115. XI.   John Cooper, b. Feb. 11, 1832; m. Lucy M. Harris+

116. XII.   Henrietta Barclay Cooper, b. Dec. 18, 1835; m. Mar. 1, 1893, Mr. Edmunds. She was a graduate of Washington Female Seminary, Washington, Pa. She taught in public schools of Ohio and Illinois for several years. The writer remembers with gratitude the impress of culture she left upon her young life. June 6, 1857, Henrietta B. Cooper united with the First Presbyterian Church of Lane (Rochelle), Ill. She d. Sept. 12, 1897, at her home in Avalon, Mo.

Two brave youths who had the courage to face the enemy in battle for liberty, during the war of the Revolution, had at the close of the war the fortitude to meet the savage in the unsettled wilds of Western Pennsylvania. One of these young men, Zebulon Cooper, a soldier in the Continental troops of New York, lured by the promise of a goodly land, crossed the Allegheny Mountains in 1777 with his father's family and his young wife, Mary White Cooper. Some of the company traveled by horseback. Moses Cooper, father of Zebulon, failed to reach the journey's end — died on the way — and was buried at Waynesburg, Pennsylvania. Zebulon Cooper reached his destination and on October 11, 1793, was enabled to purchase of George Atkinson a large tract of land on the north fork of Ten Mile Creek near Prosperity, Pennsylvania. For this tract of land he paid five hundred fifty pounds. As was customary, it was surveyed by blazing trees, the purchaser obtaining as much land for a given price as could be "stepped off," and trees blazed to mark boundaries, within a given time. The savages were not the only dangers these pioneers had to encounter: there were also the wild beasts of the forest. One day when Zebulon

Virtus omnia Nobilitat

The Armorial Bearings of

The Family of

HERRICK

Cooper and wife, with their babe Sylvanus, were returning to their home and nearing the house, they saw a huge bear in a sycamore tree in the yard. Mr. Cooper hastened into the house for his gun, shot the bear, and the skin served as a rug for several years. This babe SYLVANUS, when grown to manhood, married MARY BRYANT, daughter of DAVID BRYANT (37), the New Jersey youth who entered the Continental army at nineteen, served five years, married Catherine Woolley. About 1789 they crossed the Allegheny Mountains and settled in Morris Township, Washington County, Pennsylvania, a neighbor to Zebulon Cooper. He later removed to Buffalo Township. The marriage of Mary Bryant and Sylvanus Cooper was a social event of importance. The young ladies, of whom there were a large number in attendance, were all dressed in white. The festivities included the "infare" the following day at the home of the bridegroom. The dinner was an important part of this event, cooked in an open fireplace, the bread baked in a "Dutch oven." After the marriage they began life on a large farm called "Pheasant's Resort," an inheritance from his father. It was located on the north fork of the Ten Mile Creek adjoining lands of John and Thomas Atkinson and Charles Cracraft. In his youth Sylvanus Cooper studied for the ministry, but a growing family claimed his attention and he never entered the profession. For many years he was an elder in the Presbyterian Church. In 1864 he entered into the mercantile business in Washington, Pennsylvania. Mary Bryant Cooper was a woman of noble character who lived a life of sacrifice for her loved ones. She possessed a ripe Christian character which left its impress upon the sons and daughters who were committed to her care. Mr. Cooper was of Puritan ancestry.

NOTE.—Wm. Arthur, in his Etymological Dictionary, says the name Cooper (Copier) is of Scottish origin, derived from Co, high, a beacon fire or signal for ships; Pyre origin of pier, a wharf, landing place.

The following is the Cooper line: John Cooper[1] at the age of 41 came from Olney, Buckinghamshire, England, in 1635 in the *Hopewell* to Lynn, Massachusetts, with his wife Wibroe, and children, Mary,[2] aged 13, John[2] 10, Thomas[2] 7, and Martha[2] 5. He was one of the elders of the church when it was organized at Lynn, and owned 200 acres of land in that township. He was one of the twenty heads of families who formed the association for the

settlement of Southampton in 1639. The emigrant ancestor John[1]
had son John[2] born in England in 1625, who had son James[3] who
was made a justice of the peace in Southampton, Long Island, and
who was Judge James Cooper until his death in 1722. James[3] had
son James[4] born about 1700; died about 1753. He married Abigail
. . . ., who died about 1734, aged 32; he married, second, Mary . . . .,
and had children, James,[5] Zebulon,[5] Stephen,[5] Moses,[5] Elizabeth,[5]
Ezekial,[5] Silas,[5] Benjamin,[5] Philip,[5] Abigail,[5] Mary[5] and Selah.[5]
These are mentioned in the will of the father. Moses[5] married
Mary Coleman, or as some claim, Mary Doty. Coleman is an ancient
Anglo-Saxon name, mentioned by Bede; is in Doomsday Book.
The widow of Moses Cooper lived with her son about six miles southeast of Washington, Pennsylvania, where at an advanced age she
died and was buried in what is known as the Red Brick Churchyard near Dunn Station, Washington County, Pennsylvania.
Moses had son Zebulon, who had son Sylvanus. Twenty-four
families of the Cooper name are mentioned in Burke's General
Armory as bearing coats of arms. Zebulon Cooper,[6] son of Moses
and father of Sylvanus,[7] served in Third Company, Third Regiment, of New York troops, commanded by Colonel James Clinton,
Revolutionary War. His name appears on the muster roll of that
company dated August 9, 1775, which shows: "Time of enlistment, July 25, ...; age twenty years; born So. Hampton; stature
five feet six inches; light complexion with light hair." His name
also appears on a roll of the organization mentioned, dated Camp
at Lake George, October 15, 1775, covering the period from June
28 to October 15, 1775, with remarks: "A Private. Sick at So.
Hampton." His name last appears on a pay-roll of Captain John
Hulbert's company, "of ye 3d Regt. of New York Forces," commanded by Colonel James Clinton, for the period from September
to December 31, 17 . ., with remarks: "time of entry Sept. 1, 17 . .;
Time due four mos. A Private."— By authority of Secretary of
War. F. T. Ainsworth, Chief, Record and Pension Office.

The WHITE ancestry is as follows: "Sylvanus Cooper,[7] who married Mary Bryant, was the son of Zebulon Cooper,[6] and Mary
White.[7] Her emigrant ancestor was Thomas White,[1] born 1599
in England; lived at Weymouth, Massachusetts; died 1679. His
son, John White,[2] went to Southampton, Long Island, in 1644.
He had wife Ann, and children: John,[3] Sarah,[3] Hannah,[3] wife of

BEAU MANOR—HERRICK ESTATE

Captain Thomas Topping, James,[3] Martha,[3] wife of Captain John Howell, Abigail,[3] wife of Abraham Howell, Esther,[3] wife of Samuel Clark. James White[3] married November 24, 1675, Ruth Stratton of East Hampton, Long Island. He died August 21, 1694. He had son, Captain Ephraim White,[4] who married Sarah Herrick,[12] daughter of William Herrick.[11] Ephraim White[4] died January 2, 1752. This Captain Ephraim White[4] and Sarah Herrick White had the following descendants: John White,[5] who had son John White,[6] who had daughter Mary White,[7] who was the wife of Zebulon Cooper.[6] There are 74 English families of this name White mentioned by Burke as bearing coats of arms. Other authority makes mention of one hundred and eleven families of White name as bearing coats of arms. The name White is derived from Anglo-Saxon *hwit* (Albus) or more probably from *hwita*, a sharpener, swordsmith or armorer.—LOWER.

Descendants of Sarah Herrick, who married Captain Ephraim White[4] will be interested in the following record of Herricks (Eyryk, Eric, Erik, Ericke, Herik, Heyrick): This ancient family claim descent from Ericke, a Danish chief who invaded Britain during the reign of Alfred. They settled in East Anglia. He is recognized in history as "Ericke, king of those Danes who held the country of East Angle." The first of whom we have record in direct line is ...... EYRYK,[1] the Dane of East Anglia Britain (mentioned by early English historians) whose descendant Eric the Forester was a resident in Leicestershire, England, at the time of the Norman Invasion. This Erick the Forester was in possession of extensive domains along the sources of the Severn and on the borders of Wales. Erick raised an army to repel the invaders, and he bore a prominent and conspicuous part in dispossessing the Normans of their recent conquest. Failing in this, he was stripped of his wealth, but was taken into favor by William the Conqueror and entrusted with important offices, and in his old age permitted to retire to his house in Leicestershire, where he died. This Erick the Forester is not in our *direct* line. The second in line was HENRY EYRYK of Great Stretton, of Leicester; then JOHN EYRYK[3] of Stretton; ROBERT EYRYK[4] of Stretton, who had wife Joanna; Sir WILLIAM EYRYK,[5] Knight of Stretton, was commissioned to attend the Prince of Wales on his expedition into Gascony in 1355; ROBERT EYRICKE[6] of Houghton, 1450, wife Agnes; THOMAS EYRICK,[7] gentleman of Houghton, and is the first of the name on the books of the corporation where he is recorded as a member of that body in 1511; will proved in Leicester; buried in St. Martin's Church, Leicester; NICHOLAS EYRICK[8] of Houghton; freeman 1535; mayor of Leicester 1552. He bought a "tabernacle" where the church goods of St. Martin's were sold at the Reformation in 1547, paying 2s., 8d. for same; THOMAS EYRICK[9] was chamberlain of Leicester; will proved at Leicester 1625; buried June 8, 1625; JAMES HERRICK,[10] baptized September 11, 1603. Lucius C. Herrick in his revised Herrick Genealogy says that the date of the birth of the James Herrick,[10] son of Thomas Herrick,[9] alias Eyrick of Leicestershire, England, is identical with the date of the birth of James Herrick of Southampton, Long Island; and Jedediah Herrick Genealogy says, "No other James is found in England or America answering to the time." Howell in his History of Southampton states the following: "This (Southampton) family is without question descended from the Herricks of Leicestershire in England, as the crest of that family is engraved on the tombstone of William Herrick,[11] the son of James Herrick,[10] the first of the name in Southampton. This is said because at the time of the death of William Herrick,[11] 1736, men in this country had not begun to use arms, as they did at a later period and do now, to which they are not entitled. This William Herrick,[11] born 1654, was the father of SARAH HERRICK,[12] wife of Captain Ephraim White,[4] who died January 2, 1752. This Sarah is twelfth in line of descent; the thirteenth in the Herrick line of descent is John White,[13] son of Sarah Herrick[12] and Ephriam White.[4] John White,[13] who had wife Jerusha; fourteenth, John White,[14] who had daughter Mary White,[15] wife of Zebulon Cooper, and their son Sylvanus Cooper[16] married Mary Bryant.

Sir William Herrick, grandson of Thomas of Houghton, was a member of Parliament from 1601 to 1630; was a successful courtier and politician; was commissioned by Queen Elizabeth on an important embassy to the Ottoman Porte, and as a reward for his success with the hitherto intractable Turk, he was appointed to a situation in the Exchequer, which he held through the remainder of Queen Elizabeth's reign and the following reign of James. He acquired great wealth. He early purchased the estate of the unfortunate Earl of Essex at Beau Manor Park in the parish of Loughboro and County of Leicester, which is still in possession of

SIMEON BRYANT

his descendants in the direct line and has been for 250 years the headquarters of the Herrick race. Following is the Herrick coat-of-arms: "*to their posteritie forever*, a certeyne crest or badge, namelie: on a wreathe of their couloures a bull's head argent, yssuing forthe of a laurell garland. The mussel, eares and horncs tipped sable. To be annexed and borne with their aunciept coat-of-armes, which is silver, a fesse verray, orr and gules." The two horizontal lines composing the center of escutcheon is emblamatic of the military girdle worn around the body over the armor. Motto: "Virtus omnia nobilitat" (all virtue is noble).

James Herrick, of 1603–1687, married Martha Topping, daughter of Thomas Topping, who was in Milford in 1639 and was a rcfugee to America from religious persecution in England. Following is Topping coat-of-arms: Azure, ten lozenges, four, three, two, one argent. *Crest:* Two lion's gambs, sable holding up a roundel vair.

66

SIMEON BRYANT,[6] (David[5] [37], Simeon,[4] Cornelius,[3] Pieter Cornelisse,[2] Cornelis[1]), b. Apr. 26, 1795, Washington Co., Pa.; d. Oct. 24, 1872, at Hebron, Ind.; m., 1831, ELIZABETH MC-CAULEY, dau. of James McCauley and Margaret Reeder, of Lancaster, Ohio.

Children:

117.   I.   Willis Bryant, b. and d. in infancy.
118.   II.   Joseph Bryant, b. Aug. 20, 1834; m. Mary Lane+
119.   III.   Margaret J. Bryant, b. Apr. 16, 1837; m. John King
              Blackstone+
120.   IV.   James Edmund Bryant, b. Mar. 5, 1839; m. Sarah
              S. Pratt+
121.   V.   David L. Bryant, b. April 20, 1841; m. Ruth A.
              Barney+
122.   VI.   Elias Bryant, b. Mar. 5, 1843; m. Fanny Adams+
123.   VII.   Harriett Elizabeth Bryant, b. May 10, 1845; d. Feb.
              23, 1858.

Mr. Bryant received a common school education in Washington County, Pennsylvania; moved to Sandusky, Ohio, where he married. In the winter of 1835 he started with his family in wagons for Indiana. They came to the new country inhabited only by Indians, and for a time lived in a wigwam until a log house could be made. They settled one and a half miles from Hebron, Indiana, then only an Indian village. They had no trouble with the Indians, for Mr. Bryant and his wife were always kind to them. Before the railroads were constructed they hauled their grain and produce to Chicago and Michigan City, receiving $1.50 per hundredweight for hogs. Simeon was of a very kind disposition, always avoiding trouble and ever ready to see the bright side of life.

Mr. Bryant took up 160 acres of government land near what is now Hebron, Indiana, as shown by the following Preëmption Certificate issued June 25, 1841.

Preëmption Certificate
No. 11857

THE U. S. OF AMERICA

To All to Whom These Presents Shall Come, Greeting:

Whereas, SIMEON BRYANT, of Porter County, Indiana, has deposited in the General Land Office of the U. S. a certificate of Register of the Land Office at Laporte, whereby it appears that full payment has been made by said SIMEON BRYANT according to act of Congress of the 24 of Apr., 1820, for the South E. quarter of Section twenty-two, Township 33, North of Range 7 West, in the District of Lands subj. to sale at Laporte, Ind., containing one hundred and sixty acres according to the official plat of the survey of the said Lands returned to the General Land Office by the Surveyor General, which said tract has been purchased by the said Simeon Bryant.

Now Know Ye, That the U. S. of A., in consideration of the Premises, and in conformity with the several acts of Congress in such case made and provided, *have given and granted*, and by these presents, *do give and grant* into the said Simeon Bryant & to his heirs the said tract above described, *to have and to hold* the same, together with all rights and privileges, immunities of whatever nature, belonging unto said Simeon Bryant and to his heirs and assigns forever.

In Testimony Whereof, I, John Tyler, President of the U. S. of A., have caused these letters to be made *patent* & the *seal* of the *General Land Office* to be hereunto affixed.

DAVID BRYANT

Given under my hand at the City of W...... the 25 day of
June, 1841, and of the Independence of U. S. the 65.
[SEAL] *By the Pres.*, JOHN TYLER,— R. Tyler, Sec.
I. Williamson, Rec. of Gen. Land Office.
Rec. Vol. 25, page 33.

67
DAVID BRYANT,[6] (David,[5] [37], Simeon,[4] Cornelius,[3] Pieter
Cornelisse,[2] Cornelis[1]), b. May 12, 1797, near Washington, Pa.;
d. May 23, 1874, near Erie, Neosho Co., Kan.; m. (1st) RACHEL
ADAMS at Wyandot, Ohio, who was b. Oct. 29, 1798, in Ohio;
d. Apr., 1835; buried at Pleasant Grove cemetery, Lake Co.,
Ind. She was the dau. of John Adams. David Bryant m.
(2nd) MARGARET STEINBROOK, who died in 1849. He m. (3rd)
MERCY AMELIA RANSOM, b. Mar. 1, 1814, at Cicero, N. Y.; d.
Mar. 29, 1865; buried at Boyd's Grove, Ill.

Children 1st m.:
124.   I.   Isaac Bryant, b. Mar. 29, 1823; m. Amelia Carter+
125.   II. Nancy Bryant, b. Sept. 25, 1825; m. William Fisher+
       Children 2nd m.:
126.   III. John William Bryant, b. Apr. 27, 1839. He lived
            in his father's home until he reached manhood.
            He went across the Rocky Mountains with a
            drove of horses, and was not heard from for
            many years; finally word came that he had
            been killed by highwaymen.

127.   IV. James Harrison Bryant, b. Apr. 24, 1841; m. Minnie
            May Hodges+
128.   V.   Joseph Allen Bryant, b. May 24, 1842; m. Ida Kate
            Flanner+
129.   VI. Daniel Steinbrooke Bryant, b. Mar. 15, 1844; m.
            Frances Cooke+
130.   VII. David Bryant, b. Nov. 15, 1846; m. Laura White+
131. VIII. George Bryant, b. Apr. 5, 1849; d. July 25, 1849.
           Child 3rd m.:
132.   IX. Orah Alice Bryant, b. June 27, 1854; m. William B.
            Doddridge+

David Bryant spent the early part of his life on the farm near Washington, Pennsylvania, and later moved with his parents to Fredericktown, Ohio.

David Bryant's early life possessed much of a roving nature. He made money easily and could have amassed a fortune, but was always going into new countries, building a good home, and then a desire for a change would come, and they would move onward, usually into the frontier.

He had many experiences with Indians, who were numerous in the settlements at that time. One day he and a friendly Indian were sitting on a log, and the Indian said to Mr. Bryant, "Move along," so he moved along. "Move along," said the Indian and kept crowding against Mr. Bryant. "Why," said he, "you will push me off." The Indian then said, "That is what the white man is doing to the Indian, pushing him off all the time."

At another time when Mr. Bryant and family were moving from Illinois to Missouri, in 1837, and had almost reached their destination, they came to a large stream which they were obliged to ford; it had raised in the night until it was dangerous to cross, but the party was unaware of that and started their teams into the swollen stream. One of the horses fell, and in plunging about to extricate himself from the wagon, turned it over with all of the occupants penned in under the cover. In this wagon were Mrs. Bryant, her sister Mrs. Nevitt, Nancy, and two children (John and Mrs. Bryant's little sister). Nancy broke the cover loose and got on top of the overturned wagon, and the two women followed and held to the sides while they were fast going down stream. Shortly the little girl, Sarah Ann Steinbrooke, came to the surface and Nancy caught her by the dress and held her while they floated a quarter of a mile. She also took John from her step-mother's arms, supposing he was dead also, but he afterwards was resuscitated. Help came after they had gone nearly a mile and the lives of all were saved except that of the little girl.

At another time while living in Missouri, a large party of Indians were being taken across the Mississippi River; they camped several days near Mr. Bryant's home, and they would trade their supplies for food, etc. One day Nancy, then a child, took a basket of apples to trade for beads, and an Indian boy demanded an apple, but offered nothing in return. Nancy refused to part with her fruit without

HANNAH BRYANT MITCHELL

MATHEW MITCHELL

the necessary payment, which angered the young redskin. His sister saw his movements and called to Nancy to jump, which she did, and had no sooner gotten behind a tree when an arrow went whizzing past her, shot by the boy. He received a severe whipping from his father and did not get any apples.

Mr. Bryant encountered many hardships in new countries, but his taste for adventure seemed to be a part of his nature and he always made plenty of friends, a good living, and seemed to enjoy life to a good old age, dying at the age of seventy-seven years from paralysis.

68

HANNAH BRYANT,[6] (David[5] [37], Simeon,[4] Cornelius,[3] Pieter Cornelisse,[2] Cornelis[1]), b. Apr. 16, 1799, near Bethel, Washington Co., Pa.; m., 1818, to MATHEW BLACK MITCHELL, who was b. 1794 in Wheeling, W. Va.; d. ......, 1879; buried in Lima, Ohio. Hannah d. Jan. 1, 1879, at the home of her dau. Hannah Larminie in Chicago; buried at Lima, Ohio, in Maplewood cemetery.

Mr. Mitchell was a farmer; adherent of the Presbyterian faith. He enlisted for service in the Civil War, but was rejected by the recruiting officer because of disability. At the first draft for soldiers he offered again and was again rejected. When the Civil War broke out Mr. and Mrs. Mitchell had eight sons old enough and young enough to enlist; five offered themselves for their country's defense in the Union army, and three were accepted in the Ninth Indiana regiment. The children were all born in Richland County, Ohio. Burke's General Armory gives 25 families of the name of Mitchell as bearing coats of arms.

Children:

133. I. David Mitchell, b. Sept. 13, 1820; m. Mary Merriman+

134. II. Eliza Ann Mitchell, d. at the age of thirteen years.

135. III. Robert Mitchell, b. Sept. 8, 1825; m. Mary Forbs+

136. IV. Catherine Woolley Mitchell, b. Sept. 8, 1825; m. in 1852, Rev. Matthew Clark, who died Feb. 1, 1902. Resided in Boston and Chicago.

No children. She was an artist of ability and left many fine paintings in possession of her sister, Mrs. Hannah Larminie.

137. V. Jane Mitchell, d. aged thirteen months.
138. VI. Simeon Mitchell, b. Sept. 11, 1826; m. Isabel Mitchell+
139. VII. Joseph Mitchell, b. Dec. 31, 1831; m. Anna Catharine McVicker+
140. VIII. John Bryant Mitchell, b. Mar. 24, 1833; m. Olive Wilson+
141. IX. Torrence Mitchell, m. Sarah Martin+
142. X. Matthew C. Mitchell, b. in 1837; unm. Served in Civil War. He died at the age of thirty-nine in Nevada, O.
143. XI. Hannah Abigail Mitchell, b. Feb. 25, 1840; m. Samuel H. Larminie+
144. XII. Isaac C. Mitchell, b. Apr. 17, 1842; unm. He served as a Union soldier in the Civil War, and died soon after the close of the war and is buried at Clinton, Mo.

69

ELIZABETH BRYANT,[6] (David[5] [37], Simeon,[4] Cornelius,[3] Pieter Cornelisse,[2] Cornelis[1]), b. Mar. 13, 1801, Washington, Pa.; d. Feb. 22, 1886; m. Apr. 22, 1824, in Fredericktown, Ohio, CHARLES CRACRAFT POST, who was b. July 27, 1800, at Claysville, Pa.; d. Mar. 28, 1884; buried at Spencerville, Ohio. He was the son of Jeremiah Post and Martha Cracraft, dau. of Major Charles Cracraft, who served in the war of the Revolution. In politics, Mr. Post was a Republican; in religion a Methodist; occupation, a millwright.

Children:

145. I. Asher Taylor Post, b. Apr. 10, 1825; d. Aug. 10, 1829.
146. II. Martha Post, b. Aug. 7, 1827; m. Cyrus Hart Hover+
147. III. Bryant Post, b. July 25, 1830; d. May 11, 1831.
148. IV. Leonidas Hamline Post, b. Aug. 9, 1832; m. Eliza Jane Stewart+

ELIZABETH BRYANT POST

149.   V.   Adam Clark Post, b. Nov. 2, 1834; m. 1st Isabelle
             Martin; m. (2nd) Lucy Frost; m. 3rd Eliza
             J. Rawles+
150. VI.   Isaac Bryant Post, b. June 21, 1837; m. Emma
             Berry+
151. VII.   Charles Graham Post, b. Dec. 31, 1839; m. Maria
             Rockwell+
152. VIII. Harvey Post, b. Feb. 9, 1845; d. Mar. 31, 1846.

Mr. and Mrs. Post were among the pioneers of Ohio. Mr. Post
was a millwright and built and operated for a number of years the
present grist mill now on the Auglaize River, known in the past as
the Post mills, but at present as the Tone's mills. After disposing
of his mill he bought a large tract of land one mile west of the
Auglaize River on the Lima and Spencerville road, which he
improved, and here he resided until a short time previous to his
death, spending the last few months in the home of his daughter,
Mrs. Martha Hover. In politics Mr. Post was a Republican and
took an active part in the local and political issues of the past, and
was sent to represent Allen County in the General Assembly of
the state of Ohio in 1856-8, in which he honored himself and his
constituents. Mr. and Mrs. Post were both born in the same
neighborhood in Washington County, Pennsylvania, and thus had
known each other since childhood. They were married in Ohio,
and this marriage tie remained unbroken for almost sixty years
when death claimed the husband. Father Post, as he was familiar-
ly called, was noted for his charity. The poor never suffered in his
neighborhood. No man was turned away from his door hungry.
Mrs. Elizabeth Post was a quiet woman, domestic in her tastes,
but of very decided character. She was an excellent housekeeper
and very industrious. In person she was small, quite short of
stature, of fair complexion and blue eyes. Their home was the
stopping place of the Methodist preachers and quarterly meeting
occasions were times for the gathering of the members of the pioneer
churches. Their three younger sons served in the Union army
during the Civil War. Isaac Bryant, and Charles Graham enlisted
in the "three months' service." After being mustered out of the
service, Isaac re-enlisted in the Thirty-second Ohio Infantry and
Charles in the Fourth Ohio Cavalry. An older brother, Adam
Clark, enlisted in the Eighty-first Ohio Infantry. All served until

the close of the war, when Isaac held the rank of major, Adam Clark that of lieutenant, and Charles that of corporal. All escaped without injury except Charles, who was shot in the knee in a skirmish while in Alabama. The surgery possible was very crude, the bullet being cut out by a veterinary surgeon with a razor. After a two weeks' stay in the hospital he reported for duty.

70

JACOB BRYANT,[6] (David[5] [37], Simeon,[4] Cornelius,[3] Pieter Cornelisse,[2] Cornelis[1]), b. Jan. 15, 1803, near Washington, Pa.; d. June 22, 1870; m. in 1828, JANE ANNE WELSH, who was b. Sept. 14, 1805, near Charleston, Va. She d. Jan. 15, 1875.

Children:

153.   I. Edmund Randolph Bryant, b. Jan. 14, 1829; m. Mary Elizabeth Miller+
154.   II. Avis M. Bryant, b. ......; m. Joseph W. Stuckey+
155. III. Alford D. Bryant.
156.   IV. Isaac L. Bryant.
157.   V. Elizabeth D. Bryant.
158.   VI. Matthew M. Bryant.

Jacob Bryant removed with his parents to Knox County, Ohio, when twelve years old. They first settled in Dallas Township, then later they went to Scott Township, in Marion County. Jacob, by this time being a young man, started in the business of buying and selling stock, in which business he was successful. He used to drive large herds to Pittsburgh and Baltimore. At this time it was not uncommon to buy large herds and drive them to be fattened in the rich bottom lands of Scioto River below Columbus, where corn could then be purchased at ten cents a bushel. In 1833 Jacob and his family moved to Bucyrus, Ohio, where he entered the mercantile business on Main Street. Later he removed to La Timberville, about ten miles from Bucyrus, where he continued in the mercantile business. In 1838 he settled on his farm. It was then a portion of the Gillespie lands, which were regarded as the garden spot of the plains. Here Jacob transacted almost the whole stock business of the country and enjoyed the full confidence

NANCY BRYANT AGNEW

of the entire community. A singular illustration of the openness
of his dealings and of our peculiar financial condition at that time
is found in the account we have of an eye-witness. Mr. Bryant
would purchase from farmers their droves of hogs or herds of cattle
and having disposed of them would return with a bulky package of
several thousands of dollars in the promiscuous wild cat currency
of this and surrounding states. As farmers would call for the
money due them he would place this pile on the table and bid each
man select such money most satisfactory to himself, which each one
would proceed to do. Jacob was a good neighbor and an honorable
man in his worldly dealings. In politics he was a Whig and a
Republican, and in religion a Methodist. The last twenty years
of his life he was a partial invalid, caused by paralysis arising from
a fall from a horse while driving cattle. During these years he had
the most tender care of his wife and children. He was buried in his
family lot at Oakwood Cemetery, Bucyrus, Ohio. Mrs. Bryant
was a woman of remarkable physical vigor, retaining until within
a few months of her death the elasticity and activity of youth. She
was a faithful wife, an affectionate mother, and a woman who attended to her own affairs and was highly esteemed by all who knew
her.

72

NANCY BRYANT,[6] (David[5] [37], Simeon,[4] Cornelius,[3] Pieter
Cornelisse,[2] Cornelis[1]), b. Dec. 16, 1808, on the farm near Owl
Creek, Washington Co., Pa., which is of historical interest, for
here was founded the Campbellite or Christian Church. She
m. Dec. 5, 1827, in Mt. Vernon, Ohio, DAVID AGNEW, who d.
Apr. 15, 1835, at Pleasant Grove, Ind., and is buried at West-
ville, Ohio. She m. (2nd) JOHN GARDNER KELLER in 1840, at
Pleasant Grove, Ind. He was born in Washington Co., Pa.;
d. June 13, 1882. She d. July 4, 1884; buried in Winfield,
Iowa.

Children 1st m.:

159. I. Margaret Jane Agnew, b. Aug. 15, 1829; m. George
Henry Welsh+

160. II. Isaac Bryant Agnew, b. Sept. 11, 1831; m. Sarah
Dille+

161.   III.   Elizabeth Agnew, b. ...... 1833; m. Chester O.
Wellman+

162.   IV.   David Agnew, b. May, 4, 1835; m. Nancy E. Bright+
Children 2nd m.:

163.   V.   Martha Keller, b. Oct. ......, 1842; m. Edwin
. Lovejoy+

164.   VI.   Aurilia Keller, b. Oct. ......, 1844; m. Josiah Chapman.   She resides in Ovid, N. Y.

165.   VII.   Anna Elizabeth Keller, b. Jan. ......, 1846; m.
Henry W. Northrup+

166. VIII.   Gertrude Keller, b. Nov. ......, 1848; m. Ephriam
Cooper Andrew+ .

167.   IX.   John Keller, b. May, 1850; m. Hattie Jones+

168.   X.   Winfield Keller, b. July ......, 1852; unm.; d. 1883,
Independence, Iowa.

Agnew (from Agneau, French) means a *lamb*. Some of the
family came into England at a very early date, and some of them
accompanied Strongbow into Ireland. Others settled in Scotland,
where Sir Andrew Agnew was hereditary sheriff of Wigtonshire in
1452, which office the family retained about four hundred years.
Tradition says three brothers emigrated in the early part of the
eighteenth century to America from Great Britain. One of these
brothers settled in New Jersey, and two of them settled near
Gettysburg, Pennsylvania. The American genealogy of this
family begins with David Agnew, of Scotch descent, who was born
in New Jersey. Was a soldier of the Revolution. After the war
he moved to the vicinity of Washington, Pennsylvania; married
Ruth Maxwell; children, Jonathan, William, John, Jane, David,
and Cumie, who married Andrew Vance. A brother, William
Vance, married the above Jane Agnew.

73
JANE BRYANT,[6] (David[6] [37], Simeon,[4] Cornelius,[3] Pieter
Cornelisse,[2] Cornelis[1]), b. May 3, 1810; d. Dec. 24, 1889, at
Lathrop, Mo.; m. Nov. 13, 1828, near Fredericktown, Ohio,
MADISON WASHINGTON WELSH, who was b. Mar. 29, 1808, in
Virginia. He d. Apr. 18, 1883, in Lathrop, Mo.

JANE BRYANT WELSH

Children:

169.   I.   Bryant Welsh, b. Mar. 15, 1830; m. Sarah Margaret Stuckey+
170. II.   William St. Clair Welsh, b. July 13, 1832; m. Harriet Warner+
171. III.   George H. Welsh, b. Jan. 16, 1834; m. Amanda Foster+
172. VI.   Hannah Welsh, b. Oct. 3, 1836; m. Thomas Gillespie+
173.   V.   Emma Woolley Welsh, b. Sept. 28, 1840; d. Nov. 23, 1861.
174. VI.   Pauline Welsh, b. Apr. 1, 1842; m. John S. Stuckey+
175. VII.   John Bartrom Welsh, b. June 6, 1844; m. Louisa Flock+
176. VIII. Jane Amelia Welsh, b. July 7, 1850, Bucyrus, O; resides Woodward, Okla.; unm.

Mr. Welsh was an extensive farmer and stock-raiser; in politics a Democrat; in religious faith a Presbyterian. When five years of age, Jane Bryant removed with her parents from Washington County, Pennsylvania, to Fredericktown, Ohio, where they lived until she grew to womanhood. While attending the wedding of her brother Jacob Bryant and Jane Ann Welsh and festivities following, she met Madison Welsh, whom she married in 1828. She was eighteen years old and Madison twenty. She was of medium height, well-proportioned, very fair complexion, with rosy cheeks and even features and auburn hair. She had an unusual amount of self-respect and commanded the regard of all who knew her. It was a happy home and some of the children lingered, loath to occupy a home of their own. Her first home after her marriage was in Wyandot County, south of the town of Wyandot. At that time the Indians were numerous in that part of Ohio, they having a trail past the door, into which they rudely gazed, but never molested the young wife. In 1831 they moved to Bucyrus, which was a small town without railroads, the county seat of Crawford County. After living there a year and a half, they moved six miles south of Bucyrus. Two years later they moved onto land in Crawford County purchased from the government at a dollar and a half an acre, where they had a lovely home and a farm of eleven hundred acres. In early life, while living on the farm, the prairie

fires often raged and threatened their home and stock. The wife
by good management assisted in carrying the husband through a
financial crisis. In 1875 they moved to Upper Sandusky, at that
time a town of about five thousand inhabitants. In 1878 they
celebrated their fiftieth wedding anniversary. Two weeks later
from their home their son George was buried. Later Mr. and Mrs.
Welsh and their single daughter Jane went to Lathrop, Missouri,
where they remained until their passing away. Mrs. Welsh had
the care and raising of the children and oversight of the farm from
1834 until 1855, her husband being in the eastern cities, New York,
Philadelphia, and Lancaster, a great deal of the time. His stock
was driven over the road and he traveled by stage coach, which
consumed much time. Stock business was uncertain at that time
on account of the fluctuation of prices; also the keeping of large
droves in the city was expensive. After repeated reverses her
husband failed. It seems that the condition of their affairs finan-
cially was not known to the wife until the crash actually came.
The hard-working, saving and sacrificing companion faced poverty
with a large family, the daughters being young and unable to help
themselves and their parents. The two younger boys who were at
home came nobly to their rescue. Fortunately, Madison had
always been a liberal provider, which gave them plenty of material
with which to help along for a few years, and with the mother's
good management, and by all working together, the crisis was
passed.

76   SEVENTH GENERATION

ARTHUR VANCE BRYANT,[7] (Elias[6] [60], David,[5] Simeon,[4]
Cornelius,[3] Pieter Cornelisse,[2] Cornelis[1]), b. June 25, 1822,
near Fredricktown, Knox Co., Ohio; d. June 17, 1905, at
Peoria, Ill.; m. May 8, 1844, at Pleasant Grove, Lake Co., Ind.,
HENRIETTA HILL, dau. of Rufus Hill and Olive Humes, who
was b. Feb. 18, 1824, at Windham, Windham Co., Conn.; d.
Feb. 19, 1902; buried Lowell, Ind. In politics Mr. Bryant was
a Whig and afterwards a Republican, in religion a Methodist.
He is buried in Lowell, Ind.

Copy of land entry: "On August 14, 1845, Arthur V. Bryant
entered from the United States the southwest quarter of the south-

HOME OF SIMEON BRYANT, HEBRON, INDIANA, 1835

west quarter of section 17, township 33, range 8, 40 acres. His patent is dated May 10, 1848, but has never been recorded. He, with his wife Henrietta, conveyed this land to Elias Bryant on November 4, 1846, and on October 19, 1848, Elias Bryant conveyed the tract above mentioned to David, Robert, and John Bryant. On February 13, 1855, John Bryant of Eldorado County, California, conveyed to David Bryant and Robert Bryant the land together with another 80 acres in section 18 which they had purchased from James Andrews on March 13, 1854."

Children:

177. I. Mary M. Bryant, b. Aug. 31, 1845; d. Sept. 10, 1846.
178. II. John Arthur Bryant, b. Dec. 22, 1847; d. July 18, 1893; m. Eva Sutton.
179. III. Ann Eliza Bryant, b. Aug. 10, 1852; m. Albert Davis+
180. IV. Charles A. Bryant, b. May 2, 1854; d. Sept., 1855.
181. V. Mary P. Bryant, b. Sept. 10, 1856; d. Sept., 1857.
182. VI. Elias W. Bryant, b. Sept. 12, 1858; m. Anna E. Hayden+
183. VII. Ulysses S. Bryant, b. Oct. 17, 1868; m. Minnie K. Neehouse+

77

DAVID BRYANT,[7] (Elias[6] [60], David,[5] Simeon,[4] Cornelius,[3] Pieter Cornelisse,[2] Cornelis[1]), b. Sept. 20, 1824, in Knox Co., Ohio; d. Nov. 27, 1900; m. Oct. 21, 1858, at Hebron, Ind., MARY McGILL, who was b. Feb. 18, 1832; d. Jan., 1903; buried in Hebron Cemetery. They resided many years near Hebron, Ind. Mr. Bryant was a good farmer. Politics, Republican; religion, Presbyterian.

Child:

184. I. Annette May Bryant, b. Jan. 14, 1866; m. 1895, Charles Applegate, son of F. P. Applegate and Elizabeth Lackey. She graduated from the Valparaiso (Ind.) High School and taught in Porter Co., Ind. They reside on the old homestead where her father and mother spent their entire married lives. They have one

Child:

492.   I.   Bryant Applegate, b. Mar. 12, 1898; attending
               public school, Hebron, Ind.

78

ROBERT BRYANT,[7] (Elias[6] [60], David,[5] Simeon,[4] Cornelius,[3]
Pieter Cornelisse,[2] Cornelis[1]), b. Dec. 17, 1826, near Fredrick-
town, Knox Co., Ohio; d. Apr. 8, 1906; m. Sept. 20, 1853,
MARY JANE MERRISS, who was b. Sept. 15, 1833, in Bucyrus,
Ohio; dau. of Daniel R. Merriss and Sarah Nafus. She d.
May 8, 1867; buried Hebron, Ind. Two years later he m.
EMILY LINDLY, who d. Jan., 1905.

Children:

185.   I.   Daniel R. Bryant, b. May 9, 1854; m. Mary Lois
               Andrews+
186.   II.   Charles Bryant, b. Mar. 22, 1857; m. Endora
               Dilley+

Robert Bryant remained at home with his parents until twenty-
one years of age, after which he was employed for two years at the
low wages of $12.00 and $13.00 per month. At this early date
Ohio and Indiana were practically a tractless and almost uninhabited wilderness. When Robert was a boy of nine years his
father, Elias Bryant, accompanied by his family consisting of his
wife Ann and his five children, came to Lake County, Indiana, and
there settled. Railroads at this time had not extended so far west.
A journey which could now be made in a day was made by wagon
and required several weeks. The nearest mill was one hundred
and fifty miles distant, and it was necessary to go to Michigan City
to obtain supplies. Indians were very common and even years
later a few were to be found who were on intimate terms with their
paleface brothers. Robert's advantages were few for acquiring
an education, but he was a natural lover of books and had the
faculty of retaining what he once read; he thus became very well
informed. He and his brother purchased eighty acres of land
which were sold, together with a half interest in his father's farm,
when he moved to Porter County in 1854. Here with his brother
John he purchased 480 acres and later 100 acres more. This re-

Yours Truly
John Bryant

mained undivided until about 1861, after which he bought 40 acres
of farming land and 40 more acres of timber. He had at the time of
his death 310 acres of the finest land in the county, about a mile
and a half from Hebron. Both Mr. and Mrs. Bryant were members of the Methodist Episcopal church.

81

JOHN BRYANT,[7] (Elias[6] [60], David,[5] Simeon,[4] Cornelius,[3]
Pieter Cornelisse,[2] Cornelis[1]), b. July 20, 1833, in Richland Co.,
Ohio; m. Feb. 21, 1860, at Lowell, Ind., d. July 25, 1913,
MARY ANGELINE LAWRENCE, b. Dec. 28, 1840, in Berrien Co.,
Mich. She was the dau. of George W. Lawrence and Julia C.
Haskins. She d. Sept. 25, 1893; buried at Lowell, Ind. She
was a woman of most excellent traits of character.

Children:
187. I. Bertha A. Bryant, b. Feb. 20, 1861; m. Cassius C.
Phelps. She attended school at Lowell and
Crown Point, Ind. After the death of her
husband she entered the office as clerk of the
Baltimore and Ohio Railway, which position
she still holds. She is a member of the
Society of the Daughters of the American
Revolution. She resides at Windsor Park,
Chicago, Ill.
188. II. Luella C. Bryant, b. Aug. 22, 1862; m. (1st) John H.
Spittal; m. (2nd) Nelson H. Straight+
189. III. Marie Vance Bryant, b. July 21, 1867; m. Oscar G.
Trieglaff+
190. VI. Julia A. Bryant, b. Sept. 17, 187–; m. Ernest Hum-
mel+
191. V. John D. Bryant, b. Apr. 13, 1871; d. Mar. 6, 1874.

When Mr. Bryant removed with his parents to Indiana the
Pottawatomie tribe of Indians were about the only people in Lake
County at that time. He pursued his education in one of the
primitive log school houses found in the frontier settlements. He
attended school through the winter months until eighteen years of
age. In the summer season he was employed upon the home

farm, gaining practical knowledge and a broad experience concerning the best methods of promoting agricultural interests, which later brought him great success. In 1852 he crossed the plains to California with a horse team, traveling north of Salt Lake City on the old Kit Carson route. Here he remained until 1857 when he returned to the East by way of the Panama and Aspinwall route to New York, spending two days on the island of Cuba while en route. He went to Hebron to visit his brothers David and Robert and remained there and engaged in agricultural pursuits and merchandising in Lake County, Indiana, until 1880, when he located on a farm. In 1882 he again went to California to visit his relatives who had crossed the plains with him in 1852, thirty years before. He remained in the Golden State two months, when he again returned to Lowell and in the same year he removed to South Chicago and engaged in the grocery business, in which he continued for about three years. On the expiration of that period he again went to Lowell and resumed farming, which he has since followed. He had a valuable tract of land of one hundred and seventy acres, and the land is arable and highly cultivated, while many substantial improvements have been made on the farm which indicate his enterprising spirit. Mr. Bryant was a lifelong Republican, active in the work of his party and deeply interested in its success, yet never seeking or desiring office as a reward for party feality. He was a member of the Masonic fraternity at Lowell, Lodge No. 378, and of the Independent Order of Odd Fellows at South Chicago, Lodge No. 245; he was a member of the Methodist Episcopal church. His has been an eventful, useful, and interesting life history, for he was familiar with pioneer experiences in Indiana and in the Far West, and his mind was stored with many interesting reminiscences of his sojourn in the Golden State during the early days of its mining development.

83

KATHERINE BRYANT,[7] (Isaac[6] [61], David,[5] Simeon,[4] Cornelius,[3] Pietér Cornelisse,[2] Cornelis[1]), b. Jan. 10, 1847, Delaware, Ohio; m. Jan. 22, 1877, to RICHARD CARTER of Wellsville, Ohio, son of John Adams Carter and Mary D. Connell. Res., Upper Sandusky, Ohio. In politics a Republican; in religion a Presbyterian.

MARY A. BRYANT

Children:

192. I. May Bryant Carter, b. Nov. 27, 1877. She graduated from the High School of Upper Sandusky, Ohio, and later attended the university at Worcester, Ohio.

193. II. Martha Catherine Carter, b. June 3, 1887. She graduated from Upper Sandusky High School.

Katherine Bryant received her higher education at Steubenville Seminary, and attended the School of Design at Pittsburgh, Pennsylvania. Richard Carter was educated in Marion (Ohio) High School, at the Newell's Institute for Boys in Pittsburgh, and the Iron City Commercial College in Pittsburgh.

85
JOHN QUINCY BRYANT,[7] (Isaac[6] [61], David,[5] Simeon,[4] Cornelius,[3] Pieter Cornelisse,[2] Cornelis[1]), b. Feb. 16, 1850; m. EMMA WHEELER; d. Mar. 3, 1883.

Children:

194. I. Claude J. Bryant, b. Mar. 16, 1876; m. Bertha Smith+

195. II. Madge L. Bryant, b. May 13, 1877; m. CLARENCE MONTGOMERY of Coffeyville, Kan. Res., Asheville, N. C.

88
JEANNIE BRYANT,[7] (Isaac[6] [61], David,[5] Simeon,[4] Cornelius,[3] Pieter Cornelisse,[2] Cornelis[1]), b. Nov. 27, 1855 in Wyandot, Ohio; m. May 1, 1879, FRANK J. SHECKLER, who was b. July 14, 1857, at Bucyrus, Ohio; son of D. J. Sheckler and Charlotte. In politics a Republican. Res., Wyandot, Ohio. Mrs. Sheckler is a twin of Charles Post Bryant.

Children:

196. I. Edna E. Sheckler, b. July 6, 1880.
197. II. Maude E. Sheckler, b. Mar. 10, 1882.
198. III. Bryant V. Sheckler, b. June 15, 1888.

89

CHARLES POST BRYANT,[7] (Isaac[6] [61], David,[5] Simeon,[4] Cornelius,[3] Pieter Cornelisse,[2] Cornelis[1]), b. Nov. 27, 1855, in Wyandot, Ohio; unm.

He was educated in the public schools in Wyandot. His first teacher was his cousin Kate Grafton. He lived on the farm until 1880 when he removed to Bucyrus. In 1886 he went to Nebraska and preëmpted a tract of government land, proved up in 1887, and came back to Bucyrus. Appointed Deputy County Surveyor in May, 1893, and held the office until September, 1901, when he became County Surveyor. Also held office of City Engineer. Resides, Bucuyrus, Ohio.

91

JANE BRYANT,[7] (Joseph[6] [62], David,[5] Simeon,[4] Cornelius,[3] Pieter Cornelisse,[2] Cornelis[1]), b. ......; m. DR. SAMUEL GRAFTON, a physician of Kansas City, Mo.

Children:

199.   I.   Katherine Grafton, b. Jan. 1, 1839; m. Thomas M. Patterson+
200.   II. Mary Grafton; m. Simon Peckenpaw+
201.   III. Bryant Grafton, b. ......, 184..; m. Maria Harper+
202.   IV. Samuel Grafton; res., Denver, Colo. Member of press, Rocky Mountain News.

92

THOMAS CAMPBELL BRYANT,[7] (Joseph[6] [62], David,[5] Simeon,[4] Cornelius,[3] Pieter Cornelisse,[2] Cornelis[1]), b. 1818; m. ELIZA CHAPMAN. He was a graduate of Bethany College, Va., and a farmer in Illinois.

Children:

203.   I.   Clara Bryant.
204.   II. Jennie Bryant; m. Mr. Rathven, living in Kansas.
205.   III. Josephine Bryant.
206.   IV. Thomas Bryant, Jr.

207. V. Harry D. Bryant.
208. VI. Alexander Bryant.
209. VII. Dorothea Bryant; m. Mr. Stahl. They had two sons, Jack and Jill.
210. VIII. Frank Bryant.

93

JOSEPH WM. CULLEN BRYANT,[7] (Joseph[6] [62], David,[5] Simeon,[4] Cornelius,[3] Pieter Cornelisse,[2] Cornelis[1]), b. Nov. 12, 1824, Washington Co., Pa.; d. Aug. 26, 1911, Clifton Forge, Va.; m. ELIZABETH POSTLEWAITE, Apr. 18, 1849, in Racine. Lived several years in Tennessee. Occupation, stock-raising and farming, in Tennessee. and Ohio. He was a graduate of Bethany College. Res., Clifton Forge, Va.

Children:

211. I. Jean Carson Bryant, b. Feb. 17, 1850; m. John R. Miller, July 18, 1882+
212. II. William Postlewaite Bryant, b. Feb. 11, 1852.
213. III. Joseph Wm. Cullen Bryant, Jr., b. Jan. 28, 1854; m. Helen Bowles+
214. IV. John Isaac Bryant, b. Aug. 27, 1856; m. Paralee Lancaster+
215. V. Dorothea Lucinda Bryant, b. Apr. 5, 1861; unm.+
216. VI. James Alexander Bryant, b. Aug. 25, 1863; d. . . . .
217. VII. Elizabeth Alice Bryant, b. June 18, 1866; m. A. W. Woodward; d. Oct. 28, 1902.
218. VIII. Sidney Horace Bryant, b. Dec. 14, 1868; d. in U. S. naval service in Cuba, Aug. 18, 1899.
219. IX. Mary Emily Bryant, b. June 12, 1873; m. T. W. Cox+

94

ALEXANDER CAMPBELL BRYANT,[7] (Joseph[6] [62], David,[5] Simeon,[4] Cornelius,[3] Pieter Cornelisse,[2] Cornelis[1]), b. Oct. 8, 1828, Bethany, Va.; d. 1896; m. JENEVIEVE GALLAGHER of Fleming Co., Ky.; m. (2nd) 1861, MARY CALVERT BERRY of Fleming Co., Ky. Mary Calvert was the dau. of Wm. Calvert

Berry and Elmira Taylor. Alexander Campbell graduated at
Bethany College; studied law, but gave up his practice to enter
railroad life, holding various positions in that occupation.
Politics, Republican; religion, Campbellite.

Children 1st m.:

220.　I.　Dora Bryant; d. at age of four years.

Children 2nd m.:

221.　II.　William Henry Bryant, b. July 28, 1863; m. Birdie
May Routt+

222.　III.　Mary Lou. Bryant, b. Oct. 26, 1865, in Indianapolis,
Ind.; m. E. W. McCorkle+

﹏ 76

SARAH ANN BRYANT,[7] (Samuel[6] [63], David,[5] Simeon,[4]
Cornelius,[3] Pieter Cornelisse,[2] Cornelis[1]), b. Oct. 15, 1820, in
Washington Co., Pa.; m. HARVEY SANGER of the state of New
York; he was b. May 29, 1815. She d. May 29, 1855, near
Lowell, Ind.

Children:

223.　I.　L. W. Sanger, b. Apr. 25, 1841; m. Olive Wiley+

224.　II.　Ross Sanger, b. June 3, 1842; m. Louisa D. Hopkins+

225.　III.　Adna Sanger, b. Jan. 2, 1844; m. Phoebe Hopkins,
b. Dec. 24, 1848, dau. of Benj. Hopkins and
Elizabeth Norton; d. June 22, 1909, at Kings-
bury, Ind.

226.　IV.　David Sanger, b. Apr. 6, 1847; d. Oct. 23, 1903;
unm.; res., Lowell, Ind.

227.　V.　Mary Sanger, b. May 14, 1851; d. Aug. 28, 1869.

97

SAMUEL ROSS BRYANT,[7] (Samuel[6] [63], David,[5] Simeon,[4]
Cornelius,[3] Pieter Cornelisse,[2] Cornelis[1]), b. Nov. 27, 1822, in
Washington Co., Pa.; d. Jan. 21, 1886, at Valparaiso, Ind.; m.
Dec. 20, 1849, near La Porte, Ind., to ISABELLA LOMAX, who
was b. June 26, 1829. She was the dau. of Abel Lomax and
Elizabeth Ladd. She d. Feb. 26, 1888, at Valparaiso, Ind.

H. W. Bryant

Children:

228.   I.   Frank Jennings Bryant, b. Sept. 12, 1850; d. Feb. 3, 1854.
229.   II.   William Alfred Bryant, b. Feb. 7, 1852; m. Alla Bartholomew+
230.   III.   Mary Delight Bryant, b. Nov. 3, 1853; d. Sept. 9, 1856.
231.   IV.   Adelbert Bryant, b. Nov. 20, 1855; d. Oct. 1, 1856.
232.   V.   Hubert Ross Bryant, b. Sept. 24, 1857; d. June 12, 1881.

When Samuel Ross Bryant was an infant his mother died, leaving him to the tender care of his grandmother Ross and her daughter Elizabeth. Here he made his home until his father left Pennsylvania in 1829 for Ohio, accompanied by his second wife and children. In 1835, with his father's family, he removed to Lake County, Indiana. In 1843 he attended school in Valparaiso, Indiana, the teacher being Mr. Harvey Ball of Crown Point, Indiana, the only school in the place at that time. After leaving Valparaiso he clerked in the dry goods store of Leonard Woods in the village of Door, La Porte County. Later he engaged in the merchantile business in partnership with Mr. Warren Mason of Valparaiso, Indiana. Soon after his marriage in 1849 he bought a drug-store of Mr. William Harrison in Valparaiso. He continued successfully in this business for twenty-five years. In 1857, fearing the effects of so severe a climate on lungs already affected by its severity, he made arrangements for a home in the South. However, the unsettled condition of affairs in the South and the near approach of that terrible war-cloud deterred him from carrying out his plan. In the spring of 1879 he accompanied his son Hubert, then in poor health, to Denver, Colorado. From here he was soon compelled to return, being unable to endure the effects of the alkaline dust of that region. Previous to this time he had by unflagging and patient effort battled against the insidious disease, consumption, until he felt that he had at least gained partial victory, but it ultimately gained the mastery. As he neared the end, the deep current of his life thought came to the surface in the expression of the deep, warm affection that he felt for the loved ones who watched at his bedside. In early life he united with the Methodist church, but soon after his marriage he and his wife transferred their membership to the Presbyterian church of Valparaiso, of which he proved a faithful and efficient member, ever ready with open hand and warm heart, in his characteristic quiet manner, to help build up the kingdom of his Master, on whose rod and staff he calmly and confidently leaned, even down to the valley and shadow of death.   In business for many years, no one had cause to suspect his fidelity and integrity.   Charged with public trusts of considerable magnitude, he closed each with a correct record.

99

JACOB C. BRYANT,[7] (Samuel[6] [63], David,[5] Simeon,[4] Cornelius,[3] Pieter Cornelisse,[2] Cornelis[1]), b. Nov. 26, 1828, in Green Co., Pa.; m. Nov. 23, 1853, at Valparaiso, Ind., to ADELIA FRANCES TYLER, who was born Nov. 6, 1837; dau. of Jeremiah and Mary Ann Fitch, Rensselaer Co., N. Y.   She d. Aug. 20, 1905, at Wichita, Kan.

Children:

233.   I.   Martha Frances Bryant, b. Mar. 21, 1855; m. (1st) William H. Rogers; m. (2nd) Grear Nagle+

234.   II.   Edward Marion Bryant, b. Aug. 16, 1855; d. Sept. 15, 1857, at Pleasant Grove, Ind.; buried at Lowell, Ind.

235. III.   Samuel Tyler Bryant, b. Oct. 9, 1858+

236.   IV.   Mary Ann Bryant, b. Jan. 15, 1861; m. Henry Tucker+

When Jacob C. Bryant was one year of age his parents moved to Knox County, Ohio.   When seven years of age, he with his parents moved to Lake County, Indiana.   His education was principally acquired at the Pleasant Grove school, which was the first organized in this settlement.   The teacher was Bell Jennings, half brother of Mrs. Joanna Woodruff Bryant, who made his home with the family and who, having a love for hunting, had no trouble in supplying the family with venison during the winter, which was cooked to a queen's taste by Mrs. Bryant.   Jacob attended school at Crown Point and afterwards at Valparaiso.   Later he went to western Ohio where he engaged in business with his cousin Simeon Mitchell.   Soon after, returning to Valparaiso, he continued in

L Bryant

business for a number of years. The Tyler family removed to this vicinity from New York when the daughter was three years old. Immediately after his marriage he removed to Crown Point, Indiana. In the spring of 1860, with his wife and two children, he drove in a wagon to Franklin County, Kansas. The extreme drought of that summer compelled him to return to Indiana, where he remained until 1863, when he located at Galva, Illinois. Here he was employed by the United States government as mechanic and was stationed at Nashville, Tennessee, later being transferred to Atlanta, Georgia. Severe fighting took place about Nashville, and all mechanics were held in readiness for active service under arms. After serving the government for about six months he returned home. In 1866 he located at Chickasaw, Iowa, where he lived until 1888, going from there to Cowley County, Kansas. In the fall of 1904 he moved to Wichita, Kansas, where in August, 1905, his wife died, after a lingering illness, respected and esteemed by those who knew her. The closing years of her life were spent much in travel in an effort to regain her health, but to no avail. Since the death of his wife Jacob Bryant makes his home with his daughter, Mrs. Grear Nagle, 1501 Maple St., Wichita, Kansas. At the age of eighty-five he still enjoys a reasonable degree of health.

100

HANNAH BRYANT,[7] (Samuel[6] [63], David,[5] Simeon,[4] Cornelius,[3] Pieter Cornelisse,[2] Cornelis[1]), b. Jan. 18, 1831, at Fredericktown, Knox Co., Ohio; d. Nov. 28, 1889, at Crown Point, Ind.; m. Feb. 22, 1851, at Michigan City, Ind., to ELI MARION ROBERTSON, who was b. Jan. 24, 1829, at Charleston, Clark Co., Ind.; son of Hezekiah Robertson and Polly Teeple. He d. Nov. 16, 1896, near Hebron, Ind.

Children:

237.   I.   Mary Joanna Robertson, b. Feb. 17, 1852; m. Oscar Dinwiddie+

238.   II.   Joseph Harvey Robertson, b. Jan. 29, 1854; m. Florence Elvena Talcott+

239. III.   Fletcher Lorraine Robertson, b. Dec. 23, 1855; m. Irene Stoops+

When Hannah Bryant Robertson was nine years old her mother died. Hannah being the oldest daughter at home was of great assistance to her father in caring for the family. At the age of seventeen years she united with the Methodist Episcopal church at Westville, Indiana, and remained a member of that denomination until her death. The first ten years of her married life were spent in or near Westville, Indiana. Here her three children were born. In 1862 the family moved to Eagle Creek Township, Lake County, Indiana, where they remained for twenty years. Her next and last home was in Crown Point, Indiana. She was a farmer's daughter and a farmer's wife, devoted to her family.

101

HARVEY WOODRUFF BRYANT,[7] (Samuel[6] [63], David,[5] Simeon,[4] Cornelius,[3] Pieter Cornelisse,[2] Cornelis[1]), b. Jan. 8, 1833, at Fredericktown, Knox Co., Ohio; d. May 23, 1913, at Hebron Ind.; m. May 3, 1860, near Lowell, Ind., to LUCRETIA DOWD, who was b. Sept. 12, 1840, at Zaleski, Vinton Co., Ohio; dau. of Conner Dowd and Cynthia Pratt. She d. June 23, 1900, at Hebron, Ind.

Children:

240. I. Eva Rosella Bryant, b. Feb. 20, 1861; unm.+
241 II. Merritt Conner Bryant, b. Nov. 14, 1862; m. Effie Wilson+
242 III. Cynthia Lavinia Bryant, b. May 30, 1867; d. Jan. 1, 1868.
243. IV. Twin sister, b. May 30, 1867; d. 1867.
244. V. Milton Samuel Bryant, b. Jan. 30, 1870; d. Oct. 9, 1872.
245. VI. Ora Viola Bryant, b. June 9, 1872; unm.+
246. VII. Ada Luella Bryant, b. July 7, 1874; m. Joseph Ross Wilson+
247. VIII. Nettie Ladora Bryant, b. Apr. 3, 1877; unm.+

When Harvey Bryant was two years old his father and mother, with six children, in a party of some twenty relatives, started by wagon from the Ohio farm to Lake County, Indiana, a distance of 300 miles. As a growing boy in pioneer times he had his share of hardship. Left without a mother's care at seven, he made his home for the most part with Uncle Harvey Woodruff at Orchard Grove in the winter; and with Daniel Merris at Pleasant Grove during the summer (that he might have access to the summer schools). In these boyhood days he could be seen drowning gophers and trapping prairie chickens and quail, both as a diversion and occupation, for the chickens and quail were sent to Chicago by wagon and sold or traded for clothing. Christmas of 1848 found him — now a boy of almost sixteen — on the way back to Ohio helping Uncle David Bryant drive cattle. Others in the party were his brother Isaac and his cousin David. In Ohio he made his home with his father, who had returned in the fall of 1848, attending school or working on the farm as the season demanded. In 1852 he came to Indiana, this time by stage, boat, and rail, and spent the summer with his brother Ross and his sister Hannah and others. Four cousins, Avis Bryant, Kate Mitchell, Robert Bryant, and Harvey Bryant, made the return trip together, leaving Chicago over the Michigan Central; 1853 was characterized by a trip over the Allegheny Mountains to Lancaster, Pennsylvania, with a drove of cattle, in company with Bryant Welsh as leader. In the fall of 1854 he entered college at Oberlin, where he attended for a part of two years. Here Rev. Charles G. Finney, president of the college, commanded his respect and made a lasting impress upon his mind. The influences brought to bear upon him here no doubt culminated in his christian character of honesty and integrity. He soon entered into church relations, and has ever since been a Methodist. On December 3, 1855, he entered the rude schoolhouse at Orchard Grove, Indiana, as teacher. Among the first pupils to arrive was a girl of fifteen, in her shawl and hood — the fashion of the day — and her ten-year-old brother, wearing his faded but clean blue denim blouse and overalls tucked into his boot-tops. These two were destined to have their lives closely interwoven with that of the teacher, for the girl became his wife and the boy almost a life partner in farming and mercantile affairs. He continued teaching for four more winters — two terms at Orchard Grove and two at the Buckley school — while during the summers he farmed land owned by Jerry Kenney. In 1856 he cast his first presidential vote, which was lost, being a supporter of John C. Fremont. After his marriage in 1860 he purchased a house and lot adjoining the tract entered by his father-in-law, Conner Dowd.   These were the beginnings of the present Bryant Dowd & Company farm located five miles southwest of Hebron.   Along with his farming interests he cared for an apiary, which at one time numbered 230 hives, all having had their origin in the single swarm of bees presented by Jerry Kenney as a wedding present.   One shipment of honey — 3,000 pounds — was marketed at 27 cents per pound, while the year's yield amounted to $810.   In 1874 failing health came as a blow upon an heretofore active and ambitious life.   A change of climate and surroundings was recommended by Dr. J. K. Blackstone, hence a trip to Colorado accompanied by his kinsmen, Marion Robertson, David Fisher, and Homer DeWitt.   With health improved, after a few months he returned to his old pursuits, which in the next few years were to be supplemented by town interests, for in 1876 he built a house in Hebron, moved his family, and in 1881, in partnership with J. H. Dowd, his brother-in-law, purchased a general stock of goods of William Sturgeon, owned just previously by J. E. Bryant.   A burglary and fire in 1890 necessitated the removal of the remnant of the stock to temporary quarters, and in time the building of the corner brick, now in use and known as the Bryant Dowd & Company store.   In recent years, while in a sense Mr. Bryant had retired from store work, he had general oversight of the finances; and though a man of eighty, his pioneer life of toil and privation apparently had no effect upon later years other than to have its share in the molding of a well-rounded character of sterling worth.   He passed the fourscore years, retaining far more than usual both of physical and mental strength.   His generosity in supporting the publication of the Bryant Genealogy is highly appreciated.   A stroke of apoplexy May 19, 1913, caused his death, which occurred at the home of his son, May 23, 1913.

102

Isaac C. Bryant,[7] (Samuel[6] [63], David,[5] Simeon,[4] Cornelius,[3] Pieter Cornelisse,[2] Cornelis[1]), b. Mar. 11, 1836, at Pleasant Grove, Lake Co., Ind.; d. Apr. 15, 1908; m. Dec. 1, 1863, to Harriet Pearce, who was b. Mar. 27, 1843, near Lowell, Ind.; dau. of Michael Pearce and Margaret Dinwiddie.   She d. Nov. 12, 1912.

Children

248.   I.   Samuel Edwin Bryant, b. Apr. 14, 1865; m. Maria
             Ellen Wheeler+
249. II.   John Pearce Bryant, b. Dec. 29, 1866; d. Aug. 8,
             1868.
250. III.   Margaret J. Bryant, b. Jan. 8, 1869; d. Aug. 17, 1870.
251. IV.   Bertha L. Bryant, b. July 6, 1870; m. Harry George+
252.   V.   Jessie M. Bryant, b. Aug. 19, 1873.
253. VI.   Blanche E. Bryant, b. Aug. 3, 1878; m. May 1, 1897,
             Charles Childs, son of George Childs and
             . . . . . . Brody; Res., 230 North Ave., Chi-
             cago, Ill.

At the death of his mother, when Isaac Bryant was five years old,
he was separated from father, brothers, and sisters, and in the
years following had various homes in the neighborhood. However,
his disposition was such that, even as a child, he would not be
imposed upon by those under whose care he was placed. An ap-
proaching whipping was enough to warrant him in seeking a new
home. To his mind, boyish pranks should not be thus dealt with,
and these pranks were not foreign to his nature. The district
school was a source of annoyance, but not for long at a time; for
he gained his freedom from it in the same way that he did from a
distasteful home. His nature demanded independence and freedom. In early life he was apprenticed to one Obadiah Dunham,
in Valparaiso, to learn the tailor's trade. While he was clever at
the trade, he never entered into the business, but chose rather to
work on his father's farm in season, and hunt and trap at leisure
times. He was a remarkable shot, and many prairie chickens,
geese, and deer were the victims of his deadly aim. On at least
two different occasions he assisted in driving cattle to the East —
in one instance to Ohio, and in another across the Alleghenies to
Pennsylvania. Knowledge of the western frontier was gained by
a trip taken when he was a young man. Railroads were still in-
complete in the West, and sometimes he was obliged to go on foot.
He toured several of the states, spending some time with his sister,
Jane Stalter, then living in Kansas. On August 11, 1861, he was
enlisted in Company H, Ninth Indiana Volunteers. During the
fight at Green Briar, West Virginia, he was wounded in his left
arm; consequently he was granted a furlough and later an honorable

discharge. A Lake County paper dated October 10, 1861, says: "We notice among the wounded the name of Isaac Bryant, who is the first of Lake County's men to receive the mark of a rebel bullet." After his marriage he worked part of his father's farm on shares, but after the division of the Pearce estate they established their home on the portion falling to them, half-way between Hebron and Lowell. Here he lived uninterruptedly for years, a successful farmer devoted to the interests of his family. About ten years before his death he moved to Hebron, Indiana, where he built a roomy and comfortable home with a view to spending his closing years in retirement from active pursuits.

103

JANE BRYANT,[7] (Samuel[6] [63], David,[5] Simeon,[4] Cornelius,[3] Pieter Cornelisse,[2] Cornelis[1]), b. Jan. 26, 1838, near Lowell, Lake Co., Ind.; d. Feb. 14, 1909; m. Oct. 21, 1855, in Wyandot Co., Ohio, to JOHN STALTER, who was b. Feb. 18, 1834, son of Hiram Stalter of Pennsylvania.

Children:

254. I. Anna Stalter, b. Aug. 9, 1856; d. Aug. 26, 1856.
255. II. Mary K. Stalter, b. Aug. 18, 1857; m. Newton L. Yarbrough+
256. III. George H. Stalter, b. Oct. 20, 1859; m. Mattie Baird+
257. IV. Martha B. Stalter, b. Jan. 18, 1862; d. Mar. 5, 1862.
258. V. Elura Stalter, b. June 3, 1863; m. John K. Snyder+
259. VI. Franklin Stalter, b. Apr. 26, 1865; d. Sept. 16, 1869.
260. VII. Infant, b. Feb. 20, 1867; d. Feb. 20, 1867.
261. VIII. Samuel B. Stalter, b. Apr. 10, 1868; d. May 5, 1877.
262. IX. Delphia Stalter, b. Sept. 12, 1870; m. Feb. 2, 1893, at Rock, Kan., Ferris Dawson. Res., Pacific Grove, Calif.
263. X. Charles E. Stalter, b. Dec. 29, 1872; d. Mar. 22, 1876.
264. XI. Edwin R. Stalter, b. Dec. 3, 1874; m. Dora Moore+
265. XII. John W. Stalter, b. Dec. 4, 1876; m. Jessie E. Keats+
266 XIII. Julia J. Stalter, b. Dec. 1, 1879; d. Nov. 1, 1883.
267. XIV. Frederick L. Stalter, b. Apr. 17, 1883; m. Grace Darst+

During only two years of Jane Bryant Stalter's life did she have a mother's care; then she was left to the protection of others — of neighbors, perhaps, and of a nine-year-old sister. Her school days were passed in the old Pleasant Grove schoolhouse. When she was ten years old she was taken back to Ohio with her father's family, where because of her environment, she learned to depend upon herself and to make her own pleasures out of the simple country life. At the age of seventeen she was married to John Stalter in Wyandot County. The young couple made their home in Ohio until 1858, when they went by rail and by boat to Franklin County, Kansas. They lived on the ranch of John Brown, the noted abolitionist. On Brown's last trip through Kansas, he and a companion called one night at the Stalter home. They were on the way to the home of Brown's brother-in-law, Horace Day, who lived a half-mile away. During these troublous times, while her husband was away fighting the border ruffians, Jane was caring for her home, her family, and the ranch. In 1861 when she had charge of affairs — her husband fighting in the state militia on the Missouri and Kansas line — grasshoppers completely destroyed the crops. While they yet lived in Franklin County, they had also to contend with the ravages of fire, which wiped out their home and its contents. In 1871 with their five living children — three being left behind in the little graveyard — they moved to Cowley County by wagon to take up frontier life in southern Kansas. Here occasional hardships were interspersed with much good fortune, for they were successful in accumulating land and live stock, and owned a ranch famed for miles around. Prosperity was theirs for some fifteen years, but in 1886-7, when money matters took a bad turn, they lost all their property. However, they were a solace one to the other, for Jane Stalter was no weak, dependent woman, but one who possessed a brave, noble, and unselfish nature that knew no failure. Thoroughly Christian, she was a leader whether in church, school, or temperance movements. Because of her untiring industry and her noble Christian character, she never failed to command the respect of those with whom she mingled. Five years of her later life were spent in Woodward County, Oklahoma. Thence the couple moved to Pacific Grove, California, where in 1909 death claimed her, and where her husband still lives.

104

JOANNA BRYANT,[7] (Samuel[6] [63], David,[5] Simeon,[4] Cornelius,[3] Pieter Cornelisse,[2] Cornelis[1]), b. Apr. 2, 1840, near Lowell, Lake Co., Ind.; m. Sept. 10, 1862, at Valparaiso, Ind., to EDWIN RUTHVEN BEEBE, who was b. Nov. 30, 1835, in Tompkins Co., N. Y.; son of Samuel Clark Beebe and Currence Benedict Gregg. He d. May 14, 1906, at Princeton, Wis.

Children:

268. I. Joanna Belle Beebe, b. Oct. 8, 1878; educated in Princeton, Wis., and at Ripon (Wis.) College. Fond of reading; teacher of high school subjects in various towns of Wisconsin and Minnesota; successful in her line of work. When family lived in Chicago — earlier — she was proof-reader.

269. II. Edwin Hubert Beebe, b. Nov. 7, 1881; m. Mary Sullivan +

270. III. Ione Currence Beebe, b. Aug. 30, 1883, was educated in Princeton, Wis., the town of her birth. Later took business course in Chicago and has since been employed as stenographer in Ripon, Wis., and Princeton. Earlier she had been type-setter in her father's printing office.

When Joanna Bryant was an infant her mother died and she was left to the care of her uncle Elias Bryant, with whom she lived until she was twelve years of age. Her early education was gained in a log schoolhouse about a half-mile from her home and her first teacher was Hon. Martin Wood, of Crown Point. When she was twelve years old, her uncle and aunt both having died, she went to Valparaiso to live with her half-brother Ross Bryant, with whom she made her home until her marriage to Edwin Ruthven Beebe, a printer. In 1863 Mr. and Mrs. Beebe moved to Chicago where they lived near Halsted and Twelfth streets. Chicago, in those days before the great fire, did not bear much resemblance to the metropolis of to-day. A walk of three miles to the post-office was necessary when they wanted the mail. A public hydrant on the street corner was the only source of water supply. There were few street-

cars, an old-fashioned omnibus making the run to the business section. Farther to the south and west of where they lived was
nothing but marsh and uninhabited lowlands. In 1864 they moved
to Orchard Grove, Indiana, where they lived on a farm for four
years. They then went back to Valparaiso, where Mr. Beebe was
employed as a printer. In May, 1872, they moved to Lowell,
Indiana, and commenced the publication of the Lowell Star, the
first paper ever published in Lowell. Several years later Mr. Beebe
moved his paper to Crown Point, Indiana, where it became the
Lake County Star, still one of the prominent papers of the county.
In 1878 Mr. Beebe disposed of his business interests in Crown Point
and soon after moved to Princeton, Wisconsin. Here he soon
became the editor of the Princeton Republic, and the family
remained there until 1899 when they moved to Chicago. After
two years they returned to Princeton, which again became the
family home until Mr. Beebe's death in 1906. The following fall
Mrs. Beebe moved to Ripon, Wisconsin, where her son and her
daughter Ione were employed. After two years she returned to the
home in Princeton, Wisconsin, where she still lives. In early life
she became a member of the Presbyterian church and has always
been loyal in her support of her church and devoted to her home.

105

ZEBULON COOPER,[7] (Mary[6] [65], David,[5] Simeon,[4] Cornelius,[3]
Pieter Cornelisse,[2] Cornelis[1]), b. Nov. 2, 1813, near Van Buren,
Washington Co.; Pa.; d. Aug. 5, 1893; m. Feb., 1845, at Waynes-
burg, Pa., SARAH NICELY, who was b. July 7, 1824; dau. of
Jacob Nicely and Elizabeth McFarland.

Children:

271.   I. George Nicely Cooper, b. July 25, 1847; m. Emma
           Ainsworth. Res., Pomona, Kan.

272. II. Arabella Cooper, b. June 2, 1849; m. Thomas
           Mitchell Sellars+

273. III. Isadore Cooper, b. June 2, 1849; m. John A.
           Downey+

274. IV. David Bryant Cooper, b. Oct. 12, 1850; m. Harriet
           A. Lewis+

275.   V.   Mary Etta Cooper, b. Jan. 21, 1853; m. Marvin M.
            Roberts+
276.   VI. Eugene Norton Cooper, b. Apr. 15, 1854; m. Anna
            Wagner+
277.   VII. Elizabeth A. Cooper, b. Feb. 2, 1856; d. Apr. 9, 1856.
278.   VIII. Charles W. Cooper, b. May 1, 1858; d. Apr. 13, 1872.
279   IX. Ralph D. Cooper, b. Dec. 23, 1860; d. Feb. 1, 1872.

Zebulon Cooper resided in Washington County, Pennsylvania,
until the fall of 1863, when he removed with his family to Rochelle,
Illinois, where they remained until March, 1864, when he located
on a farm near Winfield, Iowa, where he remained until 1876, when
the pioneer spirit again took possession of him and he removed to
Miami County, Kansas. In 1885 he moved to Ottawa, Kansas.
He followed agriculture as an occupation. In politics he was a
Republican; in religious faith a Presbyterian. ·He was an extensive
reader, a well-informed man of sterling integrity of character, and
esteemed by all who knew him. He is buried in Ottawa, Kansas.
His wife is still living, at the advanced age of eighty-nine years.

106

CATHERINE COOPER,[7] (Mary[6] [65], David,[5] Simeon,[4] Cornelius,[3] Pieter Cornelisse,[2] Cornelis,[1]), b. Apr. 20, 1815, near Van
Buren, Washington Co., Pa.; d. Mar. 8, 1892; buried in Winfield, Iowa; m. Jan. 1, 1837, HARVEY GAMBLE or GAMBELL,who
was b. Jan. 24, 1815, in Shelby, Ohio; d. Dec. 18, 1868, at
Winfield, Iowa. He was an elder in the Presbyterian church of
Winfield, Iowa. He will long be remembered as a dignified,
upright citizen, an honored christian gentleman.

Children:

280.   I.   John Cooper Gamble, b. Oct. 3, 1837; m. Margaret
            Fulton+
281.   II. Sylvanus Cooper Gamble, b. Dec. 14, 1839; d. in
            the service of his country in the Civil War.
282.   III. Leroy Gamble, b. Sept. 25, 1842; m. Elizabeth A.
            Cone+
283.   IV. Charles White Gamble, b. May 8, 1847; m. Kate
            Adelaide Haight+

Obituary published in Winfield, Iowa, weekly paper: "Catherine Cooper Gamble was the second child of a family of twelve children, six of whom survive her. On January 1, 1837, at her home in Pennsylvania, she was united in marriage to Harvey Gamble, well known in this vicinity for his noble and consistent Christian character and example, and affectionally remembered for his many disinterested efforts on behalf of those who were in trouble, sorrow, and bereavement. Her husband preceded her to glory twenty-three years ago. Immediately after her marriage she and her husband moved to Shelby, Ohio, where they lived until 1845, when they moved back to Washington County, Pennsylvania. The next removal was to Iowa, where, with the exception of two years, the deceased has lived on the farm where she died. Her death took place on Tuesday, March 8, 1892, at the residence of her son John C. At the age of seventeen years she made a profession of her faith in the Lord Jesus Christ, and for the long period of threescore years has been a humble and faithful follower of her Divine Master. She was of Puritan origin and always prided herself on the fact, tracing her ancestry back to the Pilgrim Fathers who landed on Plymouth Rock. A firm adherent of the doctrines and government of the Presbyterian church, she has been in communion with it all her Christian life.

"Catherine Gamble was well known to nearly all in this vicinity, and those who were well acquainted with her will bear out the writer of this obituary in saying that she was one who studiously avoided making known her good deeds while she lived and who would not wish to be praised when she is dead. Some points in her character, however, we should mention for the imitation of those who survive. Her religion was unobtrusive, though her faith was unwavering; and she showed its reality rather in her life than in her words. Her piety was grounded on humility; her hope, through the merits of her Redeemer was as 'an anchor of the soul, sure and steadfast.' She preferred to commune with her own heart, and in her chamber; and by applying herself to God's Word and to prayer, she sought, as instructed by the Psalmist, to cleanse her ways. In the transactions of life she thought and spoke and acted as in the sight of God. Just and true in all her dealings, she endeavored to do her duty in that sphere of life into which it had pleased God to call her. To the poor she was liberal and kind, to the bereaved and afflicted, sympathetic and helpful. She was always ready, according to her ability, to lend a helping hand to those who were in trouble, and the families in this community are not few in number who have been blessed by her presence when sickness or death invaded their homes. In her the neighborhood has lost a most useful example, the church one of its most consistent members, her family a valued and beloved relative, the poor a true friend, and the world an honest and a good woman.

"Although a great sufferer for months her sun did at last go down without a cloud and she passed out of time into eternity without a struggle. Jesus was to her soul as a morning without clouds, and gave her a peaceful end. "Mark the perfect man and behold the upright, for the end of that man is peace." By her own request the funeral services were held at the residence of her son John C., and were conducted by her former pastor, Rev. James B. Butter, now of Blairstown, Iowa, assisted by Rev. David McEwan, pastor of Presbyterian Church of Winfield. Despite the inclement nature of the weather the services were largely attended, and the long procession that followed the remains to the cemetery east of town was but one more testimony to the esteem in which she was held. B."

107

DAVID BRYANT COOPER,[7] (Mary[6] [65], David,[5] Simeon,[4] Cornelius,[3] Pieter Cornelisse,[2] Cornelis[1]), b. Apr. 30, 1817, near Washington, Pa.; d. June 22, 1891; m. Apr. 11, 1839, HANNAH DILLE, who was b. June 10, 1823, Washington, Pa.; dau. of Ezra Dille and Mary McFarland.

Children:

284. I.   Mary Jane Cooper, b. Jan. 5, 1840; m. John Leach+
285. II. Milton Dille Cooper, b. May 11, 1842; unm. He is in the real estate and stock business, and mining. He is a staunch Republican; is chairman of county central committee. Res., Choteau, Mont.; lived for a time in Chicago, Ill.
286. III. Hester Ellen Cooper, b. Aug. 25, 1844; m. Andrew M. Vance+

DAVID COOPER

HANNAH D. COOPER

287. IV. Oliver Goldsmith Cooper, b. Dec. 4, 1846; m. Amanda Downing+

288. V. Emma Thrisa Cooper, b. May 11, 1849; m. James Concannon+

289. VI. Frank Darwin Cooper, b. Apr. 6, 1851; m. Alice Green+

290. VII. Linnie Brown Cooper, b. June 10, 1854; m. Jasper E. Mount+

291. VIII. Ida Arabelle Cooper, b. Feb. 4, 1857; m. James Brown+

292. IX. Charles White Cooper, b. Apr. 4, 1858; m. Mary Combs+

293. X. Edwin Stanton Cooper, b. October 28, 1861; m. October 14, 1903, at Appleton, Wis., KITTIE STUDLEY, dau. of Dr. William Harrison Studley, who was b. in Bridgeport, Conn., and Caroline Louise Heath, b. in Wanhouse Point, Conn. She was a "Daughter of the Revolution" and a "Colonial Dame." Dr. Studley was graduated an Episcopal clergyman from Trinity College, New Haven, Conn., after which he attended Rush Medical College in Chicago, Ill., and graduated from the College of Physicians and Surgeons in New York City. Dr. Edwin S. Cooper is a graduate of the Missouri Medical College of St. Louis, and of Belleview College of New York City. Politically he is a Republican, "but votes for the best man." Mrs. Cooper was educated in New York City, became a member of St. James' Episcopal Church, although she says at heart she is a member of all churches. Dr. Cooper has an extensive practice in Almond, Wis.

"Mr. David Bryant Cooper received a liberal education in the schools of Washington County, Pennsylvania, and remained on the farm until twenty-one years of age, when he engaged in merchandising with his older brother Zebulon at Washington, Pennsylvania,

and there continued for two years. He then sold out and purchased
a farm, after which he engaged in agricultural pursuits. In 1850
our subject sold his farm and moved to Lee County, Iowa, where
he farmed and also speculated in land. In the spring of 1857 he
sold out and moved to Scotland County, Missouri, where he purchased the large tract of land he owned until his death. He was
school director while in Iowa and was elected clerk of the elections. In 1862 he was elected county judge, and after two years
when all other officers were thrown out he was appointed by Governor Gamble, and at the next general election was re-elected by
the people and served eight years. He was a Republican and a
worthy and enterprising citizen." (History of Scotland County,
Missouri, 1887.)

Copied from a Memphis journal: "Judge David B. Cooper died
of paralysis at his home in this city, Monday, June 22d, 1891, after
a brief illness, aged 74 years, 1 month and 22 days. He was a man
of sterling integrity and worth, whose word was as good as his bond,
and his friendship was an honor to all on whom it was bestowed.
He was one of nature's noblemen, a born gentleman, with a great,
big, generous heart, always thoughtful of others, brave, honest,
truthful, generous and straightforward. In the home he was a
kind and devoted husband, an indulgent father, an excellent
neighbor, and, as a citizen of the town and county he was highly
esteemed and respected, and ranked among the foremost and best.
Therefore, in tendering the bereaved family our sincere sympathy
in their deep affliction, we simply voice the sentiment of a very
large circle of friends and acquaintances. The funeral services were
conducted by Rev. C. L. Hogue at the family residence in this city,
today, at 10 a. m., after which all that is mortal of our old-time
friend was tenderly and lovingly laid to rest in the Memphis
cemetery."

108

JANE COOPER,[7] (Mary[6] [65], David,[5] Simeon,[4] Cornelius,[3]
Pieter Cornelisse,[2] Cornelis[1]), b. Feb. 27, 1819, near Van
Buren, Washington Co., Pa.; d. Jan. 8, 1849; m. Apr. 18, 1839,
THOMAS HANNA, b. Oct. 7, 1816, Prosperity, Pa., son of John
Vance Hanna and Lydia McCollum. Mr. Hanna was an

CAROLINE C. VAILE

influential citizen in the community in which he lived; a valuable member of the Presbyterian Church. Died May 8, 1895, at Connellsville, Pa. Mrs. Jane Hanna died in early womanhood at the age of thirty, leaving a young family as follows:

Children:

294. I.   Adeline Hanna, b. Jan. 18, 1840; m. John Vance Smith+

295. II. Clarriet Hanna, b. Aug. 19, 1841; m. Bayard Blachly Lindly+

296. III. Mary Ellen Hanna, b. Dec. 21, 1843; m. Demas Lindly McVay+

297. IV. John Walker Hanna, b. Sept. 23, 1846; m. Caroline Elizabeth Duncan+

298. V.   Jane Hanna, b. Dec. 14, 1848; m. Frank D. Kelley+

109

MARY COOPER,[7] (Mary[6] [65], David,[5] Simeon,[4] Cornelius,[3] Pieter Cornelisse,[2] Cornelis[1]), b. Feb. 23, 1821; m. JOHN ATKINSON; he d. in the early sixties. Mrs. Atkinson resided in Washington, Penna., where she reared her family of four sons. She d. at the home of her son Charles in La Cygne, Kan., Sept. 11, 1889.

Children:

299. I.   David Bryant Atkinson, b. ......; d. in infancy.

300. II. Charles Cooper Atkinson, b. Feb. 8, 1841; m. (1st) Amelia Chapin+(2nd) Margaret Sellars+

301. III. Edwin Stanton Atkinson, b. ......; d. ....

302. IV. Dorwin Erasmus Atkinson, b. ......; d. ....

110

SARAH COOPER,[7] (Mary[6] [65], David,[5] Simeon,[4] Cornelius,[3] Pieter Cornelisse,[2] Cornelis[1]), b. Dec. 20, 1822, at Van Buren, Washington Co., Pa.; m. Nov. 11, 1841, RALPH VANKIRK, son of Arthur Vankirk and Elizabeth Parkinson, who was b. Dec. 27, 1815; d. Jan. 1, 1890. Mrs. Vankirk resides in Washington, Pa., and is an intelligent, capable woman and in good health at her advanced age of 90 years.   She is a loyal Methodist.

Children:

303.   I. Charles Cooper Vankirk, b. Oct. 10, 1842; m. ......, 1868, Elizabeth F. Gamble+

304.   II. Addison Vankirk, b. Oct. 6, 1844; d. April 6, 1845.

305.   III. Mary Jane Vankirk, b. Oct. 10, 1846; m. George W. McElree+

306.   VI. Elizabeth Ellen Vankirk, b. June 27, 1849; m. Dec. 28, 1905, in Washington, Pa., John M. Weygandt, who was b. in Nottingham Twp., Washington Co., Pa., son of Isaac Weygandt and Susanna Swickard. Res., near Washington, Pa.

112

ELIZABETH COOPER[7] (Mary[6] [65], David,[5] Simeon,[4] Cornelius,[3] Pieter Cornelisse,[2] Cornelis[1]), b. Sept. 29, 1826; d. Apr. 27, 1901; m. Nov. 6, 1845, near Prosperity, Pa., to JOHN NELSON DAY, who was b. Feb. 8, 1819, at Ninevah, Green Co., Pa., son of Stephen Day and Sarah Jolly.   He d. May 5, 1855, and was buried at Prosperity, Pa.   Elizabeth was b. near Van Buren, Washington Co., Pa.   Her life was mostly spent in Washington Co., Pa.   However, her later years were spent with her sons at Klemme, Iowa, where she d. and was buried. In religion a Presbyterian.

Children:

307.   I. Morris Reverdy Day, b. Aug. 11, 1846; m. Dora Elder+

308.   II. Mary Lavinia Day, b. Dec. 19, 1848, at Ninevah, Green Co., Pa.; m. Dec. 27, 1883, in Washington, Pa., to William Hockley, who was b. May 28, 1844, at Godalmining, Surrey, Eng., son of Thomas Hockley and ...... Cort.   In politics a Republican; in religion a Presbyterian; Res., 302 Duncan Ave., Washington, Pa.

CHARLES W. COOPER

309. III. Stephen Beveridge Day, b. June 26, 1851; m. Ida
            Alice Robbins. Res., Lynden, Wash.

113

CAROLINE COOPER[7] (Mary[6] [65], David,[5] Simeon,[4] Cornelius,[3]
Pieter Cornelisse,[2] Cornelis[1]), b. June 27, 1828, near Washington, Pa.; m. May 23, 1848, EDWARD GALLATIN VAILE, who was
b. Mar. 2, 1827, near Prosperity, Pa.; d. May 30, 1895. He
was the son of Leonard Vaile and Mary Lindley Minton.

Children:

310.   I.   Mary Elizabeth Vaile, b. April 28, 1849; unm.+
311.   II.   Clara E. Vaile, b. Jan. 9, 1851; m. Miles Joseph
             Braiden+
312. III.   Susan Maria Vaile, b. Aug. 8, 1852; m. Charles Edwin
             Cort+
313.   IV.   Anna Eliza Vaile, b. Apr. 13, 1854; m. Byron Hall+
314.   V.   Emma Caroline Vaile, b. Mar. 13, 1864; m. Eugene
             L. Cole+
315.   VI.   Edward Leonard Vaile, b. Nov. 4, 1868; m. Maude
             Eggert+

Caroline Vaile, possessing energy, enterprise, and the pioneer
spirit of her ancestors, left a home of comfort and plenty, willing to
share with her husband in giving their young lives to aid in building
up a new country on the prairies of northern Illinois. They
arrived in Lane (Rochelle), Ogle County, Illinois, in October,
1853, three months before the completion of the North Western
Railroad through to the Mississippi River. The Blackhawk War
had cleared that region of the savage, but wild animals were not
uncommon. Mr. Vaile had made a previous trip and purchased a
farm which later proved to be one of the richest and most highly
cultivated farms in the state, one and a half miles from Rochelle.
Here they continued to reside until the death of Mr. Vaile in 1895,
when Mrs. Vaile with her daughter Mary left the farm home with
its cherished memories and took up residence in Rochelle where she
still resides in remarkable strength of mind and body at the age of
eighty-six years (1913). During their early pioneer days religious
privileges were few. Colporteurs went occasionally through the
country holding meetings and distributing missionary tracts. The

Vaile home was the place of these meetings, and the well-known
hospitality of Mr. and Mrs. Vaile was always extended to these
bible agents. This worthy couple constituted a part of the first
church society organized in the village of Lane. Services were
first held in the homes, then in a car, stationed for the purpose;
later a log schoolhouse was used, which had previously been a
flouring mill. At this schoolhouse in September, 1854, a committee
from the presbytery of Chicago organized a Presbyterian church in
the town of Lane, later renamed Rochelle. A church was erected
in 1857, replaced by a larger one in 1874. Mr. Vaile had a prominent part in the erection of these church buildings and in sustaining
the best interests of the church. In politics he was Democratic
until after attending a Lincoln-Douglas political debate previous
to the Civil War. He then became a stanch Republican; always
deeply interested in the politics of his country; never willing, however, to hold any important office. He was the son of Leonard
Vaile,[4] a native of Winhall, Bennington County, Vermont, and
Mary Minton, of Washington County, Pennsylvania, b. 1808, d.
1884. Leonard Vaile,[4] in early manhood went to Washington
County, Pennsylvania, where he taught school until after his marriage, when he became a merchant in Prosperity, Pennsylvania. He
was the son of Edward Vaile[3] of Upton, Massachusetts, b. 1774,
d. 1859, who married Lois Perham of Chelmsford and Upton,
Massachusetts, b. 1777, d. 1855, who has a long line of Perham
ancestry extending into England. Edward Vaile[3] was the twelfth
child of Edward Vaile[2] and Mary Oberton, whom he married in
1772 in Bridgewater, Plymouth County, Massachusetts. This
Edward[2] was born October 20, 1746. His parents lived in Boston
at the time of a great fever, to which both were victims. Edward
Vaile served in the Continental army in the war of the Revolution, enlisting at Upton, Massachusetts, and furnishing his own
fire-arms. He served under Captain B. Reed. His military service is on record in the Secretary's office in the state of Massachusetts. The Vaile coat of arms is in the British Museum in
London, England. The name on this coat of arms is spelled *Vaile.*
This is mentioned because the name appears with other spellings.
Mary Lindley Minton,[6] the mother of Edward Gallatin Vaile,
was the daughter of Mathias Minton of Morristown, New Jersey,
b. 1783, and Sarah Lindley,[5] b. 1786, daughter of Caleb Lindley,[4]

JOSEPH BRYANT

who was the son of John Lindley,[3] son of John Lindley[2] of Morristown, New Jersey, born about 1666, who was the son of Francis Lindley,[1] the emigrant ancestor who came to Connecticut in 1639. Francis[1] married Susanna Culpepper. Caleb Lindley, grandfather of Mary Minton, served in the Continental army during the Revolution; enlisted in 1776, Captain Joseph Horton's company; military record in office of Adjutant General, Trenton, New Jersey. Caroline Vaile is a member of the Daughters of the Revolution. Both of her grandfathers served in the war of the Revolution.

114

CHARLES WHITE COOPER[7] (Mary[6] [65], David,[5] Simeon,[4] Cornelius,[3] Pieter Cornelisse,[2] Cornelis[1]), b. Mar. 18, 1830, near Washington, Pa.; d. May 10, 1886, at Middletown, N. Y.; m. Aug. 17, 1858, at New Brunswick, N. J., SARAH F. DUYCKINCK, who was b. Aug. 28, 1828; d. Sept. 24, 1876, in Bound Brook, N. J. She was the dau. of James Duyckinck and Margaret Post. M. (2nd) CHARLOTTE ELIZABETH HUNT, dau. of Rev. Holloway W. Hunt of New Brunswick, N. J. She d. Feb. 18, 1906. She was secretary of the Woman's Foreign Missionary Society of the Presbytery of Hudson.

> *Children:*
>
> 316.   I.   Mary Duyckinck Cooper, b. July 2, 1862; m. Frank M. Cummings +
> 317.   II. Charles Bryant Cooper, b. Nov. 19, 1864; m. Katherine Christie McGrew +
> 318. III. Haviland Cooper died in infancy.

Charles W. Cooper was educated at West Alexandria Academy, Pennsylvania, graduated at theological school at Princeton, N. J. Entered as a junior, 1847, Washington and Jefferson College. In 1851 he graduated. In a historical address by Prof. A. H. McCaughey of Erie, Pennsylvania, Charles Cooper was pronounced "the best looking man in the class. Pure-minded, warm-hearted, strong and faithful in his friendships — with few faults except that unusual one of not thinking as highly of himself as he ought to think — he was one whom we all loved heartily." This same history states he is related not remotely to America's most famous

novelist, J. Fenimore Cooper. In 1849–50 he studied law at
Steubenville, Ohio. In September, 1851, he entered Princeton
Theological Seminary as a student, and after a full course of study
graduated there in May, 1854. Licensed to preach, his first charge
was in Pontiac, Michigan. His next charge was the Huntingdon
South Church, Babylon, Long Island, a relation which he sustained for twelve years. In 1870 he took charge of Marlborough
Church on the Hudson River, where he remained until his death.
It was his privilege while pastor at Marlborough to receive at one
time 74 members into the church. The Duyckinck family records
with coat of arms are found in the Armoral at The Hague, Holland, published about the twelfth century.

115
JOHN C. COOPER[7] (Mary[6] [65], David,[5] Simeon,[4] Cornelius,[3]
Pieter Cornelisse,[2] Cornelis,[1]), b. Feb. 11, 1832, near Washing-
ton, Pa.; m. Sept. 27, 1860, at Jefferson, Tex., LUCY M.
HARRIS, dau. of Frank Harris and Martha Freeman. She was
b. Feb. 23, 1843, at Montgomery, Ala.; d. at Carrollton, Mo.,
Aug. 30, 1882.

Children:

319. I. St. Cloud Cooper, b. July 13, 1861; m. Dora Hud-
          son+
320. II. Maude Cooper, b. Dec. 1, 1863; m. Eugene W.
          Brown+
321. III. Texiana Cooper, b. Sept. 25, 1868; m. Stuart War-
          ner+
322. IV. ⎰ Hattie Scott Cooper, b. Oct. 5, 1873; m. Russell
      Twins ⎱ M. Kneisley+
323. V. ⎰ Harry Bryant Cooper, b. Oct. 5, 1873; m. Florence
          Thomas+

Dr. John C. Cooper was reared on a farm. His early education
was obtained in the common schools; he afterward attended the
academy of West Alexandria, Virginia. He then read medicine
with Dr. Warren Blachly and Dr. Thomas McKennan of Washington, Pennsylvania. He was a graduate of the Pennsylvania
Medical University at Philadelphia. He took a post-graduate

M. J. Blackstone

course in New Orleans. In 1856 he located in Jefferson, Texas. When the Civil War broke out he enlisted in the First Texas Partisan Rangers, and served as surgeon in the Confederate army during the war. In 1867 he moved with his wife and family to Carrollton, Missouri, where he still resides. Dr. Cooper is now past 80 years of age, tall and straight, with a gentlemanly bearing and a professional, dignified appearance.

118

JOSEPH BRYANT[7] (Simeon[6] [66], David,[5] Simeon,[4] Cornelius,[3] Pieter Cornelisse,[2] Cornelis[1]), b. Aug. 20, 1834, in Ohio; d. July 27, 1875; m. Dec. 8, 1859, MARY LANE, who d. Oct. 23, 1887.

Children:

324.   I.   Harriett Bryant, b. Oct. 18, 1860; m. E. S. Irwin+
325.   II.   Simeon Bryant, b. Apr. 11, 1862.
326.   III.   Schuyler Bryant, b. Jan. 30, 1863.
327.   IV.   Adeline Bryant, b. Aug. 31, 1865; d. Oct. 30, 1886.
328.   V.   Maryette Bryant, b. Dec. 3, 1868; d. Dec. 3, 1884.

119

MARGARET J. BRYANT[7] (Simeon[6] [66], David,[5] Simeon,[4] Cornelius,[3] Pieter Cornelisse,[2] Cornelis[1]), b. Apr. 16, 1837; m. Feb. 11, 1858, Dr. JOHN KING BLACKSTONE, son of William Blackstone and Julia Doddridge of Athens, Ohio. He was b. Feb. 12, 1827; d. Jan. 28, 1898.

Children:

329.   I.   Infant, b. Dec. 26, 1858; d. Dec. 28, 1858.
330.   II.   William Bryant Blackstone, b. Feb. 8, 1860; m. Lou Smith+
331.   III.   John King Blackstone, b. May 29, 1862; m. Ella Judson Hawkins+
332.   IV.   Lillian Elizabeth Blackstone, b. July 1, 1870; d. Nov. 21, 1900+
333.   IV.   Benjamin E. Blackstone, b. Jan. 4, 1876; attended high school, Hebron, Ind., after which he spent two years at medical school in St. Louis, Mo. Res., Hebron, Ind.

MARGARET was the first white girl born in Boone Township, Lake County, Indiana, and grew to womanhood on the old farm. Her parents often repeated their early experiences with the Indians. Once in the absence of her father the old Chief Shawne-Quoke came to the home, took a piece of chalk, made a circle on the floor, and said in the Indian language that for five miles around belonged to the Indians and ordered her to leave, threatening to kill her with a butcher knife, saying "Kin-a-bode" (kill you) if she did not leave at once. He approached her with the uplifted knife when her scream aroused two large dogs that were near by. They attacked the Indian, thus defeating his murderous intention. At another time in the absence of the family the Indians came and were trying her father's gun and inspecting things in general. Catherine Sadoris, the maid, came home while they were there. Just as she came around the corner of the house an Indian raised the gun to look through it; the girl, supposing that he intended to shoot her, ran for her life. The Indians told the family of the incident upon their return and she was not found until the next day, when she said she supposed that the family had all been slain. She stated that in the night seven deer came near to her, but she felt no fear except of the Indians. Ordinarily the Indians were civil and peaceful and gave but little trouble. At her father's home the first Methodist meeting was held and a society was organized in 1837 in Hebron, Indiana. She is a member of the Methodist Episcopal church and for many years gave valuable service to the Sunday school but has now given her place to the younger workers.

Dr. J. K. Blackstone graduated from the Western Reserve Medical College, of Cleveland, Ohio, in 1848. He practiced his profession in several places in Ohio, and in June, 1856, he located in Hebron, Indiana, where he resided until his death. Dr. Blackstone served in the Mexican War. He was appointed second lieutenant of the Ohio Volunteers, First Brigade, Twenty-second Division, of the militia of the state. He was the youngest commissioned officer of the army. His commission was signed June 4, 1846, by Governor Samuel Galloway and Secretary of State M. Barley. Dr. Blackstone served in the Civil War, was appointed captain Company E, Ninth Regiment of the Indiana Volunteer Militia, at Indianapolis, the first day of September, 1861. November 1, he

JAMES E BRYANT

was appointed regimental surgeon of the same company. He organized the above company.

120

JAMES EDMUND BRYANT[7] (Simeon[6] [66], David,[5] Simeon,[4] Cornelius,[3] Pieter Cornelisse,[2] Cornelis[1]), b. Mar. 5, 1839; d. July 23, 1903; m. Apr. 27, 1872, SARAH S. PRATT, who d. Feb. 23, 1907.

Children:

334.   I.   William Pratt Bryant, b. 1872; d. 1874.
335.   II.   Nellie M. Bryant, b. June 11, 1874; res., Chicago, Ill.
336.   III.   Florence Bryant, b. Sept. 12, 1889; res., Chicago, Ill. Florence possesses fine musical talent. She excels as a violinist. She studied music for several years in Berlin, Germany.

Mr. Bryant was one who responded to his country's call in 1862 and enlisted in Company I, Fifth Indiana Cavalry, in which he served nearly three years. During this time he was a prisoner seven months in Andersonville, having been captured at Sunshine Church, Georgia. After the war he was appointed postmaster and served twelve years. He owned a farm of five hundred acres adjoining the town of Hebron, Indiana, and a farm of one hundred sixty acres in Kansas. He was a Methodist. His daughters Nellie and Florence are in Berlin, Germany, where Florence is studying music, her specialty being the violin.

121

DAVID L. BRYANT[7] (Simeon[6] [66], David,[5] Simeon,[4] Cornelius,[3] Pieter Cornelisse,[2] Cornelis,[1]), b. Apr. 20, 1841, in Hebron, Ind.; d. June 17, 1902, at Las Vegas, N. M.; m. 1867, RUTH A. BARNEY, who was b. Aug. 9, 1843, Rotterdam, N. Y.; d. ...., 1904. David Bryant served in the Civil War, Company E, Ninth Indiana Volunteers, enlisting at the beginning of the war and serving until the close. He was a very successful farmer. Mrs. Bryant was a teacher for many years before her marriage.

Children:

337.   I.   Elizabeth R. Bryant, res., Elk City, Kan.
338.   II.   Mathew D. Bryant, res., Elgin, Kan.
339.   III.   William C. Bryant.

Mr. Bryant bought a farm near Elk City, Kansas, and lived there for many years; was a successful farmer and stock-raiser.

122

ELIAS BRYANT[7] (Simeon[6] [66], David,[5] Simeon,[4] Cornelius,[3] Pieter Cornelisse,[2] Cornelis,[1]), b. Mar. 5, 1843, near Hebron, Ind.; m. Nov. ......, 1867, FANNIE ADAMS, b. Sept. 27, 1851, dau. of George Adams and Laurentine Wattles, of Blue Island, Ill. Mr. Adams served in the Civil War.

Children:

340.   I.   Julia Bryant, b. Oct. 7, 1868; m. Hodson Morrow+
341.   II.   Emma Bryant, b. July 10, 1871; m. John Melvin Morrow+
342.   III.   Laurentine Bryant, b. Sept. 5, 1873. She is a graduate of Hebron high school. She attended University of Valparaiso after which she taught school. Later purchased a millinery business in Hebron.
343.   IV.   Edmund E. Bryant, b. May 12, 1877; m. Eva Gilson+
344.   V.   Margaret Bryant, b. Mar. 8, 1884; m. Apr. 12, 1905, Charles E. Lightfoot. Mrs. Lightfoot was appointed postmistress of Leroy, Ind., July 11, 1911. Mr. Lightfoot is a barber by trade. He is a member of the M. E. ch.
345.   VI.   George Harold Bryant, b. Apr. 12, 1887.
346.   VII.   Myra Lillian Bryant, b. July 31, 1895, at Hebron, Ind. She is a musical student.

Elias Bryant was born on the farm which his father purchased from the government, and has in his possession the deed dated June 25, 1841, and signed by President John Tyler. The house was built from timbers hewn from the native forest and its framework is still used for the present home. The Indians were friendly;

ELIAS BRYANT

Simeon, his father, had always treated them kindly and was willing to trade grain or whatever he had for their fish and some articles they had for sale. When under the influence of liquor they were troublesome. In politics Mr. Bryant is a Republican. The old homestead holds many sacred memories. Here occurred many of the births, marriages, and deaths of the family. An illustration of the old house accompanies this sketch. Residence, Hebron, Indiana.

124

ISAAC BRYANT[7] (David[6] [67], David,[5] Simeon,[4] Cornelius,[3] Pieter Cornelisse,[2] Cornelis,[1]), b. Mar. 29, 1823; d. ...... 1850; m. AMELIA CARTER.

Children:

347.   I.   Rachel Bryant; m. James Anderson; died within a few years, leaving one son:

348.   I.   William Bryant.

349.   II.   Nancy Bryant; m. Jacob Piatt; moved to Kansas, where she still lives, having raised a large family.

125

NANCY BRYANT[7] (David[6] [67], David,[5] Simeon,[4] Cornelius,[3] Pieter Cornelisse,[2] Cornelis,[1]), b. Sept. 25, 1825, near Wyandot, Ohio; d. July 24, 1913; m. May 22, 1854, WILLIAM FISHER, who was b. June 9, 1825, near Schenectady, N. Y., the son of Alexander Fisher, who was b. in Ayr, Scotland, and Agnes Brown, b. in Paisley, Scotland.

Children:

350.   I.   David A. Fisher, b. Mar. 13, 1855; m. Elizabeth Bliss+

351.   II.   Arabella F. Fisher, b. Sept. 21, 1857; m. Charles W. Hayward+

352.   III.   Ida E. Fisher, b. Mar. 7, 1860; unm.+

353.   IV.   Mary J. Fisher, b. Mar. 4, 1864; d. Feb. 26, 1878.

354.   V.   Rachel Agnes Fisher, b. May 22, 1866; d. Aug. 14, 1866.

Nancy Bryant came to Indiana with her parents in 1835, when the settlements were very few. Her mother died at Pleasant Grove, Lake County, and was buried near Valparaiso, Indiana. At this time Nancy was a child of only ten years, and with her brother Isaac was placed in school by her father in Wellsburgh, Virginia, where they lived in the home of Dr. Grafton, a son-in-law of Joseph Bryant. After about a year their father married Margaret Steinbrooke, in Illinois, and he brought them back to their western home. In 1849 her step-mother died, and Nancy was left with the care of six brothers, the youngest a mere babe. She filled the position of sister and mother to her brothers until her marriage.

In 1854 Mr. Fisher wedded this noble young woman who has proved his devoted companion and effective helpmeet during the long intervening years. They began their married life on a farm in Lake County, where, sustained by mutual affection and sympathy, and by common aims and ambitions, they toiled early and late, in order that they might gain the goal of definite independence and prosperity. With the passing of years they accumulated one of the valuable landed estates of Lake County, and the same still remains in their possession.

They remained on this homestead until 1884, when they removed to Hebron, Porter County, Indiana, where they have since resided, and have a secure place in popular confidence and venerating esteem. Soon after establishing residence in Hebron, Mr. Fisher engaged in the hardware business and later he turned his attention to the dry-goods business, in which he continued active operations until 1894, when he disposed of the stock and business, after having been one of the leading merchants of the town for a full decade. Later he here established the private banking institution which was later transformed into the present Citizens State Bank, of which he is president and of which his daughter Ida is cashier, the institution being one whose success is based alike on careful and conservative management and ample capitalistic reinforcement. Miss Fisher became cashier of the original private bank and has continued her effective services under the present régime, with the result that she is known as an especially able and discriminating business woman and as the effective coadjutor of her honored father, who has attained the patriarchal age of eighty-seven years (1912) and whose life has been one to offer both lesson and inspiration.

NANCY BRYANT FISHER

William Fisher gained his early educational training in the common schools of his native county and thus laid the foundation for the comprehensive knowledge which he was later to acquire through active association with men and affairs. At the age of twenty-five years, his youthful ambition responded to the lure of the West, which offered superior opportunities for the winning of success through individual effort. He had kinsfolk in Indiana and thus was led to make that state his destination, while his resourcefulness was shown by careful preparation for business activities in the new home. He came west with the means and intention of engaging in the manufacture of brooms, and he brought with him not only a supply of broom-corn seed, but also the requisite drill for the cultivation of the product. Upon his arrival in Lake County he formed a partnership with his cousins, the late William and John Brown, and engaged in the raising of broom-corn, in the manufacturing of which they employed a skilled broom-maker. They continued in this line of enterprise for several years and at one time had nearly one hundred acres of land under effective cultivation for the propagation of broom-corn. The products were shipped to Detroit, Chicago, and other places in the Middle West, and the industry was made a profitable venture.

He has been a loyal adherent of the Republican party from the time of its organization and while a resident of Lake County he served with marked ability and zeal as a member of the board of county commissioners. He held this office for seven years and within that time he earnestly fostered the movements which resulted in the erection of the county court house, jail, and infirmary, the buildings of each of which were erected during his incumbency of office. He and his family are devoted members of the United Presbyterian church in Hebron and all who remain here show a lively interest in everything that tends to advance the moral, educational and social welfare of the community. A substantial fortune stands as the concrete evidence of the excellent labors of Mr. Fisher in the years that have passed, and his career has been one unblemished by injustice or selfishness. He and his estimable wife have shown sympathy for those in affliction and have been animated by a spirit of helpfulness that ever indicates a high sense of stewardship. Secure in the high regard of all who know them, they may well look back into the perspective of the years and find satisfaction in the goodly fruitage which has crowned their efforts, as well as the faith and confidence which their earnest labors and kindly deeds have inspired in those about them. Forty-three English families of Fisher name bear coats of arms. (Burke's General Armory.)

127

JAMES HARRISON BRYANT[7] (David[6] [67], David,[5] Simeon,[4] Cornelius,[3] Pieter Cornelisse,[2] Cornelis,[1]), b. Apr. 24, 1840, in Gentry Co., Mo., near St. Joseph. Moved to Illinois with family soon after birth where he lived until he was 19 years old. In 1859 went across the plains with his brother John to California. He lived in different parts of California until 1865, when he returned to his old home. In 1867, went to Kansas with his three brothers, Daniel, David, and Allen. All four brothers took up claims about four miles north of Erie, Kan.; m. Jan. 1, 1873, MINNIE MAY HODGES in Erie, Kan. She was b. Feb. 23, 1855; dau. of Norman W. Hodges and Eliza J. Britt.

Children:

355.   I.   Belle Bryant, b. Dec. 30, 1876; d. Jan. 9, 1899.
356.   II. Harry Allen Bryant, b. Aug. 20, 1883, in Neosho Co., Kan.; m. Lelia Parks Ewing, who was b. July 14, 1909, in Los Angeles, Cal. Res., Parsons, Kan.

In 1879 Mr. Bryant moved to Colorado Springs, Colorado, and was engaged in railroad contracting until 1883. He returned to Kansas and located in Parsons, his present home. For eight years he was Street Commissioner of Parsons. He then engaged in the street paving business until 1906, when he established a wholesale coal and feed business, which he is now conducting.

Belle Bryant attended the Parsons public schools from 1884 to 1896, when she became an invalid and was such until her death.

Harry A. Bryant attended the Parsons public schools, and also Parsons Business College, and in 1901 entered the employ of the Missouri, Kansas and Texas Railway Company, where he remained two years and then took a position as assistant cashier of the Parsons Commercial Bank, and was afterwards promoted to cashier, which position he still holds.

J. H. Bryant

128

Joseph Allen Bryant[7] (David[6] [67], David,[5] Simeon,[4] Cornelius,[3] Pieter Cornelisse,[2] Cornelis[1]), b. May 24, 1842, d. ......; m. Dec. 21, 1871, at Olathe, Kan., Ida Kate Flanner, who was b. Oct. 19, 1848, at Pleasant Grove, Belmont Co., Ohio, dau. of William Flanner and Elizabeth Ross. William Flanner was the son of Jacob Parker Flanner and Charity Beeson. Jacob was son of Wm. Flanner. Charity Beeson was the dau. of Henry Beeson of Uniontown, Pa. Elizabeth Sparks Ross was the dau. of James A. Ross and Martha Ackeley Watson, dau. of William Watson, who served in the war of the Revolution, a member of the Jersey Blues. His wife was Sarah Akeley of Mayflower descent.

Children:

357. I. Bessie Bryant, b. Dec. 6, 1872, at Olathe, Kan. She attended the home schools and also received a college education, and taught for a few years. While in California she had supervision over clerks in a publishing house. She is a member of the Daughters of the American Revolution. Res., Chicago, Ill.

358. II. Orah Bryant, b. Nov. 19, 1874; d. Feb. 7, 1882.

359. III. John Bryant, b. Feb. 21, 1877; d. June 26, 1878.

360. IV. William Harrison Bryant, b. Dec. 1, 1878, in Neosho Co., Kan.; m. Sept., 1899, at Middletown, N. Y., Genevieve Lynn. He was educated at Olathe, Kan., and was employed by the American Felt Co. in Chicago, Ill., for a number of years. He is now manager of the Felters Co., Chicago.

361. V. Joseph Allen Bryant, b. June 6, 1882; m. Margaret Anderson+

Joseph Allen Bryant served as a soldier during the Civil War. He enlisted when about eighteen years of age, August 10, 1861, at Oneida, Illinois. He was mustered into service as a private in Company C, Forty-second Illinois Volunteer Infantry, for the period of three years. He re-enlisted on the first day of January,

1864, as a veteran volunteer for a period of three years, at Stone's Mills, Tennessee. He was mustered into service as a veteran February 16, 1864, at Chattanooga, Tennessee. Received his appointment as sergeant in Company C, Forty-second Regiment of Volunteer Infantry, on the 30th day of April, 1864. His residence at date of first enlistment is stated as Altoona, Knox County, Illinois. He was in service from the time of his first enlistment until the close of the rebellion, and was credited as a brave and loyal soldier. After his return from the war he went to Erie, Neosho County, Kansas, and from there to Arizona, where, while working on the construction of the Atlantic & Pacific Railway, he was also deputy United States marshal, and was shot while arresting a desperado. The following clipping was taken from an Arizona paper, the *Arizona Miner*:

"A man from San Bernardino, Cal., named Miller, *alias* Grizzly, had threatened the life of Railroad Contractor King, who swore out a warrant for the arrest of said Miller, and placed same in the hands of Allen Bryant, railroad contractor and deputy United States marshal. A man by the name of Holmes, a United States marshal from Albuquerque, New Mexico, armed with a Remington rifle, accompanied Mr. Bryant in making the arrest of Miller. Bryant read the warrant and commanded the accused to surrender his revolver, which he pulled and shot Bryant twice, one ball passing through the breast, the other through the abdomen. Holmes, the assistant, was posted behind a tree, and like the coward he was, allowed his brother officer to be murdered. The assassin, after mortally wounding Bryant, took his arms and then demanded of Holmes his gun, which the United States marshal threw to him and begged mercy at his hands. Miller, after coming off victorious, mounted a fine horse and started off into the mountains, waving his hat at the enraged people of Flagstaff, who followed in hot pursuit. Holmes also left, to avoid being lynched by the citizens, who were rightly incensed at his beastly cowardice. Mr. Bryant died about six hours after the shooting. He was an honest, law-abiding citizen, with an excellent wife and three little children."

129
DANIEL STEINBROOKE BRYANT[7] (David[6] [67], David,[5] Simeon,[4] Cornelius,[3] Pieter Cornelisse,[2] Cornelis[1]), b. Mar. 15, 1844; m.

J. H. Bryant

FRANCES COOK. He lived some years in Illinois, and moved to Kansas in 1869 where he bought a farm near Erie in Neosho Co., Kan. Mr. Bryant d. Jan. 24, 1894, at his home at Erie, Kan.

Children:

362. I. Maude Bryant, b. in Neosho Co., Kan.
363. II. Ora Dell Bryant, b. 1870; d. young.
364. III. Fred Bryant, b. Mar. 19, 1880, in Neosho Co., Kan.; d. Mar. 14, 1904.

130

DAVID BRYANT[7] (David[6] [67], David,[5] Simeon,[4] Cornelius,[3] Pieter Cornelisse,[2] Cornelis[1]), b. Nov. 15, 1846, in Ill., moved to Neosho Co., Kan., where he married LAURA WHITE in 1878. Mr. Bryant followed farming and dealing in real estate. Has been a constant sufferer from rheumatism for many years, yet, notwithstanding, has accumulated quite an income.

Child:

365. I. Bertie Bryant, b. Aug. 7, 1879; d. Apr. 27, 1888.

Mr. Bryant has in his possession the stock of the gun that our common ancestor, David Bryant, carried in the Revolutionary War and Mrs. Joseph Allen Bryant has the bullet moulds used by David Bryant. (37.)

132

ORAH ALICE BRYANT[7] (David[6] [67], David,[5] Simeon,[4] Cornelius,[3] Pieter Cornelisse,[2] Cornelis[1]), b. June 27, 1854, near Hebron, Ind.; m. Oct. 18, 1871, to WILLIAM B. DODDRIDGE, who was b. Sept. 20, 1846, in Salem, Ohio, son of Alexander Doddridge and Rebecca Flemming.

Children:

366. I. William Bryant Doddridge, b. Aug. 23, 1872; m. Myrtle Sarber.
367. II. Charles Parker Doddridge, b. Feb. 23, 1874; d. Aug. 25, 1889; buried in Hebron, Ind.

368. III. Mabel Alberta Doddridge, b. Sept. 13, 1877; m.
            Adelbert P. Meredith+
369. IV. Phillip Harrison Doddridge, b. May 15, 1888; unm.+

Orah Alice Bryant attended the public schools, and also the
Valparaiso College. She moved to Illinois with her parents, and
when she was eleven years of age her mother died and she with her
father came to Indiana, where they made their home with her sister,
Nancy Bryant Fisher, until her marriage. Orah and her father
lived a short time in Kansas with her brothers. After her marriage
she assisted her husband in the drug business, and then she engaged in the photograph business, which she carried on very successfully for several years until she went to Lafayette, Indiana, where
she placed their son Phillip in Purdue University. She remained
there four years, then returned to Mentone, and is now a registered
pharmacist. In politics, Mr. Doddridge is a Republican; religion,
Methodist; occupation, druggist and jeweler. They have resided
in Hebron, Indiana; Galva, Illinois, and at present in Mentone,
Indiana. She is a member of the Daughters of the American
Revolution.

William Bryant Doddrige [366] lived with his parents in Hebron
and attended the public schools, and moved with them to Galva,
Illinois, and then to Mentone, Indiana. He studied the jewelry
and drug business, and assisted his father. He worked for some
time in Chicago. In 1895 he went into the jewelry business for
himself in Claypool, Indiana, where he was living at the time of his
untimely death, which occurred on New Year's night, 1896, when,
going home with a young man from a "watch night" prayer-
meeting, cold and overcome with sleep, the horse went upon the
railroad tracks in front of an express train. Willie and his companion were dashed into eternity without a moment's warning.

133
DAVID MITCHELL[7] (Hannah[6] [68], David,[5] Simeon,[4] Cornelius,[3] Pieter Cornelisse,[2] Cornelis[1]), b. Sept. 13, 1820; m. June
14, 1855, MARY MERRIMAN, who was b. at Bucyrus, Ohio.

            Children:
370.   I. Mathew Mitchell, b. Sept., 1859; m. Mary J.
            Ihrie+

DAVID BRYANT

371.   II.   Lettie M. Mitchell, b. ......; m. Jasper A. Mc-
Millan+

Copied from the Historical Edition of Amanda Church, the
following: "The late David B. Mitchell of Amanda Church was a
man whose daily life was a most excellent example for the Christian
to follow, yet he himself wisely pointed out the Master as the only
perfect man.   His earlier life was spent in Richland County, Ohio.
After his marriage they located on a farm near Amanda Church in
Allen County, Ohio.   His good wife was a member of the Baptist
Church and a most devoted Christian.   Mr. Mitchell said his wife
never failed to pray before retiring and that her devotion was
largely the means of bringing him into the fold.   He was converted
on May 19, 1867, united with the Amanda Baptist Church, where
he became an active worker and was elected deacon.   Mrs. Mitchell was called from this life on the 12th day of May, 1881, and
in her death Amanda Church lost a most highly esteemed member.
David B. Mitchell was a great bible student as the well-marked
pages of his favored book mutely testify.   Having quietly and
peacefully laid down the burdens of life, with his work completed,
after fourscore years, he cheerfully entered into the joys of a better
life on the 8th of May, 1901.   He was conscious until the last
moment and had even dictated his own modest obituary shortly
before the end came.   During the long period of failing health he
frequently called his little grandchildren to his side and told them
of the better life that awaited him; of the mansions God had prepared in heaven.   He was honored and respected by all who knew
him."

135
ROBERT MITCHELL[7] (Hannah[6] [68], David,[5] Simeon,[4] Cornelius,[3] Pieter Cornelisse,[2] Cornelis[1]), b. Sept. 8, 1825; m. (1st)
MARY FORBES, near Bucyrus, Ohio; m. (2nd) MARIA MARTIN,
of Pittsburg, Kan.

By his first wife he had four children, all of whom died young
except:
372.   I.   Anna Mitchell, who is living with her step-mother
at Pittsburg, Kan.

138

SIMEON MITCHELL[7] (Hannah[6] [68], David,[5] Simeon,[4] Cornelius,[3] Pieter Cornelisse,[2] Cornelis[1]), b. Sept. 11, 1826; d. Jan.
22, 1907; m. ISABELLE MITCHELL, who was b. Nov. 8, 1828;
d. Oct. 8, 1904.

Children:

373.   I. William Torrence Mitchell, b. July 15, 1852; m.
          Ella Jane Gibson+
374. II. Katherine Clark Mitchell, b. Oct. 29, 1854; m. July
          24, 1876, George Herod Ashley, of Ash-
          bourne, Eng. Mrs. Ashley is a woman of
          education and culture and has traveled ex-
          tensively. No children.
375. III. Robert Mitchell, b. Nov. 23, 1856; unm.
376. IV. Mathew Mitchell, b. Nov. 17, 1858; m. Nettie
          Amanda White+
377.   V. Mary Bryant Mitchell, b. Sept. 10, 1864; m. Richard
          Alston Metcalf+
378. VI. Jane Mitchell, b. Jan. 6, 1866; d. in infancy.
379. VII. John Mitchell, b. Jan. 6, 1866; d. in infancy.

We believe that a sketch of the life of Mrs. Isabelle Mitchell
should not be omitted in the history of this family, for she not only
fulfills the proverb, "She looketh well to the ways of her household," but by a life of usefulness she left a radiance of lasting influence in bringing about reforms that tend toward the betterment
of humanity. She assisted in providing churches and organizing
Sunday schools for the colored people of the South. Her work in
the temperance cause covered a wide territory, particularly in the
state of Missouri, where she spent twenty years associated with the
Woman's Christian Temperance Union organization. Her attention was attracted toward the condition of prisons. She found
that the prison cells throughout the South were under ground, and
through her solicitation prison cells were placed above ground.

In 1890 Mr. and Mrs. Mitchell and family removed to Iowa.
Mrs. Mitchell was appointed state organizer of Bible Reading
Societies under the state Woman's Suffrage Association. These
bible study clubs were organized in many cities and towns throughout the state. Later, going to Wisconsin, she became a member of

Orah Bryant Doddridge

the National Prison Reform Association. She traveled extensively and visited many prisons in the United States. She gave brief addresses to the prisoners. She had a special gift in reaching the hearts of the people. While in the line of prison work she made the acquaintance of Mrs. Eva Booth, "the little mother of the prisoners." Mrs. Mitchell excelled as an organizer. During her residence in Wisconsin she organized night schools and bible study classes among the women of the Fox River Paper Mills. She was engaged in this work when one evening, while returning to her home, her strength gave out on the way, and soon her useful life passed away.

139
JOSEPH R. MITCHELL[7] (Hannah[6] [68], David,[5] Simeon,[4] Cornelius,[3] Pieter Cornelisse,[2] Cornelis[1]), b. Dec. 31, 1831, in Richland Co., Ohio; d. Oct. 29, 1864; m. Sept. 17, 1857, ANNE CATHARINE MCVICKER, who was b. May 29, 1834, at Bedford, Pa.; dau. of John McVicker and Nancy Dennison. Anne Catharine McVicker was of Scotch-Irish descent. She d. June 22, 1896, in Monmouth, Ill. In politics Mr. Mitchell was a Republican; in religion a Presbyterian.

Children:

380.   I.   Frances Lettie Mitchell, b. July 15, 1858; m. Millard A. Burrell+
381.   II. Nancy Kate Mitchell, b. Sept. 27, 1859; m. William E. Johnson+
382.   III. Martha M. Mitchell, b. Dec. 8, 1861; d. Feb. 13, 1864.

On the 9th day of August, 1862, Joseph Mitchell enlisted in what was known as the Railroad Regiment, being the Eighty-ninth Regiment, Illinois Volunteers; First Brigade, Third Division, Fourth Army Corps, of the Army of the Cumberland. His first engagement was at Perryville, Kentucky; then at Stone River, followed by Liberty Gap, Tullahoma, Chickamauga, Mission Ridge, Knoxville, Rocky-face Ledge, and Dallas in succession; these being the regular battles, with fifteen or twenty heavy skirmishes scattered between.

At Dallas on the 27th day of May, 1864, he was wounded and taken prisoner, his wound being in the side. After lying on the battlefield for two nights and one day he was removed to a field hospital, where he laid on the ground five days with nothing done for him except being given a little corn bread, and coffee made from burnt beans. Then, on a dark, rainy night, he was taken to Marietta in a wagon train, with sixteen hundred other prisoners, and placed for the night in a church, in beds of straw, which seemed like beds of down to the poor torn bodies. Here the Union ladies came with tea, wine and other good things, and insisted upon feeding the men. The next day they were loaded into freight cars and taken into Atlanta, where they were met and again fed by the Union ladies, before being taken to the prison hospital.

No one can tell of the suffering endured during these days and nights on the battlefield and during the removal into Atlanta, but while there in the prison hospital they were treated as well as the rebels, with their limited resources, could treat them, which was very different from their after-treatment at Andersonville. Before Atlanta fell, the prisoners were all sent to Andersonville where Mr. Mitchell soon died, a victim to the horrors of that terrible place. He is buried in the National Cemetery at Andersonville, Georgia, the number of his grave being 11,617.

The highest praise can be accorded his memory. He lived and died a Christian soldier. He was always in the front rank and ready for duty; full of patriotism and love of country, but always remembering the loving wife and little daughters at home; always thinking and planning for their welfare, and daily praying and longing for the time of returning to them. His life went out a sacrifice to his country. He has slept away the years of his manhood, far from his home and loved ones, but surely he will receive his reward from the Great Commander.

140

JOHN BRYANT MITCHELL[7] (Hannah[6] [68], David,[5] Simeon,[4] Cornelius,[3] Pieter Cornelisse,[2] Cornelis[1]), b. Mar. 24, 1823, near Ontario, Ohio; d. June 12, 1913; m. July 15, 1856, OLIVE WILSON, who was b. July 1, 1836, on the Wyandot Indian Reservation; d. Jan. 6, 1913, at Cleveland, Tenn.; dau. of Daniel Wilson

W. B. DODDRIDGE

of Plattsburg, who was b. July 4, 1804; d. Wyandot Co., Ohio, Feb. 19, 1902, living to the good old age of ninety-eight years.

Children:

383.   I.   Hannah Mary Mitchell, b. April 28, 1857; d. July 24, 1877, at Lima, Ohio.
384.   II.   Clark Mitchell, b. Nov. 1, 1862; d. Dec. 24, 1876.
385.   III.   John Franklin Mitchell, b. Dec. 23, 1866; m. Estella McClandish+

Mrs. Mitchell's mother's maiden name was Johanna French. She died September 19, 1906. Mr. Mitchell's early childhood was spent on a farm. His father, however, in connection with his farming carried on milling, a mill for grinding flour, a sawmill, and a carding and fulling mill for making cloth. In 1842 his father removed with his family to Crawford County, Ohio, where he purchased a farm. John Bryant Mitchell's education was received in the public schools. At the age of twenty he entered Oberlin College. He did not finish the college course because of ill health. While there he believes that his future character was formed through the preaching of Rev. Charles G. Finney, president of the college. After leaving college Mr. Mitchell spent twelve years as agent of the American Bible Society, distributing bibles and collecting funds for that society. Many thousands of bibles were distributed by him throughout the newly-settled frontier where usually no churches existed. He reluctantly gave up this service and was connected with the American Tract Society, his field of labor being the middle and southern states. While in Tennessee near the mountains he heard much about the destitution and poverty of the people living in the mountain district. He became interested to know the truth of the matter. He arranged with a friend to go with him. They loaded a spring wagon with bibles, testaments and other good literature and spent a month traveling through the mountains of Tennessee and North Carolina. He was astonished and distressed by what he saw, both of destitution and ignorance, existing there. He gave up all other plans and vowed with the aid of his Master to give up the remainder of his life for the benefit of these poor, neglected people. He has spent twenty-one years in this service. He placeed among these people 115,000 bibles and testaments and 300,000 gospel books and tons of other literature and of clothing. Mr. Mitchell gave largely of his own money and also was assisted in his work through his solicitations with donations from churches and missionary societies. He received $15,000 in money with which to purchase bibles.

141
TORRENCE MITCHELL[7] (Hannah[6] [68], David,[5] Simeon,[4] Cornelius,[3] Pieter Cornelisse,[2] Cornelis[1]), b. ......; d. ......; buried in Dallas, Tex.; m. SARAH MARTIN.

> *Children:*

386.   I. Bertha Mitchell.
387.   II. Georgia Mitchell, who m. JOHN WATSON of Perth Amboy, N. J. Mr. and Mrs. Watson live in New York City.

> *Child:*

772a.   I. Eunice Watson.

143
HANNAH ABIGAIL MITCHELL[7] (Hannah[6] [68], David,[5] Simeon,[4] Cornelius,[3] Pieter Cornelisse,[2] Cornelis[1]), b. Feb. 25, 1840, near Mansfield, Ohio; m. at Bloomington, Ill., Aug. 1, 1863, SAMUEL H. LARMINIE, who was b. Oct. 13, 1838, at Westport, Mayo Co., Ireland; d. May 9, 1885, at 5006 Washington Ave., Chicago, Ill. He was the son of Charles Larminie and ...... Ferel. Mr. Larminie was a member of the board of trade; in politics a Republican; adherent of the Episcopalian faith. Mrs. Larminie resides in Chicago. No children.

146
MARTHA POST[7] (Elizabeth[6] [69], David,[5] Simeon,[4] Cornelius,[3] Pieter Cornelisse,[2] Cornelis[1]), b. Aug. 7, 1827, at Fredericktown, Knox Co., Ohio; d. Sept. 8, 1912; m. Aug. 4, 1847, at Spencerville, Ohio, to CYRUS HART HOVER, who was b. Mar. 5, 1822, at Trumhill, Warren Co., Ohio; d. Mar. 8, 1896. He was the son of Joseph Hover and Caroline Adgate. Mrs.

JOSEPH R. MITCHELL

Hover was a member of the Methodist Church of Spencerville, Ohio.

Children:

389. I. Caroline Elizabeth Hover, b. June 27, 1848; m. Philip LeMasters+
390. II. Lora Inez Hover, b. Feb. 24, 1850; d. Feb. 28, 1852.
391. III. Joseph Oscar Hover, b. Feb. 28, 1852; d. July 25, 1853.
392. IV. Mary Eliza Hover, b. Mar. 26, 1854; m. Robert Henry Gamble+
393. V. Charles Alfred Hover, b. Oct. 25, 1856; m. Mercy Ellen Sunderland+
394. VI. Kate Pauline Hover, b. Apr. 13, 1859; m. Daniel Hicks Crites+
395. VII. Bryant Graham Hover, b. Dec. 1, 1861; m. Mercy Naomi Bice+
396. VIII. Minnie Lorene Hover, b. Sept. 10, 1864; m. James Green Cochran, who was born Mar. 27, 1847, Lima, Ohio, son of Simon Cochran and Lucinda Miller. Mr. Cochran is a dealer in coal, building supplies, and ice; in politics Republican; in religion a Baptist. Res., Spencerville, Ohio.
397. IX. Florence Edna Hover, b. Apr. 3, 1867, at Spencerville, Ohio; m. June 5, 1901, Frederick W. Newell, who was b. Apr. 28, 1860, at Mattawan, Mich., son of William Henry Newell and Marrilla Butler. Mr. Newell is an electrician; in politics a Republican; res., Hammond, Ind.
398. X. Addie Luella Hover, b. Jan. 26, 1870; d. Sept. 13, 1874.
399. XI. Martha Jane Hover, b. July 14, 1872; m. Frank Austin Hitchcock+

Martha Post lived in the home of her childhood at Fredericktown, Ohio, until about nine years of age. Her parents then removed to Shelby, Richland County, Ohio, where they remained until 1838. In that year her father was sent by the government to Upper Sandusky to build there a sawmill and a gristmill on the Indian reservation. During their residence at this place Martha taught a school composed of six Indians and eight white children. She taught this school before she was fourteen years of age. In 1842 the family removed to Amanda Township, Allen County, Ohio. Martha attended school in Shelby and in Lima, Ohio. She taught several terms in Amanda Township. A few of the pupils are still living (1912). After her marriage to Mr. Hover in 1847 they lived in Lima, Ohio, until 1850, when they removed to Delphos County, where they remained until 1863, when they moved to a farm five miles east of Spencerville. In 1887 they made their residence in Spencerville and there remained until the death of Mr. Hover in 1896. Mrs. Hover was a remarkable woman in mind and personal charm. She was a fine conversationalist. Her mind was well stored through the various experiences she encountered from the early pioneer days and through the rapid and marked development of her native state during the nineteenth century. Much is due to her and those who lived, as she did, for the present degree of civilization, in a country recently in possession of savages. She represented an important link between the past and the present. Mrs. Hover possessed a strong religious temperament. She united with the first society of Methodists formed in Hartford, Ohio, when she was fifteen years old. Her public life was modest, but her home life was very wholesome and pronounced. During her long life she has left a good and illustrious record. She has left her posterity a rich heritage and has been a great blessing in example to her associates. It is said of her, with the privilege of a college education she would have made her mark in the religious and literary world. She would have stamped the printed page with the same sunny and cheerful glow she did her home life. Mr. and Mrs. Hover are buried in the Woodlawn cemetery at Lima, Ohio.

148

LEONIDAS HAMLINE POST[7] (Elizabeth[6] [69], David,[5] Simeon,[4] Cornelius,[3] Pieter Cornelisse,[2] Cornelis[1]), b. Aug. 8, 1832, at Fredericktown, Ohio; d. Oct. 4, 1904; m. Aug. 2, 1854, in Urbana, Ohio, ELIZA JANE STEWART, who was b. Oct. 13, 1830; d. Sept.

Hannah Mitchell Larmun

16, 1912. She was the dau. of Samuel Stewart and Mary Thomas. In politics he was a Democrat; in religion a Baptist.

Children:

400.   I.   William Stewart Post, b. July 7, 1855; d. Sept. 19, 1856.

401.   II.   Samuel Alven Post, b. Nov. 22, 1856; m. Alice Crites+

402.   III.   Charles Cyrus Post, b. Oct. 8, 1858; m. Ida Crites ⊢

403.   IV.   Edward Grant Post, b. Sept. 11, 1867; m. Jennie Whetstone+

404.   V.   Mary Elizabeth Post, b. June 20, 1870; d. Oct. 22, 1872.

405.   VI.   Martha Jane Post, b. Apr. 27, 1872; d. Feb. 27, 1874.

406.   VII.   Leonidas Hamline Post, Jr., b. Sept. 11, 1875; m. Altha Moorman+

Leonidas Hamline Post, when a child, moved with his father's family to Shelby, Richland County, and from there to Upper Sandusky, Wyandot County, where for three years the father— a millwright by profession—was engaged in constructing a grist and sawmill, and also a council house for the Wyandot Indians. He had much commerce with this tribe by whom he was held in high esteem on account of his just dealings. In March, 1841, the family moved to Allen County, where the father built a sawmill for his cousin, Chas. Marshall, near the old town of Hartford. In 1843 he moved four miles east of Spencerville on the Auglaize River where he built the Post Mill, which he operated until 1849, when he bought over 500 acres of land about one and a quarter miles west of his former location, and here the subject of our sketch grew to manhood.

When a young man L. H. Post learned the molder's trade, working both in Delphos and Lima. Later he attended Oberlin College, and in 1852 he made a trip to California, via New York, crossing the Isthmus of Panama, and thence up the coast to San Francisco. Here he engaged in gold-mining, returning to Ohio in 1854 via Nicaragua and New Orleans. After his marriage he settled on a farm in Amanda Township, Allen County, where he continued to reside until his death October 3, 1904. His farm home was one of the best in his community and the farm one of the best equipped as to other buildings, farming machinery, and all that goes to make a first-class farm.

Among other agricultural interests he devoted much time and attention to the careful breeding of draft horses and probably to his interest and work in this direction is due the excellence of this stock in Amanda Township, he having owned several imported French horses, in company with Mr. James Hover of Lima. He took great pride in his fine Shorthorn cattle, and is credited with introducing this breed into the township.

Mr. Post was a member and ardent supporter of the Amanda Baptist Church. He was a man widely known, highly respected wherever known, having several times been elected to office in his home township. In the last few years of his life, after he had quit work, he was fond of relating incidents of his childhood, especially of the few years he had only Wyandot Indian children for his playmates. They played with bows and arrows much as any children of that time would have done. A few years prior to his death, while on a visit to his brother at Carthage, Missouri, he went into the Indian Territory to see if he could find some of his old-time playfellows, but found only a few of them, and was told that most of the tribe had died (no doubt of grief, as was frequently the case) after they had been forced to leave their old home in Wyandot County, Ohio, for their new home in the Red Man's State.

Eliza Jane Post was reared under the care of her uncle William Stewart, her mother having died when she was four years old. Her childhood was spent in Champaign County where she was educated in the common schools. At the age of nineteen she united with the King's Creek Baptist Church. She was married in 1854 to Leonidas H. Post, of one of the prominent families of Allen County. Returning with her husband to their future home in Amanda Township, she became a charter member of the Amanda Baptist Church, to the interests of which she ever remained loyal and where she was a regular attendant at all of the services until hindered by the infirmities of old age. She was faithful in the home, nothing being too arduous for her to undertake for her loved ones. She was a granddaughter of Captain Arthur Thomas, a brave soldier of the War of 1812, who with his company had been ordered to Fort Findley to guard the public stores. He and his son, on

MARTHA HOVER

their return to their home near Urbana, Ohio, were killed and scalped by the Indians near Bellefontaine and the bodies, which had been badly mutilated, were carried to Urbana in sacks by a deputation of citizens sent out from that place.

149
ADAM CLARK POST[7] (Elizabeth[6] [69], David,[5] Simeon,[4] Cornelius,[3] Pieter Cornelisse,[2] Cornelis[1]), b. Nov. 2, 1834, at Shelby, Richland Co., Ohio; d. June 27, 1908; m. Nov. 22, 1855, at Lima, Ohio, ISABEL MARTIN, who was b. June 1, 1834, at Fort Amanda, Allen Co., Ohio; dau. of Archelaus Martin and Catherine Russel. She d. June 11, 1869. Mr. Post m. (2nd) Jan. 1, 1871, at Carthage, Mo., LUCY ANN FROST, b. at Quincy, Ill.; dau. of Worthy Frost and Julia Runnels. He m. (3rd) Oct. 16, 1885, at Carthage, Mo., ELIZA J. RAWLES, who was b. Mar. 15, 1835, at Marion, Ohio; dau. of John Rawles and Clarissa Pangburn.

Children:
            1st marriage —
407.   I. Martha Post, b. Aug. 14, 1856; m. Andrew Clark Ale+
408.   II. Charles Archelaus Post, b. Oct. 20, 1857; m. Cora A. Bowman+
409.   III. Katie Elizabeth Post, b. Aug. 16, 1861; d. Jan. 7, 1878.
            2nd marriage —
410.   IV. Winfred Bryant Post, b. Oct. 19, 1871; m. Elizabeth Elenor Luscombe+
411.   V. Margaret Gertrude Post, b. Aug. 12, 1873.
412.   VI. Mary Maude Post, b. Mar. 9, 1875, Carthage, Mo.; m. Nov. 26, 1902, DANIEL ROBERT SMITH, who was b. Sept. 14, 1869, at Rowlets, Hart Co., Ky., son of Daniel E. W. Smith and Mary Francis Whitehurst. In politics Mr. Smith is a Republican. Mr. and Mrs. Smith are adherents of the Methodist faith. Res., Carthage, Mo.

413. VII.   Mabel Post, b. Jan. 15, 1877; m. Curtis R. Hixson;
        d. Nov., 1907.

414. VIII.   William Frank Post, b. Nov. 21, 1878; d. Feb. 6, 1879.

Adam Clark Post enlisted on July 21, 1862 from Allen County,
Ohio, to serve three years or during the war, and was mustered into
the United States service at Camp Lima, Ohio, as orderly sergeant
of Captain W. H. Hill's Company A, Eighty-first Regular Ohio
Volunteer Infantry; Colonel Thomas Morton Commander. He
was promoted to Second Lieutenant of Company D, June 14, 1864;
to First Lieutenant of Company A, February 14, 1865, and was
mustered out with his command, at Louisville, Kentucky, July 21,
1865. March 2, 1862, the regiment was ordered to St. Louis,
Missouri, and there was armed with Enfield rifles. It was assigned
to the Second Brigade, Second Division, Sixteenth Corps, Army of
the Tennessee, and with it he participated in the following engagements: Shiloh or Pittsburg Landing, Seige of Corinth, Mississippi;
also battle of Corinth; Iuka, Mississippi; Tuscumbia, Alabama;
Snake Creek Gap, Georgia; Leey's Ferry, Georgia; Resaca, Georgia;
Rome Cross Roads; Dallas or New Hope Church; battle and seige
of Atlanta, Georgia; Jonesboro; Sherman's March to the Sea;
Savannah, Georgia; Bentonville, North Carolina; Goldsboro,
North Carolina; Raleigh, North Carolina.

He marched to Washington, District of Columbia, by way of
Richmond and participated in the Grand Review, May 24, 1865.
He was a member of Station Post No. 16, Department of Missouri,
Grand Army of the Republic, of which he was Senior Vice-Com-
mander. He was a member of the Masonic order. After the war
Mr. Post entered extensively into farming. Residence, Carthage,
Missouri. In politics he was a Republican; in religion, a Methodist.
In 1902, while on a visit to Wyandotte, Indian Territory, Captain
A. C. Post of Carthage, Missouri, found several old Wyandotte
Indian friends with whom he studied in their government schools
when a boy of eight, sixty years ago, at Upper Sandusky, Ohio.

AFTER SIXTY YEARS APART — CAPTAIN A. C. POST MET AND
      KNEW INDIAN SCHOOLMATES — STUDIED WITH SPLIT-
      LOG, OLD MUDEATER, AND OTHER WYANDOTTE IN OHIO,
      AND WILL HUNT WITH SURVIVORS.

"While at Wyandotte, Indian Territory, Thursday Captain A. C.
Post, of Carthage, found several old Wyandotte Indian friends

A. C. POST AND FAMILY

with whom he studied in their government schools when a boy of eight, sixty years ago, at Upper Sandusky, Ohio.

"The tribe was moved from its Ohio reservation to a point just west of Kansas City in the forties. The Kansas City suburb of Wyandotte was named for them. In 1868 these Indians were moved to their present reservation in the Territory, southwest of Carthage. One of the old Indian schoolmates was the well-known Mathias Splitlog, who built the old Splitlog, or P. & G., Railroad through this country. Another was the father of Ex-Chief Albert Mudeater, and such others as Black Sheep, Between-the-Logs and Gray Eyes.

"These are all dead now, but Captain Post ran across several old fellows whom he actually had gone to school with, and they remembered him, even after sixty years, during which time they had never met. Among them were Isaac Zane and Isaac Long, halfbloods. Of course he also met Albert Mudeater, and Shoto Armstrong, brother of the present chief, and was invited by them to go down this fall and join in a hunt. Captain Post will accept. All are now growing old and this may be their last opportunity before the 'happy hunting grounds' are reached."

150

ISAAC BRYANT POST[7] (Elizabeth[6] [69], David,[5] Simeon,[4] Cornelius,[3] Pieter Cornelisse,[2] Cornelis[1]), b. June 21, 1837, at Shelby, Ohio; m. Oct. 22, 1874, at Delphos, Allen Co., Ohio, EMMA E. BERRY, who was b. Aug. 7, 1851, at Delphos, Ohio; dau. of John Berry and Eunice A. Griffin. Occupation, banker; politics, Republican; religion, Methodist; Res., Spencerville, Ohio.

Child:

415.   I. Ira B. Post, b. Oct. 14, 1875; m. Ida M. Robbins+

Isaac Bryant Post was educated in local schools and graded school in Delphos, Ohio. Enlisted in Fifteenth Ohio Volunteer Infantry in April, 1861; re-enlisted in Thirty-second Ohio Volunteer Infantry, and served in West Virginia during 1862. In 1863 he led a company of men in General Grant's campaign against Vicksburg, Mississippi, and in 1864 as Captain of company served with General Sherman in campaign against and capture of Atlanta, Georgia; later accompanied General Sherman's army "from Atlanta to the sea," then leaving Savannah crossed the Savannah river into South Carolina, moving east along the coast and cutting off Charleston, South Carolina; then turning north captured Columbia, South Carolina, and marched further north to Greensboro, North Carolina, where Sherman's army encountered the Confederate army under General Johnston. Toward the close of the war was appointed major of regiment and assigned to staff duty as division inspector. At the close of the Civil War he returned to his parents' home and remained with them until they were past their fourscore years, when he came to Spencerville, Ohio, and started a private bank.

151

CHARLES GRAHAM POST[7] (Elizabeth[6] [69], David,[5] Simeon,[4] Cornelius,[3] Pieter Cornelisse,[2] Cornelis[1]), b. Dec. 31, 1839, at Shelby, Ohio; m. Nov. 15, 1865, at Columbus, Ohio, MARIA ROCKWELL, who was b. Apr. 24, 1844, in Columbus, Ohio; dau. of Elkanah Rockwell and Mary Bowen; d. Mar. 27, 1901.

> *Children:*

416.　I. Adelaide Post, b. Sept. 12, 1867, at Spencerville, Ohio; d. June 8, 1909, Parma, Mo. She was a graduate of Ohio Wesleyan University.

417.　II. Harold Rockwell Post, b. Nov. 27, 1870; m. Lillian Kieth in 1892.

418.　III. Vernon Bryant Post, b. Dec. 23, 1873; m. Alice Hanley+

419.　IV. Corwin Hover Post, b. Dec. 10, 1874, at Spencerville, Ohio. Soldier and farmer; in politics, Republican; religion, Methodist. He served during the Spanish War, stationed at Chickamaugua Park, Knoxville, Tenn., and Macon, Ga. Res., Parma, Mo.

420.　V. Helen Marr Post, b. Oct. 14, 1879; d. June 21, 1890.

Mr. Charles G. Post enlisted under the first call of President Lincoln for 75,000 volunteers to suppress rebellion. He was mustered into service in Company E, Fifteenth Ohio Volunteer Infantry, May 23, 1861, for three months. He was mustered out August 8, 1861 at Columbus, Ohio. He re-enlisted October 2,

1861, in Company I, Fourth Ohio Volunteer Cavalry. Re-enlisted in 1864; was mustered out as Sergeant July 22, 1865. He was wounded in action in Alabama, May 2, 1862. A brave soldier, an honor to his country and to the name of Bryant, a useful citizen, a Christian gentleman.

153

EDMUND RANDOLPH BRYANT[7] (Jacob[6] [70], David,[5] Simeon,[4] Cornelius,[3] Pieter Cornelisse,[2] Cornelis[1]), b. Jan. 14, 1829, at Bucyrus, Ohio; d. Oct. 4, 1879; m. Oct. 13, 1850, MARY ELIZABETH MILLER of Detroit, Mich.

Children:

421.   I. Franklin W. Bryant, b. Sept. 29, 1851; unm.; belonged to U. S. Militia; is in employ of Kimball Brick Co., 6229 Justine St., Chicago, Ill.
422.   II. Jennie B. Bryant, b. Sept. 12, 1853; unm.
423. III. Edmund R. Bryant, b. Feb. 9, 1855; m. Emily Elizabeth Sweeney+
424.   IV. Sarah G. Bryant, b. Jan. 4, 1857; d. Aug. 28, 1866.
425.   V. William C. Bryant, b. June 11, 1858; m. Lulu Stensell+
426.   VI. Lulu Bryant, b. Dec. 3, 1859; m. Harry J. Sheldon+
427. VII. Elmer E. Bryant, b. Dec. 11, 1861; unm. Res., Kankakee, Ill.
428. VIII. Lincoln C. Bryant, b. Dec. 6, 1864; d. Aug. 12, 1910; unm.
429.   IX. Geary D. Bryant, b. Aug. 8, 1866; d. Sept. 11, 1866.

This marriage occurred at the home of an aunt of the bride in La Timberville, Ohio. Mary Elizabeth Miller was born December 25, 1829, near Philadelphia, Pennsylvania; died October 4, 1871. She was of Quaker descent. Her grandfather was a Quaker minister. Her parents removed to Detroit, Michigan, when she was a child. Edmund Randolph attended the public school of Bucyrus, Ohio. In 1843 he entered Bethany College, Virginia. While there he boarded in the home of Bishop Alexander Campbell, who was president of Bethany College and the founder of the Campbellite or Christian Church. Mr. E. R. Bryant has still in his possession the bible purchased of Bishop Campbell. After leaving college he entered into the business of buying and selling of stock, and later extensive farming. Soon after his marriage he purchased forty acres of land, to which he added until he owned three hundred acres. In the fall of 1875 he sold the farm and with his family moved to Bucyrus, Ohio, where he remained until 1877, when he removed to Hebron, Indiana. His death occurred two years later. He was buried in Bucyrus, Ohio, the place of his birth. In 1891 his family became residents of Chicago, Illinois. In religious faith Mr. Bryant was a Methodist; in politics, a Republican.

154

AVIS M. BRYANT[7] (Jacob[6] [59], David,[5] Simeon,[4] Cornelius,[3] Pieter Cornelisse,[2] Cornelis[1]), b. ......, 1830; d. 18 ......; m. Mar. 7, 1879, JOSEPH W. STUCKEY.

Children:

154a. I. Alfred Bryant Stuckey, b. July 13, 1857; m. Mar. 17, 1879, Mary C. Hazelbalker+

154b. II. John S. Stuckey, b. ......; d. Dec. 2, 1884, at Fairmount, Neb.

We regret that we have so meager a record of Avis Bryant Stuckey. She was a person of more than ordinary charm of person and manner, and of a bright intellect.

154a

ALFRED BRYANT STUCKEY[8] (Avis[7] [154], Jacob,[6] David,[5] Simeon,[4] Cornelius,[3] Pieter Cornelisse,[2] Cornelis[1]), b. July 13, 1857, near Bucyrus, Ohio; m. Mar. 17, 1879, MARY C. HAZELBALKER, in Delaware Co., Ind.; occupation stock-raising; Res., Bingham, Neb.

Children:

154c. I. Avis A. Stuckey, b. May 30, 1880.

154d. II. Asa W. Stuckey, b. July 8, 1882.

154e. III. Joseph E. Stuckey, b. Oct. 24, 1887; d. Nov. 10, 1899, at Hyannis, Neb.

154f. IV. Elizabeth C. Stuckey, b. May 15, 1887; m. Frank
W. Yeast.
154g. V. Grace Stuckey, b. Nov. 22, 1889.
154h. VI. Frances E. Stuckey, b. Aug. 22, 1892.
154i. VII. Hazel Stuckey, b. July 24, 1897.
154j. VIII. Katherine J. Stuckey, b. June 14, 1900.

Alfred B. Stuckey spent his childhood in the home of his parents
near Bucyrus, Ohio. He went west in 1872. At the age of seventeen he went on a government survey through the western part of
Nebraska, which was then principally inhabited by Indians.
After his marriage in 1879 he located in Custer County, and engaged in the cattle business. Later, while living in Grant County,
he served three terms as commissioner of that county, and several
years as school treasurer. He is a member of the Masonic order,
is a man of good reputation, and strong Christian character. An
author made the statement a person is judged by his reputation in
this world, and by his character in the next. Residence, Bingham,
Nebraska.

159
MARGARET JANE AGNEW[7] (Nancy[6] [72], David,[5] Simeon,[4]
Cornelius,[3] Pieter Cornelisse,[2] Cornelis[1]), b. Aug. 15, 1829, at
Mt. Vernon, Ohio; d. Apr. 4, 1856; m. May 29, 1855, at
Wyandot, Ohio, GEORGE HENRY WELSH, who was b. Apr. 15,
1829. .
Child:
430. I. Agnew Welsh, b. Apr. 11, 1856; m. Cora E. Hous-
stater+

She spent several years of her life in teaching, making her home
with her uncle Isaac Bryant in Wyandot, Ohio, from whose home
she was married. After her marriage she and her husband moved
to a farm a few miles east of Wyandot, Ohio, where her only child,
Agnew Welsh, was born. Seven days after this journey into the
valley of the shadow of death, she laid her life upon the altar of
motherhood. Rev. Silas Johnston who performed her marriage
ceremony also officiated at the funeral.
G. H. Welsh was the youngest of five sons of Zachariah Welsh and

Nancy Steen and was born near the village of Wyandot, Ohio, on
April 15, 1826; he also had six sisters, one of whom, Jane Ann,
married Jacob Bryant.   Madison W. Welsh, an older brother of
G. H. Welsh, married Jane Bryant, and Bryant became a family
surname, there being Bryant Agnews and Bryant Welshes.

160

ISAAC BRYANT AGNEW[7] (Nancy[6] [72], David,[5] Simeon,[4]
Cornelius,[3] Pieter Cornelisse,[2] Cornelis[1]), b. Sept. 11, 1831, at
Mt. Vernon, Ohio; m. Sept. 9, 1856, SARAH R. DILLE of Val-
paraiso, Ind.   Res., at Otterville, Iowa.

Children:

431.   I.   Frank Vilroy Agnew, b. Oct. 30, 1857; d. 1880.
432.   II.   Ward Bryant Agnew, b. May 13, 1860; Res., Fair-
              bank, Iowa.
433.   III. Mary E. Agnew, b. Oct. 16, 1862; m. Samuel L.
              Wilson; she d. Mar., 1901.
434.   IV.   Nanetta Eva Agnew, b. Oct. 12, 1864; m. Arthur H.
              Wallace.   She was a teacher.
435.   V.   Sarah Gertrude Agnew, b. May 18, 1876; a teacher.
              Res., Independence, Iowa.
436.   VI.   Fred F. Agnew, b. June 5, 1874; a medical student.
              Res., Philadelphia, Pa.
437.   VII. Herbert Ross Agnew, b. . . . . . ., 1881.

Mr. and Mrs. Agnew are pioneer residents of Buchanan County,
Iowa, going there in 1854, Mrs. Agnew making her wedding trip
from Indiana there in 1856.   The entire country was sparsely
settled, and when Mr. Agnew located on his farm in Fairbank
Township there was not a house on the prairie between his place
and West Union.   The early settlers had a tendency to take to the
woods.   Mr. Agnew preferred the prairie land and entered 160
acres, which he still owns, which is the only land in the county
which has never been transferred from the original patentee.   At
various times Mr. Agnew added to his possessions.   When building
his house it was necessary to haul the lumber from Dubuque, the
trip each way taking three or four days.   Those were the days of
deer and Indians.   For the first two years, many deer were daily

GEORGE HENRY WELSH   MARGARET JANE WELSH

seen on the trail between Otter Creek and the river. The winter
of 1856, however, was one of heavy snows, and the deer were nearly
all slaughtered that season. Indians were plenty in the spring and
fall on their migrations north and south. They constantly begged
for "squaw chicken," absolutely refusing the roosters. Their
requests were usually granted, as the fowls were stolen if the demand
was denied. In 1901 the family moved to Independence, Iowa, where
they now reside. September 9, 1906, this worthy couple celebrated their golden wedding. Both Mr. and Mrs. Agnew have
been lifelong members of the Methodist Church, and generous in its
support.

161

ELIZABETH AGNEW[7] (Nancy[6] [72], David,[5] Simeon,[4] Cornelius,[3] Pieter Cornelisse,[2] Cornelis[1]), b. 1833; m. CHESTER OBED
WELLMAN, who was b. 1829, at Littleton, Iowa; d. Aug.
16, 1864. Elizabeth d. 1866.

Children:

438. I. Eugene B. Wellman, b. 1854.
439. II. Margaret Jane Wellman, b. Sept. 2, 1856; m. James
          O. Vincent+

162

DAVID BRYANT AGNEW[1] (Nancy[6] [72], David,[5] Simeon,[4] Cornelius,[3] Pieter Cornelisse,[2] Cornelis[1]), b. May 4, 1835, at Pleasant
Grove, Ind.; d. Feb. 6, 1890, at Independence, Iowa; m. ......,
1860, NANCY E. BRIGHT, who was b. Apr. 30, 1843, at Pleasant
Grove, dau. of David Bright and Lucinda Logan. He moved
to Iowa at the age of nineteen.

Children:

440. I. Gertrude M. Agnew, b. Jan. 11, 1861; m. Dec., 1896,
          George M. Baird of Butler, Pa. She was ed-
          ucated at Upper Iowa University and Iowa
          State Normal School. She taught in public
          schools until her marriage. They now reside
          at Sumner, Iowa.

441. II. Fay D. Agnew, b. Dec. 24, 1866; m. Minnie B. Greenwood+

442. III. Jesse Winfield Agnew, b. Sept. 9, 1868; m. Kittie M. Nalbert+

443. IV. Isaac Agnew, b. Dec. 26, 1870; educated at Upper Iowa University. Res., Fairbanks, Iowa.

444. V. Arthur Grant Agnew, b. Dec. 11, 1873; m. Laura Francis in January, 1903. He was educated at Upper Iowa University. Res., Denver, Col.

445. VI. Anna Naomi Agnew, b. Jan. 4, 1876; m. in 1896, J. H. Manning. She was educated at Independence, Iowa, and Upper Iowa University. After graduating she taught school until her marriage. Res., Independence, Iowa.

446. VII. Minnie Dorothy Agnew, b. Nov. 4, 1879. She was educated at Independence (Iowa) High School and Iowa State Normal, and spent one year at the Musical Conservatory at Cedar Rapids, Iowa.

447. VIII. Lela Inez Agnew, b. July 4, 1881. She pursued the same course of instruction as that of her sister Minnie Dorothy. Res., Cedar Rapids, Iowa.

448. IX. Guy Owen Agnew, b. Dec. 11, 1883. He is a student at Coe College, Cedar Rapids, Iowa.

163
MARTHA KELLER[7] (Nancy[6] [72], David,[5] Simeon,[4] Cornelius,[3] Pieter Cornelisse,[2] Cornelis[1]), b. Oct. 1842; d. Mar. 15, 1897; m. EDWIN LOVEJOY.

Child:

449. I. Claude B. Lovejoy; in railroad employment in Mexico.

165
ANNA ELIZABETH KELLER[7] (Nancy[6] [72], David,[5] Simeon,[4] Cornelius,[3] Pieter Cornelisse,[2] Cornelis[1]), b. Jan. 20, 1846, at Valparaiso, Ind.; d. Sept. 12, 1876, at Dubuque, Iowa; m. Jan.

15, 1864, at Independence, Iowa, HENRY WANTON NORTHRUP, who was b. June 11, 1839, at Braintrem, Wyoming Co., Pa. He is an express messenger on the Illinois Central Railroad, a position he has held for thirty-five years. Res., Dubuque, Iowa.

Children:

450.   I.   James H. Northrup, b. 1865; d. 1865.
451.   II.   Anna Gertrude Northrup, b. Aug. 18, 1869, at Dubuque, Iowa; m. in June, 1898, WILLIAM BENNETT, who was b. Oct., 1868, in La Fox, Ill., the son of Richard Bennett and Hannah Shaw. His parents were born in England. He was one of nine children. He is express messenger on the fast mail of the North Western Railroad running between Chicago and Omaha. Res., Austin, Ill.

166

GERTRUDE KELLER[7] (Nancy[6] [72], David,[5] Simeon,[4] Cornelius,[3] Pieter Cornelisse,[2] Cornelis[1]), b. Mar. 18, 1848, at Valparaiso, Ind.; m. Oct. 12, 1880, at Independence, Iowa, EPHRAIM COOPER ANDREW, who was b. Oct. 2, 1844, at Bucyrus, Ohio; son of Samuel Andrew and Nelly Cooper. He is a farmer; in politics, a Republican; in religion, a Presbyterian. Res., St. Petersburg, Fla.

167

JOHN KELLER[7] (Nancy[6] [72], David,[5] Simeon,[4] Cornelius,[3] Pieter Cornelisse,[2] Cornelis[1]), b. May 21, 1850; d. Mar. 1, 1906, in Iowa City; m. HATTIE JONES. Res., Winfield, Iowa.

Children:

452.   I.   Clara Keller; m. Mr. Allen.
453.   II.   Maude Keller; m. Mr. Reagan, Winfield, Iowa.
454.   III.   Winnie Keller.
455.   IV.   Winfield Keller.
456.   V.   Henry Keller.

In 1855 Mr. John Keller located on a farm adjoining the town of
Independence, Iowa, where he resided, with the exception of three
years in Missouri, until his death. He was a consistent member of
the Presbyterian Church. He was the grandson of a Revolutionary
soldier.

169

BRYANT WELSH[7] (Jane[6] [73], David,[5] Simeon,[4] Cornelius,[3]
Pieter Cornelisse,[2] Cornelis[1]), b. Mar. 15, 1830, near Wyandot,
Ohio; d. Apr. 19, 1906; m. Mar. 1, 1853, SARAH MARGARET
STUCKEY, of Bedford Co., Pa., who was b. Mar. 7, 1832; dau. of
Samuel S. Stuckey and Anna Silvers.

Children:

457.   I.   Alice Elmira Welsh, b. Jan. 1, 1854; m. Aaron M.
             Holler+
458.   II. Jane Welsh, b. Dec. 25, 1855; m. William Z. Thomp-
             son+
459.   III. Emma Welsh, b. Aug. 10, 1858; d. Mar. 20, 1870.
460.   IV. Anna Welsh, b. Sept. 23, 1861; m. Cecil Woodward
             Brown+
461.   V.   George St. Claire Welsh, b. Sept. 15, 1864; m. Emma
             Bohart of Lathrop, Mo.   Mr. G. S. Welsh
             is a merchant of Apache, Okla.
462.   VI. Harry Madison Welsh, b. Sept. 7, 1866; m. Lillian
             May Bohart+
463.   VII. Albert Clay Welsh, b. Nov. 6, 1869; m. Ida Lena
             Perry+
464. VIII. Margaret Bryant Welsh, b. July 13, 1874; m. Seth
             Carson George+

Bryant Welsh attended the country schools near where he lived,
and afterwards Bethany College. His father was a stockman and
sold in the markets at Philadelphia and other eastern towns, remaining at those cities sometimes several months till he sold the
cattle or sheep. There being no railroads, the animals were
driven, and, being ready for market, it was necessary that they
should not be hurried on the way, and it took a long time to reach
their destination. Drovers were hired to drive them, and they

BRYANT WELSH

had what they called the "boss" who had the management of the men and cattle, and would ride in advance of the herd and engage water and pasture for the cattle and board and lodging for the men for the night and over Sundays. Bryant, being a trustworthy lad, and old beyond his years, seemed to have responsibility thrust upon him before the usual time, for at the age of twelve he was a "boss." Hotels or inns were far apart and farmers were frequently forced to accommodate these herds, or see them and the men suffer for want of food or water. So people having fine springs on their places on the road to the market would feel driven to have a room to accommodate these men. It would usually be a large room in the upper story of these large log houses where they would place as many as four beds. The boss must sleep here in the room with these big rough men, and this lad, who had been brought up by a refined mother, dreaded these long, dangerous trips. It was necessary for him to always carry a good deal of money to pay the expenses of the trip, and sometimes his father had him carry large sums of money, usually in gold, in a belt strapped around his waist under his clothing. Having to ride ahead and engage the pasture, and then to return to the herd and see that they were brought to the right place, caused him to ride more than the others. It was a feeling of relief to be alone and lest one of these men might follow him he would spur his horse on and away from them. There was a stretch of woods on the road and, boylike, he peered among the shadows, fearing he knew not what, but something to be dreaded.

All this tended to develop courage. On one of his semiannual trips when he had arrived at manhood he met Margaret, the young daughter of Samuel Stuckey, of Bedford County, Pennsylvania, whom he married in 1853. The Stuckeys were thrifty people, and in addition to the well-filled chests her father gave the young couple a new rockaway, a then generally used carriage. The young people started in this on their wedding trip to their home in Wyandot County, Ohio. Here they lived two years, when they thought it well to go west. With their little daughter Alice, then a year old, in the same carriage they started, and settled on a farm near Altona, Illinois. Here they lived for fourteen years, and here three other daughters, Jane, Emma, and Annie, and two sons, George and Harry, were born. About this time (1866) Missouri was attracting attention and being advertised by railroad companies. Bryant Welsh with his brother St. Clair went on the first train over the then just completed road, Hannibal and St. Joseph route, and bought a large farm at Lathrop, Missouri, where he brought his family March 20, 1867. At this place two other children, Albert and Margaret, were born, and here his family was reared. One of the daughters, Emma, died at the age of twelve. Three of the daughters, Alice, Jane, and Annie, were married here. In 1901 he disposed of most of his possessions at Lathrop, and on November 20 moved to Apache, Oklahoma, then a town but a few months old, in order that he might live in a mild climate, and at the same time be near members of his family, some of his children having lived in the Indian Territory many years previous to this time. During his residence here he was ill most of the time, died April 19, 1906, and was buried at Lathrop, Missouri. It can truly be said that his was a life of practical Christianity, integrity, and usefulness. He was one of the peacemakers of the community. When a dispute arose between neighbors and was left to arbitration he was usually the first man selected. He was just, and his judgment was good. He held the Sabbath day sacred and never allowed anything to be done on that day that could be done at other times. He was a consistent member of the Presbyterian Church. He was jovial and kind-hearted and had a host of friends wherever he lived.

170

WILLIAM ST. CLAIR WELSH[7] (Jane[6] [73], David,[5] Simeon,[4] Cornelius,[3] Pieter Cornelisse,[2] Cornelis[1]), b. July 13, 1832, in Bucyrus, Ohio; d. Nov. 28, 1892, at Lathrop, Mo.; m. Feb. 17, 1857, in Bucyrus, Ohio, HARRIET E. WARNER, who was b. Jan. 18, 1836, Bucyrus, Ohio; dau. of Benj. Warner and Mary Walton.

Children:

465.   I.   William Madison Welsh, b. Apr. 21, 1858, at Bucyrus; m. Emma Kelley, dau. of Richard T. Kelley and Mellissa Peavy, of Lathrop, Mo. She was b. July 7, 1863; politics, Democrat; occupation, farming. Res., Denver, Col.

466. II.   Mary L. Welsh, b. Sept. 16, 1862; unm. She devoted her life in kindness for others.

467. III. Anson S. Welsh, b. Jan. 21, 1865; m. Bertha Duval. They have two sons and one daughter.

468. IV.   Gertrude P. Welsh, b. June 7, 1871; m. Frank P. Brown. They have three children, two sons and a daughter. The two younger are twins. Res., Lathrop, Mo.

After their marriage Mr. and Mrs. Welsh lived in Ohio near Bucyrus on the Scioto River for one year, then moved to the Pike. From there they moved to Altona, Illinois. In 1867 they bought land two miles northeast of Lathrop, Missouri, where they built up a most pleasant home. Later they traded this property for a tract of land in Caldwell County, Missouri, where their son Anson now lives on the land which is the dower interest of his widow.

171

GEORGE H. WELSH[7] (Jane[6] [73], David,[5] Simeon,[4] Cornelius,[3] Pieter Cornelisse,[2] Cornelis[2]), b. Jan. 16, 1834; m. Nov., 1876, AMANDA FOSTER, Indiana. For years Mr. Welsh bought and sold stock extensively in Indiana. In Ohio he had a fine farm from which he shipped stock to the eastern cities. The first year of his married life he spent in Upper Sandusky, Ohio; the second year he lived at Kokomo, Ind. The climate affecting his health unfavorably, he with his family went in Nov., 1878, to Upper Sandusky to attend the golden wedding of his parents. Being taken ill with a congestive chill, he passed away within a week of pneumonia.

Child:

469.   I.   Emma Eugene Welsh, b. Sept. 2, 1877; m. 1897, Thomas Gaddes+

172

HANNAH WELSH[7] (Jane[6] [73], David,[5] Simeon,[4] Cornelius,[3] Pieter Cornelisse,[2] Cornelis[1]), b. Oct. 3, 1837, near Bucyrus, Ohio; d. Mar. 31, 1875, at Newman, Ill.; m. Feb. 12, 1862,

THOMAS GILLESPIE, who was b. July 16, 1837; son of James M. Gillespie, who was the son of Thomas M. Gillespie.

Children:

470.   I.   Bryant W. Gillespie, b. Jan. 26, 1863; m. Laura A. Milan+

471.   II.   Emma Gillespie, b. Nov. 17, 1864; d. 1866.

472.   III.   Luella Jane Gillespie, b. Oct. 16, 1866; m. Oliver O. Hockett+

473.   IV.   Alice Gillespie, b. Dec. 3, 1867; m. James Edwards.

474.   V.   Kate Gillespie, b. Mar. 23, 1868; m. David P. Akers.

475.   VI.   Pauline W. Gillespie, b. Aug. 25, 1871; m. Clarence W. Funk+

476.   VII.   Ralph M. Gillespie, b. Nov., 1872; d. 1874.

477.   VIII.   Lela Gillespie, b. 1874; d. 1874.

The following sketch was taken from "American Ancestry," a book in the Chicago Public Library, page 157: The Gillespie family belong to the Campbell clan. Their home was in the Highlands of Scotland. They were strong adherents of the Calvinistic doctrine, and one of them helped to frame the "Confession of Faith." They fought for religious liberty. About the close of the seventeenth century three brothers crossed into Ireland, settling in County Antrim. Their names were David,[1] John,[1] James.[1] During the Revolution of 1690 James[1] fought under William III, Prince of Orange, with whom he crossed the Boygne, July, 1690. His sword is still kept as a relic by one of his descendants. After this decisive battle the Gillespies moved to County Monaghan, Banbridge, Ireland, where they owned a large tract of land. In 1895 Elizabeth, a descendant, was living in the old home place where her people had lived for over two hundred years. The Gillespies were linen drapers. James[1] married Elizabeth Riddle about 1700; children: James,[2] John,[2] Mathew,[2] Elizebeth,[2] Letitia,[2] Sarah.[2] James[2] came to America about 1750. It was reported that he was killed in the war of the Revolution. John[1] married Jane Stewart; children: James,[2] Isaac,[2] Jane,[2] Elizabeth,[2] Agnes,[2] Letitia.[2] Isaac,[2] son of John,[1] married Jane Boyd; children: seven sons and three daughters. One son, William,[3] emigrated to America about 1830; settled in Jo Davies County, Illinois. John[4] was a Presbyterian minister, educated in Belfast, Ireland. The

PAULINE STUCKEY

first mentioned David[1] married Isabella Wilson; had son Joseph,[2] who married Sarah Breakey; children, five; one, David,[3] fled to America to escape British yoke.

174

PAULINE WELSH,[7] (Jane[6] [73], David,[5] Simeon,[4] Cornelius,[3] Pieter Cornelisse,[2] Cornelis[1]), b. Apr. 1, 1842, at Bucyrus, Ohio; m. Oct. 18, 1866, at Wyandot, Ohio, JOHN S. STUCKEY, who was b. Apr. 24, 1834, at Bedford, Pa. He d. Feb. 23, 1897, at Eddyville, Neb. He was a banker; in politics, a Republican; in religion, a Presbyterian.

Children:

478.   I.   Bryant Stuckey, b. Sept. 3, 1867; d. Mar. 3, 1873.
479.   II. Madison Welsh Stuckey, b. Jan. 24, 1869; m. Kate Ray Daniels+
480.   III. Anna Stuckey, b. Jan. 28, 1872; m. Benton Maret+
481.   IV. Infant daughter, b. Sept. 16, 1874; d. Sept. 19, 1874.
482.   V.   Ruby Stuckey, b. Sept. 15, 1876; m. Edwin S. Eves+

John S. Stuckey was born in Bedford County, Pennsylvania, April 24, 1834, living in his native state until he enlisted in the Civil War in August, 1862, in Company D, One Hundred and Thirty-eighth Pennsylvania Volunteers. For distinguished bravery he was made captain of the company, participating in the battles of Brandy Station, Wilderness, Spottsylvania, Cold Harbor, Fishers Hill, and Winchester. In 1872 Mr. Stuckey with his family moved to Plum Creek, Nebraska, where they lived two years. He was elected county treasurer and engaged in stock-raising and farming.

Mr. Stuckey helped organize and was the first president of the Plum Creek (now Lexington) Bank; his son Madison was chosen assistant cashier. Mr. Stuckey's death occurred February 23, 1897, from an affection of the heart. The death of the son Madison followed on the 27th of June, 1898, resulting from an operation performed at Denver, Colorado, where he had gone on business. The marriage of the daughter, Ruby, left Mrs. Stuckey alone in the world and she has since resided with her daughters in the state of Washington.

The following reminiscences are from the pen of Mrs. Pauline Welsh Stuckey:

"My parents lived six miles south of Bucyrus, Crawford County, Ohio, on the Bucyrus and Marion road at the time of my birth. My early childhood enjoyments were greatly enhanced by the lively, stirring boyhood of brother John, who was two years my junior. By perseverance I succeeded in forming a taste for refining and elevating thought and speech. Our home was a two-story house situated on a farm of eleven hundred acres. On the south and joining the yard was the orchard, beyond it was pasture land, and, farther south, cultivated lands, reaching east to the river. Intervening between the orchard and the pasture was a rivulet, which ran swiftly from the pasture to the highway, then down the slightly rolling plain to the Scioto River.

"Well do I remember the overflow of the river when brothers Bryant and St. Clair barely escaped drowning in their efforts to rescue the live stock. It rose and surged madly, flowing down the pasture towards the barn and house but did not reach them because of the low hills in the rear. The frenzied sheep sought higher ground for protection, but one by one they fell into the surging waves and were drowned. On the west side of the road our land extended north nearly a half-mile where the landscape effects were beautiful, the various tints of blue grass varied with the lovely white and red clover. Beyond this, in the distance, were trees; one, with its mammoth dignity, lingers in my memory. It was large, well proportioned, and commanding in appearance. South of this was a meadow, rolling gradually downward in front and away from the house, in front of which was a beautiful grove of trees. A mile distant was the little schoolhouse where we were given six months schooling each year. Later my education was continued at Wyandot and Springfield, Ohio.

"In the spring of 1856 we moved to Wyandot, where we had a large home with fruit and flowers in abundance. I was favored with two loyal, kind, and attentive brothers, George and John, who were always ready to take me to places of enjoyment. About this time in my life, my sympathies were drawn to the one whom I afterwards married, Captain John Stuckey, who lost a limb in the service of his country in the Union Army in the Civil War. I had known him early in life through the intermarriage of the two families, but it was after he came home from the Civil War that I cared particularly for him. Sympathy ripened into love and we were married October 18, 1866, in Wyandot, Ohio. In 1872 my husband sold the farm and his interest in the old home, took a soldier's homestead near the little town of Plum Creek, Dawson County, Nebraska (now Lexington), on the Union Pacific Railroad.

"In this great western country I was always in great fear of the Indians but was not a coward, as the following incident will show:

"One warm afternoon a Pawnee Indian wearing a red turban and a red blanket unceremoniously stepped into the room where I was working. In blunt speech he asked me for goods wherewith to line an unfinished cap and insisted I could give him the goods. Thinking to frighten me he walked to the table where I was standing, and picked up a butcher knife; I immediately picked up a sharper one. He drew his finger along the blade, at the same time looking at me with a cynical smile. I said, 'That knife is worthless, this is the sharp knife,'—holding up the one I held. With a look that showed defeat he sullenly departed."

A friend of Mrs. Stuckey says of her, that her artistic ability is of the most excellent quality. Now, at the age of seventy, as a pleasant pastime, her work in china painting and fine embroidery would be a credit to one half her age.

175
JOHN BARTROM WELSH[7] (Jane[6] [73], David,[5] Simeon,[4] Cornelius,[3] Pieter Cornelisse,[2] Cornelis[1]), b. June 6, 1844, near Bucyrus, Ohio; m. Oct. 13, 1870, LOUISA FLOCK of Wyandot, Ohio; she was b. June 22, 1849, at Bucyrus, Ohio. Mr. Welsh is a successful farmer; in politics a Democrat; Res., Woodward, Okla.

Children:

483.   I.   Georgia S. Welsh, b. Nov. 22, 1874; m. Walter B. Thompson+
484.   II.   Grace Welsh, b. Nov. 24, 1879.
485.   III.   Harry Madison Welsh, b. Apr. 27, 1881.
486.   IV.   Frances Welsh, b. Aug. 15, 1889.
487.   V.   Daniel Ralph Welsh, b. Oct. 4, 1891.

He is a man of bright intellect and remarkable memory. The first years of their married life were spent on the Isaac Bryant farm near Upper Sandusky, Ohio. Then, after living for a time near Bucyrus, they removed in 1883 to Lathrop, Missouri, and later to Caldwell County, same state. In 1901 he took a homestead of one hundred and sixty acres ten miles from Woodward, Oklahoma. In 1902 they took up residence there.

Grace Welsh was educated at the Kirksville Normal School. In 1901 she filed on one hundred and sixty acres of land in Oklahoma which joins her father's fine homestead, their house being located so as to hold both claims, and with her father she uses her land for farming and grazing purposes. She has fenced her land and improved it, using her school money. She is energetic and persevering and very successful as a teacher.

179   EIGHTH GENERATION

ANN ELIZA BRYANT[8] (Arthur[7] [76], Elias,[6] David,[5] Simeon,[4] Cornelius,[3] Pieter Cornelisse,[2] Cornelis[1]), b. Aug. 10, 1852, at Pleasant Grove, Lake Co., Ind.; d. Sept. 13, 1895; buried at Orchard Grove, Ind.; m. Feb. 25, 1875, at Lowell, Ind., WALBERT DAVIS, who was b. Feb. 28, 1850, at Orchard Grove, Ind. He was the son of Samuel Davis and Sarah J. McSparrin. In politics, Republican. Res., Orchard Grove, Ind.

Children:

488.   I.   Cora Jane Davis, b. Dec. 26, 1875; m. Nicholes Wheeler.
489.   II.   George Nelson Davis, b. June 3, 1880; d. 1897, at Lowell, Ind.
490.   III.   Ethel May Davis, b. Nov. 12, 1885. Res., Peoria, Ill.

182

ELIAS W. BRYANT[8] (Arthur[7] [76], Elias,[6] David,[5] Simeon,[4] Cornelius,[3] Pieter Cornelisse,[2] Cornelis[1]), b. Sept. 12, 1858, Lowell, Ind.; m. Nov. 20, 1880, at Kankakee, Ill., ANN E. HAYDEN, who was b. Oct. 25, 1861, at Momence, Ill.; dau. of

ELIAS BRYANT

Joseph Hayden and Maria P. Green. Mr. Bryant is a traveling hardware salesman; is a staunch Republican; a member of
the Baptist Church. He has resided in Peoria, Ill., Boston,
Mass., Indianapolis, Ind., and LaFayette, Ind.

Children:

491. I. Percy J. Bryant, b. May 25, 1884; m. Nov. 18, 1909,
LOLA E. WHITSEL, dau. of William Whitsel and
Lucinda Payne. Percy Bryant is a graduate of
the LaFayette (Ind.) High School of the class
of 1903; also graduated from the Purdue University as mechanical engineer in class of 1908.
He accepted a government position at Jefferson, Ind., May 1, 1909, as chief engineer of
the government depot. Res., 329 Meigs Ave.,
Jeffersonville, Ind. *Child:* 491a, William
Whitsel Bryant, b. Mar. 17, 1913.

492. II. Edith May Bryant, b. July 17, 1886; d. Oct. 14,
1898, at Indianapolis, Ind.

183

ULYSSES S. BRYANT[8] (Arthur[7] [76], Elias,[6] David,[5] Simeon,[4]
Cornelius,[3] Pieter Cornelisse,[2] Cornelis[1]), b. Oct. 17, 1868, in
Lowell, Ind; m. Oct. 22, 1893, in LaFayette, Ind., MINNIE K.
NIEHAUS, who was b. July 3, 1870; d. Feb. 22, 1908, buried in
Peoria, Ill. She was dau. of Charles Niehaus and Ann Rowley.
Ulysses received a common school education at Lowell and
Crown Point, Ind.; worked in the hardware and implement
business at LaFayette, Ind., and Peoria, Ill. Afterward he
learned the barber trade, and by his clever and congenial ways
won the confidence of the people and established a good busi-
ness in Peoria, Ill.

Child:

493. I. Charles A. Bryant, b. Aug. 20, 1895.

185

DANIEL R. BRYANT[8] (Robert[7] [78], Elias,[6] David,[5] Simeon,[4]
Cornelius,[3] Pieter Cornelisse,[2] Cornelis[1]), b. May 9, 1854, at

Hebron, Ind.; m. June 24, 1875, MARY LOIS ANDREWS, who was b. Oct. 16, 1856, at Hebron, Ind.; dau. of Solomon Andrews and Sarah Stholp. He was a farmer and owned a fine property near Hebron, Ind. In politics he was a Republican; in religion, a Methodist.

Children:

494.   I.   Otto Deforest Bryant, b. July 7, 1881; m. July 3, 1904, Grace Stewart.

495.   II.   Carl Clayton Bryant, b. June 21, 1886; m. June 25, 1907, Mary Sweney, b. Mar. 2, 1889.

496.   III.   Winfred A. Bryant, b. Nov. 3, 1890; m. June 26, 1912, FLORENCE TURNER, dau. of James Turner and Cora Dunn. Mr. Turner is a successful farmer and dealer in imported stock. Winfred was educated in Hebron, a graduate of the high school and also of DePauw University.

186

CHARLES BRYANT[8] (Robert[7] [78], Elias,[6] David,[5] Simeon,[4] Cornelius,[3] Pieter Cornelisse,[2] Cornelis[1]), b. Mar. 22, 1858; m. Oct. 15, 1878, ENDORA DILLE.

Children:

497.   I.   Floyd Bryant, b. July 31, 1880.

498.   II.   Ray Bryant, b. Mar. 8, 1883; m. Gladys Stewart+

499.   III.   Charles Roy Bryant, b. Aug. 25, 1885; d. Sept. 25, 1886.

500.   IV.   Earl Bryant, b. Mar. 24, 1889.

501.   V.   William Sterling Bryant, b. Aug. 9, 1895.

188

LUELLA C. BRYANT[8] (John[7] [81], Elias,[6] David,[5] Simeon,[4] Cornelius,[3] Pieter Cornelisse,[2] Cornelis[1]), b. Aug. 22, 1862, in Lake Co., Ind. She is the widow of JOHN H. SPITTAL, who was b. Aug. 31, 1860, in Scotland. She was educated at Lowell and Crown Point, Ind.; m. (2nd) Nelson H. Straight. She is a member of the Society of the Daughters of the American Revolution. Res., Chicago.

Children:

502. I. Bertha M. Spittal, b. Oct. 9, 1886, in Chicago; m. Nov., 1908, Frank M. Pierson+
503. II. Cassius Duncan Spittal, b. Feb. 11, 1889, in Chicago; student.

189

MARIE VANCE BRYANT[8] (John[7] [81], Elias,[6] David,[5] Simeon,[4] Cornelius,[3] Pieter Cornelisse,[2] Cornelis[1]), b. July 21, 1867, Lake Co., Ind.; m. June 26, 1911, OSCAR G. TRIEGLAFF, who was b. in Rockford, Ill. She is a member of the Society of the Daughters of the American Revolution. Res., Windsor Park, Chicago, Ill.

Child:

504. I. Helen Amelia Trieglaff, b. Sept. 20, 1912, in Chicago, Ill.

190

JULIA A. BRYANT[8] (John[7] [81], Elias,[6] David,[5] Simeon,[4] Cornelius,[3] Pieter Cornelisse,[2] Cornelis[1]), b. Sept. 17, 1876; m. Dec., 1897, EARNEST HUMMEL, son of Earnest Hummel, Sr., city treasurer of Chicago. Res., Chicago. Member of the Society of the Daughters of the American Revolution. Res., Chicago.

Child:

505. I. Marie Angeline Hummel, b. Mar. 25, 1899, in Chicago. She is entering upon her second year as a student at Ferry Hall, Lake Forest.

194

CLAUDE J. BRYANT[8] (John Q.[7] [85], Isaac,[6] David,[5] Simeon,[4] Cornelius,[3] Pieter Cornelisse,[2] Cornelis[1]), b. Mar. 16, 1876, at Wyandot, Ohio; m. BERTHA SMITH, June 25, 1902, who was b. Nov. 9, 1880, at Waterloo, Iowa; dau. of Wilford M. Smith and Della Hass. Claude Bryant graduated from Northwestern University in 1901. Is practicing law at Independence, Kan.

Child:

506.   I.   Winifred E. Bryant, b. Jan. 17, 1909.

199

KATHERINE GRAFTON[8] (Jane[7] [91], Joseph,[6] David,[5] Simeon,[4] Cornelius,[3] Pieter Cornelisse,[2] Cornelis[1]), b. Jan. 1, 1839, in Wellsburg, W. Va. She was a graduate of Berien College. M. in 1863, THOMAS M. PATTERSON. Removed to Colorado in 1872. She was a grandniece of Alexander Campbell, and was herself an adherent of the Campbellite faith. She was a leader for several years in club and charitable circles in Denver. Mr. Patterson, b. in Ireland, lived in Denver, where he was a leader in Democratic politics and a lawyer of eminence. He was nominated for governor of Colorado but his party was defeated. He is a proprietor of the Rocky Mountain News. Mr. Patterson was U. S. Senator from Colorado.

Children:

507.   I.   James Patterson, b. ......; d. young.
508.   II.   Jennie Patterson, b. ......; d. young.
509.   III.   Margaret Mountjoy Patterson; m. Richard Campbell.

200

MARY GRAFTON[8] (Jane[7] [91], Joseph,[6] David,[5] Simeon,[4] Cornelius,[3] Pieter Cornelisse,[2] Cornelis[1]), b. ......; m. Simon Peckinpaw. They had one child, who died in infancy. She m. (2nd) Ernest Campbell.

Children:

510.   I.   Bryant Campbell.
511.   II.   Samuel Campbell, b. ......; m. Mary ......;
           child: Mary Campbell.

211

JEAN CARSON BRYANT[8] (Joseph W.[7] [93], Joseph,[6] David,[5] Simeon,[4] Cornelius,[3] Pieter Cornelisse,[2] Cornelis[1]), b. Feb. 17,

1850; m. July 18, 1882, JOHN R. MILLER. Res., Birmingham, Ala.

Children:

211a. I. Margaret Elizabeth Miller.
211b. II. John R. Miller, Jr.
211c. III. Horace C. Miller.

213

JOSEPH WM. CULLEM BRYANT, JR.[8] (Joseph W. C.[7] [93], Joseph,[6] David,[5] Simeon,[4] Cornelius,[3] Pieter Cornelisse,[2] Cornelis[1]), b. Jan. 28, 1854; m. HELEN BOWLES.

Child:

513. I. Henry Alexander Bryant; d. at the age of 13 years.

Mr. Bryant has been in the employ of the Chesapeake & Ohio Railway Company for thirty-five years; for last seventeen years, general yard master for the company.

214

JOHN ISAAC BRYANT[8] (Joseph W.[7] [93], Joseph,[6] David,[5] Simeon,[4] Cornelius,[3] Pieter Cornelisse,[2] Cornelis[1]), b. Aug. 27, 1856; m. PARALEE LANCASTER.

Child:

514. I. Sidney E. Bryant, who, in 1882, m. ELIZABETH
         TALBOT; they had one child:
871. I. Elizabeth Campbell Bryant.

215

DOROTHEA LUCINDA BRYANT[8] (Joseph W.[7] [93], Joseph,[6] David,[5] Simeon,[4] Cornelius,[3] Pieter Cornelisse,[2] Cornelis[1]), b. Apr. 5, 1861; graduate of a high school and of normal, Shelbyville, Tenn.

She was a very successful teacher in Tennessee, Kentucky, and Virginia. For twenty years principal of a young ladies' seminary at Clifton Forge, Virginia. She is a woman of strong characteristics, fine stature, having inherited the Bryant physique, a woman of fine mental and moral attainments, who has in her life-work directed many young women into useful and cultured lives.

219

MARY EMILY BRYANT[8] (Joseph W.[7] [93], Joseph,[6] David,[5] Simeon,[4] Cornelius,[3] Pieter Cornelisse,[2] Cornelis[1]), b. June 12, 1873; m. T. W. Cox of Virginia.

Children:

515.   I.   T. W. Cox, Jr., b. Mar. 20, 1902.
516.   II.   Dorothea Bryant Cox, b. June 14, 1905.
517.   III.   Elizabeth Postelwaite Cox, b. June 14, 1905.

221

WILLIAM HENRY BRYANT[8] (Alexander C.[7] [94], Joseph,[6] David,[5] Simeon,[4] Cornelius,[3] Pieter Cornelisse,[2] Cornelis[1]), b. July 28, 1863, in Indianapolis, Ind.; m. Nov. 1, 1888, BIRDIE MAY ROUTT, b. Apr. 4, 1868, Bloomington, Ill.; dau. of John L. Routt and Hester Anne Woodson.

Children:

518.   I.   Routt Alexander Bryant, b. Aug. 15, 1889.
519.   II.   Minnie Lou Bryant, b. Dec. 9, 1890; m. Sept. 24, 1910, J. W. HUTCHINSON of Oxford, Miss. They have a son b. Aug. 3, 1911.
520.   III.   Dorothea Campbell Bryant, b. Apr. 24, 1896.
521.   IV.   Lila Routt Bryant, b. Nov. 30, 1901; d. 1906.

Mr. Routt was the third assistant postmaster under President Grant and appointed by him as the first territorial governor of Colorado and elected as state governor in 1876. Afterward he was twice elected to the same office. Was one of the state's most prominent men and a leader of the Republican party. A county of the state is named for him. William Henry graduated at the University of Virginia in 1886 and was admitted to the bar. Was assistant district attorney one term and has been very successful as a lawyer in Denver and Goldfield, Nevada. At present he is attorney for city and county of Denver.

222

MARY LOU BRYANT[8] (Alexander[7] [94], Joseph,[6] David,[5] Simeon,[4] Cornelius,[3] Pieter Cornelisse,[2] Cornelis[2]), b. Oct. 26, 1865; graduated 1863 from Stanford Female College, Ky. She was a successful teacher in public and private schools in Virginia and Colorado. She taught for eight years in the Clifton Forge Seminary in connection with her cousin, Dora L. Bryant. She m. in Clifton Forge, Va., in 1899, REV. EMMETT W. McCORKLE, a son of a prominent Scotch-Irish family of Lexington, Va. He was a minister of the Presbyterian Church in Rockbridge Baths, Va.

Child:

522. I. Emmett Wallace McCorkle, Jr.

223

L. W. SANGER[8] (Sarah Ann[7] [96], Samuel,[6] David,[5] Simeon,[4] Cornelius,[3] Pieter Cornelisse,[2] Cornelis[1]), b. Apr. 25, 1841, near Lowell, Ind.; d. Mar. 4, 1893; m. Feb. 2, 1875, at Orchard Grove, Ind., to OLIVE WILEY, who was b. Sept. 1855; dau. of Wilson W. Wiley and Clarinda Craft. He was a respected farmer, honorable and upright; in politics a Republican. After four years of patient suffering he died of tuberculosis, and was buried in the Orchard Grove Cemetery, Lowell, Ind.

Children:

523. I. Violetta Pearl Sanger, b. Nov. 2, 1875; m. June 29, 1899, William Buckley+
524. II. Elnora Sanger, b. May 6, 1882.
525. III. Hazel Clarinda Sanger, b. June 25, 1890, Lowell, Ind.; m. Apr. 29, 1908, Charles Kenney, who was b. Oct. 21, 1883, son of George W. Kenney, grandson of Jerry M. Kenney.
526. IV. Sarah Ann Sanger, b. Feb. 2, 1892.

224

ROSS SANGER[8] (Sarah Ann[7] [96], Samuel,[6] David,[5] Simeon,[4] Cornelius,[3] Pieter Cornelisse,[2] Cornelis[1]), b. June 3, 1842,

Lowell, Ind.; d. Feb. 10, 1901, at Crown Point, Ind., a victim
of tuberculosis; m. Dec. 31, 1865, at Ross Station, Lake Co.,
Ind., to LOUISA D. HOPKINS, b. Mar. 20, 1846, at Hobart, Ind.;
dau. of Benj. Hopkins and Elizabeth Norton.

Children:

527.   I. Benjamin Harry Sanger, b. Jan. 11, 1867; m. Julia
            A. Wall+
528.   II. Sarah Elizabeth Sanger, b. June 9, 1868; d. May,
            1880.
529. III. Edith May Sanger, b. Mar. 21, 1877; m. Charles
            Sidney Fullmer+

Of a roving disposition, he allowed no business interests to tie
him to one place, but the scenes of his earlier years attracted him
in his closing life.   In politics he was a Republican, in religion a
Disciple since 1896.   Funeral was held at his brother Adna's
home in Crown Point, and burial was made in the Lowell Cemetery.

229

WILLIAM ALFRED BRYANT[8] (Samuel R.[7] [97], Samuel,[6] David,[5]
Simeon,[4] Cornelius,[3] Pieter Cornelisse,[2] Cornelis[1]), b. Feb. 7,
1852, at Valparaiso, Ind.; d. Sept. 3, 1886; m. Sept. 23, 1874,
at Englewood, Ill., ALLA BARTHOLOMEW, who was b. May 9,
1854, at Valparaiso, Ind.; dau. of Stephen Leroy Bartholomew
and Eusebia Fravel.

Children:

530.   I. Infant, b. Oct. 12, 1876; d. in infancy.
531.   II. Caryl Hubert Bryant, b. Aug. 29, 1878; d. Jan. 12,
            1879.
532. III. Ross Leroy Bryant, b. Oct. 22, 1881, in Valparaiso,
            Ind.

Ross Leroy Bryant was educated in the home school, and at
Purdue University, where he took a course of study in civil, mechanical, and electrical engineering.   On leaving school he found work
in the West, where he has been successful, working at different
times in all of these lines.   Since 1903 he has been employed in

California. He has the same quiet, retiring disposition that characterized both his father and grandfather. He finds his chief diversion in out-of-door sports and in music.

William Alfred when only 17 entered his father's drug-store and continued in the drug business until his death. Although he spent two years in Chicago as bookkeeper in a commission house he still retained his drug business at home. He was regarded by those who best knew him as a man whose word and business integrity were never questioned. Retiring, quiet and studious by nature, he was a man of deeds rather than words. He was true and loyal to those who proved themselves worthy of his friendship. Thus endowed with natural gifts and attainments he seemed only entering upon a useful life when death claimed its own. In politics he was a Democrat; in religion, a Presbyterian.

233

MARTHA FRANCES BRYANT[8] (Jacob[7] [99], Samuel,[6] David,[5] Simeon,[4] Cornelius,[3] Pieter Cornelisse,[2] Cornelis[1]), b. Mar. 21, 1855, at Crown Point, Ind.; m. Dec. 9, 1872, WILLIAM H. ROGERS; ancestors from New Jersey; m. (2nd) Grear Nagle; b. 1849, in Williamsport, Pa., son of John Nagle and Mary A. Bennett. Res., 1501 Maple St., Witchita, Kan.

> *Children*, 1st m.:

533.   I.   Della Adelia Rogers, b. Oct. 9, 1873; m. Albert A. Lindley+

534.   II. Elea May Rogers, b. Dec. 28, 1875; m. Loren H. Bump+

> 2nd m:

535.   III. Samuel Grear Nagle, b. Oct. 21, 1883; d. Oct. 29, 1884.

536.   IV. Infant daughter, b. Mar. 17, 1886; d. Apr. 25, 1886.

235

SAMUEL TYLER BRYANT[8] (Jacob[7] [99], Samuel,[6] David,[5] Simeon,[4] Cornelius,[3] Pieter Cornelisse,[2] Cornelis[1]), b. Oct. 9, 1858; d. Nov. 19, 1880, as the result of an accident occurring at Rudd, Iowa, while he was in the employ of the Chicago, Milwaukee and St. Paul Ry. He was buried at New Hampton, Chickasaw Co., Iowa.

His untimely death occasioned the writing of "Down Brakes," by John B. Kaye, and published by G. P. Putnam's Sons in their collection of poems, "Songs of Lake Geneva." Permission to publish it in this volume has been granted by Vashti Bayshaw Kaye, son of John B. Kaye, the author, and by G. P. Putnam's Sons, publishers.

DOWN BRAKES

By John B. Kaye

The night was dark, a lurid gleam
   Lit up the trailing cloud of smoke,
And whirling sparks and 'scaping steam,
   Which from the black-mouthed engine broke
In fleecy masses murky-gray,
   As rolling o'er the iron way
The heavy freight train, like a flood,
   Swept down the steep grade nearing Rudd.

Down brakes! the iron-hinged monster screamed;
   Down brakes! and starting to his feet,
While hot sparks fall like burning sleet,
   The brakeman quick his lantern takes,
And mounting to the frosty deck
   Of the first car, turns on the brakes
The downward thundering train to check,
   While the long, smoky banner streamed
About him, and the fire-box's glare
   Broke fitful on the wintry air.

Down brakes! and hast'ning toward the rear
   He leaps each moving chasm that yawned,
Like gaping death 'twixt car and car,
   And musing as he onward strode
He mutely thanked his lucky star,
   Which thus far brought him safe and clear,

For he had planned to leave the road,
  And this was his last run,
And ere another morning dawned,
  As promised to his mother dear,
His braking would be done.

  Down brakes! the iron cyclop shrieked,
His one great eye's malignant gleam
  Darting ahead a ruddy beam,
While throbbing jets of vapor reeked
  Along his palpitating sides,
As on a trestle bridge he glides,—
  A bridge with cross beams overhead.

Down brakes! The brakeman deftly mounts
  The tall deck of a "foreign" car —
A crushing blow! his lucky star
  Sank like a falling meteor.
Ah! surely he had truly said
  'Twas his last run! The man who counts
His chain of life off into links
  Ofttimes counts truer than he thinks,
Though nothing in his mind forecast
  The link he's counting is the last.

Down brakes! He's silent now, and still.
  No more those stentor signal tones
The brakeman's rugged frame shall thrill
  With action. On his face, laid prone,
They found him on the car that night,
  Beneath the cold and clouded skies,
His lantern on his arm still burning,
  But all the glow of life and light
Had faded from the brakeman's eyes,
  And crimson streamers of his blood
(Life's offering and Nature's mourning)
  Draped the tall car that entered Rudd
An altar and its sacrifice.

236

MARY ANN BRYANT[8] (Jacob[7] [99], Samuel,[6] David,[5] Simeon,[4] Cornelius,[4] Pieter Cornelisse,[2] Cornelis[1]), b. Jan. 15, 1861, at Lowell, Ind.; d. July 4, 1910, at Wichita, Kan., and buried beside her mother at Douglas, Kan. She m. May 6, 1877, at Ionia, Iowa, HENRY TUCKER, who was b. July 8, 1857, in Chickasaw Co., Iowa, son of William Tucker and Julia Johnson.

Children:

537. I. Grace Mildred Tucker, b. July 26, 1878; m. Frank Cagley+

538. II. Martha Frances Tucker, b. Apr. 25, 1883; m. John Parsons+

539. III. Roy Henry Tucker, b. Feb. 13, 1885.

540. IV. Lloyd Bryant Tucker, b. Feb. 14, 1887; m. Apr. 2, 1912, Emma May Myers, dau. of Abraham Myers and Minnie . . . ., of Bloomington, Kan.

541. V. William Clair Tucker, b. Sept. 15, 1890; m. June 5, 1909, Bertha Toole, dau. of Roy Toole and Annie . . . . .

237

MARY JOANNA ROBERTSON[8] (Hannah[7] [100], Samuel,[6] David,[5] Simeon,[4] Cornelius,[3] Pieter Cornelisse,[3] Cornelis[1]), b. Feb. 17, 1852, at Westville, La Porte Co., Ind.; m. Feb. 2, 1874, in Eagle Creek Twp., Lake Co., Ind., OSCAR DINWIDDIE, b. Sept. 2, 1844, at Minooka, Will Co., Ill., son of John Wilson Dinwiddie and Mary Jeanette Perkins.

Children:

542. I. Marion Elmer Dinwiddie, b. Nov. 18, 1874; m. Edna Irene Gromann+

543. II. Joseph Perkins Dinwiddie, b. Feb. 3, 1876; m. Alice Ermina Shurte+

544. III. Belle Irene Dinwiddie, b. June 21, 1879, at Plum Grove, Lake Co., Ind.; m. Feb. 28, 1900, at Crown Point, Ind., FOREST MARO GORMLEY, who was b. Oct. 27, 1876, at Upper Sandusky, Ohio, son of John Milton Gormley and Isabel

Nye. Mrs. Gormley has in her possession a
mahogany bureau brought from Ohio by her
grandparents in 1835. Res., Lowell, Ind.

545.   IV. Edward Loraine Dinwiddie, b. Nov. 17, 1882.
546.   V. Edith Jeanette Dinwiddie, b. June 9, 1884, at Plum
Grove, Ind.; m. Jan. 27, 1910, SAMUEL COR-
NELIUS BAIRD, who was b. Sept. 11, 1884, son
of Andrew Baird and ...... Knox. Res.,
Billings, Mont.

Child:

890.   I. Donald Dinwiddie Baird, b. Jan. 22, 1911.

The Dinwiddie clan has records of the family for several genera-
tions. There were five Davids in succession. Our data begins with
the fourth David, who died in 1744. David, fifth, born 1724 in
Ulster, Ireland, married December 17, 1745, Jean McClure, who
died June 22, 1781; married (second) November 20, 1783, Elizabeth
Kerr. He died 1802, Gettysburg, Pennsylvania. Thomas, son of
David, was born March 27, 1787; married October 20, 1808, Mary
Ann Wilson. Thomas died September 17, 1862. He and his
wife are buried near Hebron, Indiana. John Wilson, son of
Thomas, born October 1, 1813, in Trumbull County, Ohio. The
day he was born his father Thomas killed fifteen turkeys, four deer,
and one bear. John W. came with his father to Porter County,
Indiana, in 1836, while the Pottawatomie tribe of Indians still lived
near Hebron, on land now owned by Charles Bryant. Thomas and
John each bought one hundred acres of land of the Indian reservation. Mary Janette Perkins went May 5, 1818, from Rome, New
York, her native place, to Grundy County, Illinois, to teach school.
Here she met Mr. John W. Dinwiddie, whom she afterward married. Mr. Dinwiddie had a contract to construct two sections of
the Illinois and Michigan Canal near Morris, Illinois. After finish-
ing his contract he with his young wife went to Crown Point,
Indiana, to live, where he engaged in merchantile business. Having
purchased one thousand acres of land in Eagle Creek Township, he
moved in 1852 onto the land, and adding more land until he had
thirty-seven hundred acres, he entered into extensive farming.
Among his enterprises he dug a ditch two miles long to change the
channel of Eagle Creek. He engineered another ditch twenty-five

feet deep, to drain the Cady Marsh into the Calumet River. This ditch is now (1913) nearly fifty feet deep. Oscar Dinwiddie, son of John W., possesses the sturdy character and enterprising spirit of his ancestors. He and his wife are staunch Presbyterians, as were the ancestors. The esteem in which Mr. Dinwiddie is held by his friends and neighbors is shown in the offices of trust with which they have honored him. Mrs. Dinwiddie is of the class of wives and mothers who fill a part in making this nation which we are proud to call great — modest, quiet, but with the fortitude of the pioneer and the dignity of Christian womanhood. They have both traveled extensively.

238

JOSEPH HARVEY ROBERTSON[8] (Hannah[7] [100], Samuel,[6] David,[5] Simeon,[4] Cornelius,[3] Pieter Cornelisse,[2] Cornelis[1]), b. Jan. 29, 1854, at Westville, La Porte Co., Ind.; m. Mar. 15, 1882, at Crown Point, Ind., FLORENCE ELVENA TALCOTT, b. Mar. 20, 1860, at Valparaiso, Ind.; dau. of Henry Talcott and Elizabeth Martin.

Children:

547.   I.   Elizabeth B. Robertson, b. Jan. 8, 1883, Eagle Creek, Lake Co., Ind. Educated in Crown Point High School. She is a successful teacher.

548.   II. Francis M. Robertson, b. July 6, 1889, Crown Point, Ind.

549.   III. Joseph Alfred Robertson, b. Dec. 5, 1891, Blaine, Wash.

550.   IV. Eva Bryant Robertson, b. June 23, 1900, Eagle Creek, Lake Co., Ind.

Mr. Robertson is a farmer, also engaged in fruit-growing on Vashon Island, Washington. He owns timber land that he entered as a government claim; in politics, a Democrat; in religion, a Methodist. Has resided in Crown Point and Hebron, Indiana, Benton, Washington, and Plummer, Idaho.

239

FLETCHER LORRAINE ROBERTSON[8] (Hannah[7] [100], Samuel,[6] David,[5] Simeon,[4] Cornelius,[3] Pieter Cornelisse[2] Cornelis[1]), b.

Dec. 23, 1855, Westville, La Porte Co., Ind.; m. Sept. 17, 1889, at Blaine, Whatcom Co., Wash., IRENE STOOPS, b. Dec. 23, 1868. Residences, Hebron, Ind., and Custer, Wash. In early manhood he went West. Was a contractor at Blaine, Wash.

Children:

551. I.   Clifford Lorraine Robertson, b. Sept. 9, 1890.
552. II.   Glen Robertson, b. Mar. 3, 1892.
553. III. Emil Marion Robertson, b. May 22, 1895.
554. IV.   John Herbert Robertson, b. June 23, 1897.
555. V.   Wendel Robertson, b. June 21, 1903.
556. VI.   Clara Leona Robertson, b. Jan. 25, 1905.
557. VII. Irene Joan Robertson, b. May 1, 1907.

240

EVA ROSELLA BRYANT[8] (Harvey W.[7] [101], Samuel,[6] David,[5] Simeon,[4] Cornelius,[3] Pieter Cornelisse,[2] Cornelis[1]), b. Feb. 20, 1861, near Orchard Grove, Ind.

Her early childhood was spent on the farm five miles southwest of Hebron, where she attended the Eagle Creek country school, but later was student in Hebron, where the family resided after 1876. A year later, under the influence of the "tent meeting," she became a member of the Methodist Episcopal Church. To her, Christianity is nothing visionary, but a reality of part of her daily life. Her interest in missions has led her to have her life insured for the benefit of the Methodist Episcopal Foreign Missionary Society. The winter of 1891–2, accompanied by her mother, who was in poor health, she spent in Colorado. After her return she became engrossed with duties in the Bryant, Dowd & Company store, from which she did not release herself for sixteen years, with the exception of a winter spent in Mississippi and one in California. Since 1908 she has been in and a part of the home of her father.

241

MERRITT CONNER BRYANT[8] (Harvey W.[7] [101], Samuel,[6] David,[5] Simeon,[4] Cornelius,[3] Pieter Cornelisse,[2] Cornelis[1]), b.

Nov. 14, 1863 in Eagle Creek township, Lake Co., Ind.; m. Feb. 11, 1896, EFFIE WILSON, b. Apr. 20, 1865; d. Mar. 21, 1913; dau. of John Wilson and Caroline Gregg.

Children:

558.   I.   Glenn Wilson Bryant, b. Oct. 26, 1886, d. Apr. 6, 1887.
559.   II.   Leland Dowd Bryant, b. Feb. 2, 1888.
560.   III.   Bernard Ross Bryant, b. Nov. 13, 1890.
561.   IV.   Edith Miriam Bryant, b. Mar. 27, 1900.
562.   V.   John Harvey Bryant, b. May 14, 1906.

His early education began when, as a bashful boy, accompanied by his mother and hired by his grandfather, he entered the Eagle Creek country school. After the family moved to Hebron he attended the town school for a time, but the routine of the work, especially that of a literary nature, did not appeal to him. In 1884 he was sent to Troy, Missouri, to sell out a stock of goods in which his father had an interest. Though there for less than a year, he learned to mingle with different classes of people, thus gaining a needed experience in his development. After his marriage in 1886 he settled in Hebron, where he soon built a home. In 1889 he, with his wife, entered into relations with the Methodist Episcopal Church. For a number of years he was engaged with Bryant, Dowd & Company, later giving his attention almost entirely to the selling of farm machinery. However, the need of some one to look after the interests of the Bryant, Dowd & Company farm gave the desired opportunity to develop his instinct for farming and stock-raising. Persevering, practical, and up-to-date in his methods, with the aid of his two sons he is making improvements that stamp the present-day successful farmer. He possesses a dry humor, broad sympathy, and unquestionable honesty that make for him many and lasting friends.

245

ORA VIOLA BRYANT[8] (Harvey[7] [101], Samuel,[6] David,[5] Simeon,[4] Cornelius,[3] Pieter Cornelisse,[2] Cornelis[1]), b. June 9, 1872, in Eagle Creek Twp., Lake Co., Ind.

As a girl of thirteen, she became identified with the Methodist Episcopal Church of Hebron. She was a member of the first class to graduate from the Hebron High School in 1890. After a year's experience teaching school, she attended at different times the normal school at Valparaiso, devoting part of the time to the study of music. She gained a practical knowledge of this subject at the Chicago Musical College, but on account of a nervous temperament she was unable to make a musical education practical. In 1900 she suffered a nervous collapse, which was counteracted to some extent by a winter spent in the South. Home-loving, she devotes much of her time to the needs of her father's home, while at other times she finds employment in the store, for the most part doing clerical work. Whether a duty is pleasant or disagreeable, she is faithful in its performance.

246

ADA LUELLA BRYANT[8] (Harvey W.[7] [101], Samuel,[6] David,[5] Simeon,[4] Cornelius,[3] Pieter Cornelisse,[2] Cornelis[1]), b. July 7, 1874, at Eagle Creek, Lake Co., Ind.; m. Sept. 12, 1893, at Crown Point, Ind., JOSEPH ROSS WILSON, who was born Dec. 23, 1867, near LeRoy, Ind., son of Joseph Wilson and Jane McCay.

Delicate as a child she aroused the sympathy of parents and grandparents and won many a point in her favor. She was a favorite among her playmates, but not because they dominated her. In 1885 she united with the Methodist Episcopal Church. Her education was obtained at the Hebron school. Because of ill health she did not finish the prescribed course of study. In 1893 she became a partner in a millinery concern in Hebron of Sweet, Bryant & Company, but disposed of her interest immediately after her marriage in September, 1893. Dr. Joseph Ross Wilson is a practicing physician and has an extensive practice in Hebron and surrounding vicinity.

247

NETTIE LADORA BRYANT[8] (Harvey W.[7] [101], Samuel,[6] David,[5] Simeon,[4] Cornelius,[3] Pieter Cornelisse,[2] Cornelis[1]), b. Apr. 3, 1877, Hebron, Ind.

After her graduation from high school in 1894 she attended the

normal school at Valparaiso, Indiana, for two terms, preparatory to
entering Northwestern University at Evanston, Illinois.   Previous
to this time she had united with the Methodist Church.   After her
graduation from college in 1900, she spent five and one half years
teaching high school subjects, the last four being spent in the home
school at Hebron.   Any success in teaching that she possessed was
due more to her love of, and sympathy for, the pupils than to mere
scholarship.   Since 1907 she has been with Bryant, Dowd & Company, engaged in store duties of a general nature and especially as
wholesale buyer of dry-goods.

248

SAMUEL EDWIN BRYANT[8] (Isaac[7] [102], Samuel,[6] David,[5]
Simeon,[4] Cornelius,[3] Pieter Cornelisse,[2] Cornelis[1]), b. Apr. 14,
1865, Lake Co., Ind.; m. May 8, 1890, MARIA ELLEN WHEEL-
ER, who was b. Aug. 8, 1869, near Lowell, Ind.   Mr. Bryant is
a large dealer in thoroughbred stock and is a successful agricul-
turist; in politics, a Republican.

Children:

563.   I.   Alice Alvira Bryant, b. Mar. 4, 1891.
564.   II.   Clara May Bryant, b. May 20, 1892.
565.   III.   Chistopher Wheeler Bryant, b. Nov. 28, 1893.
566.   IV.   Lelia Marie Bryant, b. Mar. 31, 1897.
567.   V.   Rúth Bryant, b. Sept. 4, 1900.

251

BERTHA L. BRYANT[8] (Isaac[7] [102], Samuel,[6] David,[5] Simeon,[4]
Cornelius,[3] Pieter Cornelisse,[2] Cornelis[1]), b. July 6, 1870, near
Orchard Grove, Lake Co., Ind.; m. July 6, 1890, HARRY
GEORGE, who was b. Jan. 9, 1867, in Clifton, Houghton Co.,
Mich.; son of Thomas George and Anne Muffat.   He d. Jan.
24, 1894, at LeRoy, Lake Co., Ind.   Res., 546 Wieland Ave.,
Chicago, Ill.

Children:

568.   I.   Grace May George, b. Dec. 24, 1891, in Calumet,

Mich.; m. Dec. 29, 1910, in Chicago, JOHN
YOUNG, son of Frank Young and Anna Brough.

569.   II.   Effie George, b. May 31, 1893; d. Sept. 27, 1893.

570.   III. Helen Louise George, b. Aug. 14, 1894; m. Dec. 31,
            1912, Myron L. Armantrout. Res., 3441
            N. Troy St., Chicago, Ill.

Bertha Bryant George received a common and high school education. She was a teacher in a public school until her marriage to Mr.
George. He was employed in the copper mines of Calumet, Michigan. About two years and a half after their marriage Mr. George
contracted typhoid fever and died. Mrs. George with her two little
daughters then made her home in Hebron, Indiana, where she served
as clerk for several years in the dry-goods store of Bryant, Dowd &
Company. Later she went to Chicago where she clerked for Carson Pirie Scott & Company. At present she is engaged with a
ladies' tailoring establishment in Chicago. Mrs. George is an
adherent of the Methodist faith. Residence, 1949 Larabee Street,
Chicago, Illinois.

255

MARY K. STALTER[8] (Jane[7] [103], Samuel,[6] David,[5] Simeon,[4]
Cornelius,[3] Pieter Cornelisse,[2] Cornelis[1]), b. Aug. 18, 1857,
near Little Sandusky, Ohio; m. Nov. 7, 1875, at Rock, Cowley
Co., Kan., NEWTON L. YARBROUGH, who was b. Mar. 20, 1850,
Warrensburg, Mo.; Res., Guerneville, Cal.

Children:

571.   I.   Ernest E. Yarbrough, b. Feb. 12, 1879; m. Sadie
            Riggan.

572.   II. Charles Roy Yarbrough, b. July 3, 1886.

256

GEORGE HERVEY STALTER[8] (Jane[7] [103], Samuel,[6] David,[5]
Simeon,[4] Cornelius,[3] Pieter Cornelisse,[2] Cornelis[1]), b. Oct. 20,
1859, at Ottawa, Kan.; m. Sept. 25, 1881, in Winfield, Kan.,
MATTIE BAIRD, who was b. Feb. 25, 1862, in Roaring Springs,
Ky.; dau. of Volney Baird and Emily E. Griffin. Res., Fargo,
Okla.

Children:

573.   I.   Emma Jane Stalter, b. May 14, 1883, at Winfield, Kan.; m. Sept. 3, 1902, at Woodward, Okla., WILLIAM ALEXANDER WRIGHT, who was b. Aug. 30, 1873, in Texas; son of John Griffin Wright and Sally Elizabeth Perkins.
574.   II.   Ethel C. Stalter, b. Oct. 3, 1889.
575.   III.   Lottie M. Stalter, b. Aug. 30, 1892.
576.   IV.   John Frank Stalter, b. May 24, 1895.
577.   V.   Volney J. Stalter, b. Apr. 1, 1900.

In early life Mr. Stalter was a herdsman, later a farmer and stock-raiser. He also ran a blacksmith shop. He assisted in settling three new countries. Resided in California, Kansas, and Oklahoma, now resides at Aberdeen, Texas. In politics he is a Democrat.

258

ELURA STALTER[8] (Jane[7] [103], Samuel,[6] David,[5] Simeon,[4] Cornelius,[3] Pieter Cornelisse,[2] Cornelis[1]), b. June 3, 1863, in Franklin Co., Kan.; m. June 27, 1879, in Cowley Co., Kan., to JOHN K. SNYDER.

Children:

578.   I.   Maude Snyder, b. Aug. 9, 1880; m. F. T. Wisley+
579.   II.   Pearl E. Snyder, b. June 21, 1882.
580.   III.   Jesse B. Snyder, b. Sept. 5, 1884.
581.   IV.   Lucy Snyder, b. July 28, 1886; d. ....
582.   V.   Sophia J. Snyder, b. June 27, 1888.
583.   VI.   Wildie M. Snyder, b. Dec. 13, 1889; m. May 14, 1910, A. L. Parish.
584.   VII.   Paul J. Snyder, b. Mar. 8, 1896.
585.   VIII.   Hoyt P. Snyder, b. Mar. 8, 1898.

264

EDWIN R. STALTER[8] (Jane[7] [103], Samuel,[6] David,[5] Simeon,[4] Cornelius,[3] Pieter Cornelisse,[2] Cornelis[1]), b. Dec. 3, 1874, near Rock, Cowley Co., Kan.; m. June 9, 1895, DORA MOORE, who was b. Feb. 8, 1876. Res., Pacific Grove, Cal.

Children:

586. I.   Verne Stalter, b. Nov. 13, 1896.
587. II. Harold Stalter, b. Oct. 15, 1902.

265

JOHN W. STALTER[8] (Jane[7] [103], Samuel,[6] David,[5] Simeon,[4] Cornelius,[3] Pieter Cornelisse,[2] Cornelis[1]), b. Dec. 4, 1876, near Rock, Kan.; m. JESSIE E. KAATS, who was b. June 29, 1876.

Children:

588. I.   Gladys Y. Stalter, b. Mar. 10, 1897.
589. II. Morita Lois Stalter, b. Mar. 26, 1902.

267

FREDERICK L. STALTER[8] (Jane[7] [103], Samuel[6]), b. Apr. 17, 1883, at Rock, Kan.; m. Mar. 15, 1904, to GRACE DARST, who was b. Apr. 2, 1888. Res., Pacific Grove, Cal.

Children:

590. I.   Mabel Grace Stalter, b. Oct. 2, 1905.
591. II.   Chester L. Stalter, b. Nov. 20, 1906.
592. III. Eunice Viola Stalter, b. Jan. 20, 1908.

269

EDWIN HUBERT BEEBE[8] (Joanna[7] [104], Samuel,[6] David,[5] Simeon,[4] Cornelius,[3] Pieter Cornelisse[2], Cornelis[1]), b. Nov. 7, 1881, at Princeton, Wis.; m. 1909, at Hartford, Wis., MARY SULLIVAN. Occupation, printer; educated public schools of Princeton, Wis. Employed in Princeton, Ripon, and Hartford, Wis., and Kankakee, Ill.

Children:

593. I.   Ruthvin Sylvester Beebe, b. May 2, 1910.
594. II. Edwin Beebe, b. July 23, 1911.

272

ARABELLA COOPER[8] (Zebulon[7] [105], Mary,[6] David,[5] Simeon,[4] Cornelius,[3] Pieter Cornelisse,[2] Cornelis[1]), b. June 2, 1849, near

Washington, Pa.; m. Feb. 27, 1873, in Mt. Pleasant, Iowa, to
THOMAS MITCHELL SELLERS, who was b. Aug. 7, 1845, Waynesburg, Pa.   Res., Aldine, Texas.

Children:

595.   I.   Charles Walter Sellers, b. July 18, 1874.
596.   II.   Robert Donald Sellers, b. July 29, 1878; m. Alberta
                Johnson.
597.   III.   Clyde Cooper Sellers, b. Aug. 30, 1881.
598.   IV.   Mary Etta Sellers, b. Sept. 25, 1886.
599.   V.   Katharine Sellers, b. Mar. 7, 1893.

273
ISADORA COOPER[8] (Zebulon[7] [105], Mary,[6] David,[5] Simeon,[4]
Cornelius,[3] Pieter Cornelisse,[2] Cornelis[1]), b. June 2, 1849, near
Washington, Pa.; m. 1879, JOHN A. DOWNEY, who was b. Feb.
2, 1857, in Athens, Ohio, son of John Downey and Eliza Buchanan.   In politics a Republican; owns extensive tract of land
in Oregon.   Res., Knappa, Ore., or Stella, Wash.

Children:

600.   I.   Ralph Downey, b. July 7, 1880.
601.   II.   John A. Downey, Jr., b. Oct. 16, 1881.
602.   III.   Blanch E. Downey, b. Jan. 20, 1883.
603.   IV.   Alfred Downey, b. Oct. 10, 1884.
604.   V.   Raymond Downey, b. Feb. 11, 1886.
605.   VI.   Maude Downey, b. Oct. 3, 1888.
606.   VII.   Issie Belle Downey, b. Jan. 23, 1891.
607.   VIII.   Sarah Esther Downey, b. Dec. 6, 1893.

274
DAVID BRYANT COOPER[8] (Zebulon[7] [105], Mary,[6] David,[5]
Simeon,[4] Cornelius,[3] Pieter Cornelisse,[2] Cornelis[1]), b. Oct. 12,
1850, near Washington, Pa.; m. Sept. 25, 1879, HARRIET A.
LEWIS, dau. of W. L. Lewis and Deborah .... Res.,
Fontana, Kan.

Children:

608.   I.   Carrie B. Cooper, b. Aug. 18, 1881; m. O. C. Peterson, who is in the employ of the Missouri Pacific Railway Co. Res., Paola, Kan.

Child:

899.   I.   Paul Peterson, b. Feb. 28, 1911.
609.   II.   Charles B. Cooper, b. June 29, 1884; m. Feb. 3, 1910, MAE STROUP. Res., Denver, Colo., where he is in the employ of an electric light company.
610.   III. Earl C. Cooper, b. Feb. 3, 1888; employee of government mail service.
611.   IV.   William Y. Cooper, b. Oct. 19, 1889.
612.   V.   Russel R. Cooper, b. Dec. 31, 1892.
613.   VI.   Hollis M. Cooper, b. Jan. 16, 1898.

275

MARY ETTA COOPER[8] (Zebulon[7] [105], Mary,[6] David,[5] Simeon,[4] Cornelius,[3] Pieter Cornelisse,[2] Cornelis[1]), b. Jan. 21, 1853, near Washington, Pa.; m. Feb. 22, 1878, in Fontana, Kan., MARVIN M. ROBERTS, who was b. Jan. 31, 1855, in Fulton, Iowa. Res., Villisca, Iowa.

Children:

614.   I.   Maude E. Roberts, b. June 13, 1879; m. Theodore Frans. They have three children:
900.   I.   Cleova Lorene Frans, b. July 23, 1899.
901.   II.   Eva Elene Frans, b. Sept. 2, 1900.
902.   III. Clara Frans, b. Sept., 1906.
615.   II.   Volney W. Roberts, b. Feb. 15, 1882; d. Feb. 23, 1882.
616.   III. Mary Roberts, b. Oct. 19, 1883.
617.   IV.   Leona Pearl Roberts, b. Mar. 22, 1886; d. Aug. 24, 1886.
618.   V.   Grace Belle Roberts, b. Oct. 19, 1887; m. Samuel W. Barker, who d. May 8, 1912.

276

EUGENE NORTON COOPER[8] (Zebulon[7] [105], Mary,[6] David,[5] Simeon,[4] Cornelius,[3] Pieter Cornelisse,[2] Cornelis[1]), b. Apr. 15,

1854, in Washington, Pa.; m. Dec. 27, 1877, in Hillsdale, Kan., ANNA WAGNER, who was b. Sept. 20, 1856, in Independence, Mo.; dau. of David Wagner and Sara Moore Rayburn.

Children:

619.   I.   Arthur Lester Cooper, b. Jan. 28, 1879.
620.   II.   Clara Cooper, b. Apr. 10, 1881; d. Dec. 13, 1885.
621. III.   Edward Cooper, b. Mar. 12, 1883; d. July 17, 1885.
622.   IV.   George Millard Cooper, b. Oct. 22, 1886.
623.   V.   Mabel Cooper, b. Mar. 4, 1890; d. Nov. 25, 1892.
624.   VI.   Earl Noble Cooper, b. Nov. 10, 1892.
625. VII.   Eugene Randall Cooper, b. May 25, 1895; d. Jan. 24, 1904.
626. VIII.   Floyd Bryant Cooper, b. Aug. 7, 1897.

Eugene Norton left Pennsylvania with his parents for the West in 1863; remained one winter near Rochelle, Illinois; moved in 1864 on a farm near Winfield, Iowa. In 1876 this family again removed to Miami County, Kansas, near Paola. In the spring of 1886 he moved to Pawnee County, Kansas, and recently moved to Steller, Alberta, Canada, where he followed extensive farming. Politics, Republican; religion, Baptist.

280

JOHN COOPER GAMBLE[8] (Catherine[7] [106], Mary,[6] David,[5] Simeon,[4] Cornelius,[3] Pieter Cornelisse,[2] Cornelis[1]), b. Oct. 3, 1837; m. Apr. 16, 1862, MARGARET J. FULTON.

They resided for many years on the Gamble homestead until November, 1901, when they moved into Winfield, Iowa. He has been elder and trustee in the Presbyterian Church of Winfield, and for more than twenty years has been clerk of Scott Township, and secretary of the Scott Township school board.

Children:

627.   I.   Sylvanus Cooper Gamble, b. Mar. 8, 1863; m. Nellie Webster+
628.   II.   Anna Gamble, b. Mar. 19, 1865; m. James B. Butter+
629. III.   Herbert Fulton Gamble, b. June 10, 1868; M. Helen Swain+

630.   IV. Francis Harvey Gamble, b. Apr. 3, 1870; m. Helen
                 Fernstrom+
631.   V. Catherine Gamble, b. Sept. 9, 1872; m. Jerome L.
                 Rawhouser+
632.   VI. Elizabeth Gamble, b. Oct. 25, 1876; m. Fred C.
                 Berks+

282

LEROY GAMBLE[8] (Catherine[7] [106], Mary,[6] David,[5] Simeon,[4]
Cornelius,[3] Pieter Cornelisse,[2] Cornelis[1]), b. Sept. 25, 1842, at
Shelby, Ohio; m. Dec. 5, 1867, ELIZABETH A. CONE, dau. of
Isaac P. Cone of New London, Iowa.   She was b. Aug. 5, 1844;
Mr. Gamble enlisted Aug. 13, 1862, in Co. B, Iowa Vol. Inf.;
was honorably discharged June 6, 1865, at Washington.   He
was with Gen. U. S. Grant at Vicksburg and with Sherman
on march from Atlanta to the Sea.   Res., Indianola, Iowa.

        Children:
633.   I. Harvy C. Gamble, b. Feb. 15, 1870; m. Minnie Fos-
                 ter+
634.   II. Walter Gamble, b. Apr. 8, 1872; d. Mar. 11, 1904, of
                 appendicitis.
635.   III. Edwin R. Gamble, b. Aug. 11, 1876; m. May Vig-
                 lenny+
636.   IV. Caroline E. Gamble, b. Aug. 28, 1879; m. Lewis E.
                 Hawes+

283

CHARLES WHITE GAMBLE[8] (Catherine[7] [106], Mary,[6] David,[5]
Simeon,[4] Cornelius,[3] Pieter Cornelisse,[2] Cornelis[1]), b. May 8,
1847, Washington, Pa.; m. Mar. 31, 1874, KATE ADELAIDE
HAIGHT, who was b. Mar. 21, 1857, in Ithaca, N. Y.

Mr. Gamble started in service for the public by filling the office
of constable for six years.   He now holds the office of justice of the
peace, which office he has held for twelve years.   He is also a
county supervisor of Henry County, Iowa.   He is well known in
his part of the state because of his interest in the political welfare

of his county. He is a leading official of the Eastern Iowa District Fair Association. His residence is at Winfield, Iowa.

Child:

637.   I.   Charles Oscar Gamble, b'. Jan. 1, 1875; m. Mary Almina Hewett+

284

MARY JANE COOPER[8] (David[7] [107], Mary,[6] David,[5] Simeon,[4] Cornelius,[3] Pieter Cornelisse,[2] Cornelis[1]), b. Jan. 15, 1840, Washington Co., Pa.; d. Aug. 21, 1903, in Conrad, Montana; m. Sept. 15, 1861, JOHN P. LEECH, eldest son of James Leech and Nancy A. .... Mr. Leech d. in 1865; m. (2nd) Aug. 18, 1870, THOMAS H. LEECH, who was also a son of James and Nancy A. Leech.

Children, 1st m.:

638.   I.   Ida M. Leech; m. George H. Vincent. They have six children.
639.   II.   Eugene E. Leech; m. .... Two children. Res., Dupuyer, Mont.

2nd m.:

640   III..   John F. Leech; m. Pearl Brockman. Res., Dupuyer, Mont. They have two children.
641.   IV.   Don C. Leech; m. Willa Dorsey. Child; a son.
642.   V.   Lloyt C. Leech; m. Pearl Humble. Res., Dupuyer, Mont.
643.   VI.   Bert C. Leech.
643a.   A daughter, d. in infancy.

Mrs. Leech when nine years of age went with her parents in a boat down the Ohio River. They settled in Lee County, Iowa, where the family lived for several years, and later removed to Memphis, Missouri. Mrs. Leech was the oldest of ten children. She was a dutiful daughter, a faithful wife and a devoted mother. The welfare of home was always near to her heart.

286

HESTER ELLEN COOPER[8] (David[7] [107], Mary,[6] David,[5] Simeon,[4] Cornelius,[3] Pieter Cornelisse,[2] Cornelis[1]), b. Aug. 25,

1844; m. ANDREW N. VANCE, who is a merchant and real estate dealer in Des Moines, Iowa.

Children:

644.   I.   Grace Vance, b. ......; m. Judge Erickson, who is judge of the district court of Flathead Co., Mont. Res., Kalispell and Chouteau, Mont.
645.   II. Lloyt Vance, b. ......; m. N. M. Shields. Res., Afton, Iowa.
646.   III. Bert C. Vance, b. ......; m. Sept. 10, 1903, Ethel Rice. Res., Chicago, Ill.

287

OLIVER GOLDSMITH COOPER[8] (David[7] [107], Mary,[6] David,[5] Simeon,[4] Cornelius,[3] Pieter Cornelisse,[2] Cornelis[1]), b. Dec. 4, 1846, near Washington, Pa.; m. Jan. 17, 1882, to AMANDA M. DOWNING, who was b. Dec. 23, 18—, at Memphis, Mo.; dau. of Henry Hawkins Downing and Perineia Goldsberg.

Mr. Cooper is a successful stock trader. He, with the inherited pioneer spirit, went when a mere youth into the new territory of Montana where he, with other members of his father's family, have aided materially in building up a new country. Mr. Cooper is a Republican. Res., Chouteau, Montana.

Children:

647.   I.   Downing Bryant Cooper, b. April 25, 1885; d. Oct. 6, 1895.
648.   II. Frances Downing Cooper, b. Mar. 5, 1887; m. Elbert Kline. Mr. Kline is president of the Continental Fire Insurance Company. Res., New York City.

288

EMMA THERESA COOPER[8] (David[7] [107], Mary,[6] David,[5] Simeon,[4] Cornelius,[3] Pieter Cornelisse,[2] Cornelis[1]), b. May 11, 1849; m. JAMES CONCANNON.

Child:

649.   I.   J. Lloyt Concannon, who m. Hugh Ute, Sept. 11, 1907. Res., Mansfield, Wash.

289

FRANK DARWIN COOPER[8] (David[7] [107], Mary,[6] David,[5] Simeon,[4] Cornelius,[3] Pieter Cornelisse,[2] Cornelis[1]), b. Apr. 6, 1851; m. Apr. 24, 1884, in Memphis, Mo., ALICE GREEN, who was b. Apr. 20, 1859; dau. of Thomas W. Green and Nancy Priest. Res., San Diego, Cal.

Children:

650. I. Linnie Cooper, b. Dec. 10, 1887; graduate of Great Falls (Mont.) High School.
651. II. Nelson Cooper, b. Oct. 8, 1891.
652. III. Frances Cooper, b. Apr. 8, 1894; student at National Park Seminary, Washington, D. C.
653. IV. Alice Cooper, b. Sept. 3, 1899.

Frank Darwin Cooper was educated at Memphis, Missouri, and also graduated in Helena High School. He made a specialty of the study of surveying. In politics a Republican, he was a member of the state legislature of state of Montana, 1882–1883; appraiser of property of Cascade County, twice appointed; school trustee; commissioner of Cascade County two terms; chairman of board of commissioners when a $300,000 courthouse was erected in Great Falls, Montana. He is dealer in real estate, an extensive stock trader, owner of twenty thousand acres of land in Cascade County, Lewis and Clarke County, and Jefferson County; has city property in Helena, Great Falls, Boulder, Cascade, and Sun River. Resides in San Diego, California. He is a member of the Order of Odd Fellows.

Mrs. Cooper's father, Thomas W. Green, who was born in Kentucky, is a prominent citizen of Memphis, Missouri; is treasurer of Scott County, Missouri; was a member of the state legislature; is a Democrat in politics; in religious faith a Baptist. Alice Green Cooper is a sister of Dr. John P. Green, president of West Jewel College, Liberty, Missouri, who was also pastor of Second Baptist Church of St. Louis. Alice Green attended school in Louisville, Kentucky, graduated at La Grange, Missouri; was a music teacher in Louisville.

290

LINNIE BROWN COOPER[8] (David[7] [107], Mary,[6] David,[5] Simeon,[4] Cornelius,[3] Pieter Cornelisse[2], Cornelis[1]), b. June 19,

LINNIE C. MOUNT

1854; m. Jan. 18, 1882, JASPER E. MOUNT, who was b. July 17, 1847, son of Jasper E. Mount and Sarah A. ...... Mr. Mount is a Republican. They are of the Presbyterian faith.

A sketch of the life of Linnie Cooper Mount, born in a humble cottage in the little village of Mount Sterling, Iowa: While still young, her parents emigrated to a farm near Memphis, Missouri. Being the seventh of a family of ten children, she was not basked in the luxuries of fortune, nor favored with surroundings of beauty, but acting upon the principle that every inheritance has a purpose, she sought opportunities; and with the guidance of wise and sympathizing parents she secured a good education in the public school and in a private seminary, and acquired many accomplishments which embellish her character, giving her a nobility worthy of her aspirations. While her goal may not have been attained, she looks back over the years, inspired with the feeling that notwithstanding the privations her pathway has been strewn with flowers and overarched with the beauties of heaven. She found much happiness in the panorama of the farm and in the association of father, mother, five brothers and four sisters. Residence, Memphis, Missouri.

291

IDA ARABELLA COOPER[8] (David[7] [107], Mary,[6] David,[5] Simeon,[4] Cornelius,[3] Pieter Cornelisse,[2] Cornelis[1]), b. Feb. 4, 1857; m. Feb. 4, 1885, at Bowler, Mont., JAMES BROWN, who was b. July 6, 1847, at Geneva, Ill. Res., 1011 South Wyoming St., Butte, Mont.

Children:

654.   I.   James Hugh Brown, b. Nov. 5, 1885.
655.   II.   Hannah Marie Brown, b. July 27, 1888.

292

CHARLES WHITE COOPER[8] (David[7] [107], Mary,[6] David,[5] Simeon,[4] Cornelius,[3] Pieter Cornelisse,[2] Cornelis[1]), b. Apr. 4, 1858; m. MARY COMBS, who was b. Sept. 1, 1864, in Louisville, Ky.; dau. of Charles Combs and Catherine Cornelius. Mr. Cooper is engaged in real estate business and stock-raising; in politics, a Progressive. He was educated at the Memphis (Mo.) Academy. Res., Glasgow, Mont.

Children:

656. I.   Catherine Cooper, b. Aug. 5, 1887; d. Apr., 1899,
           while attending school at Kansas City, Mo.
657. II. David Charles Cooper, b. Feb. 14, 1889; graduated
           from high school of Great Falls and from
           Commercial College of Great Falls.
658. III. Leslie Lamb Cooper, b. May 4, 1890; student in
           high school, Kalispell, Mont.
659. IV. Homer Cooper, b. ......, 189–.
660. V.   Grace Cooper, b. Apr. 1, 1886; d. June, 1886.

294

ADELINE HANNA[8] (Jane[7] [108], Mary,[6] David,[5] Simeon,[4] Cornelius,[3] Pieter Cornelisse,[2] Cornelis[1]), b. Jan. 18, 1840, Prosperity, Pa.; m. Nov. 27, 1862, JOHN VANCE SMITH, who was b. June 6, 1836, in Carrollton, Ohio; son of David Smith and Elenor Hanna. In politics, a Democrat; in religion, a Presbyterian. Res., Carrollton, Ohio.

Children:

661. I.   Martha Jane Smith, b. Apr. 29, 1867; m. Frank
           White+
662. II. Thomas D. Smith, b. Feb. 18, 1870; d. Aug. 26, 1870.
663. III. Lulu N. Smith, b. Dec. 1, 1873; m. George Kurfiss+

295

CLARRIET HANNA[8] (Jane[7] [108], Mary,[6] David,[5] Simeon,[4] Cornelius,[3] Pieter Cornelisse,[2] Cornelis[1]), b. Aug. 19, 1841, at Prosperity, Pa.; m. May 21, 1863, BAYARD BLACHLY LINDLY, who was b. Aug. 20, 1841, son of John Milton Lindly and Eliza Blachly.

Children:

664. I.   John Milton Lindly, b. Nov. 17, 1864; unm.
665. II. Jennie Franc Lindly, b. Oct. 27, 1867; m. William
           Bailey Ridgeway+

WILMA J. RIDGEWAY

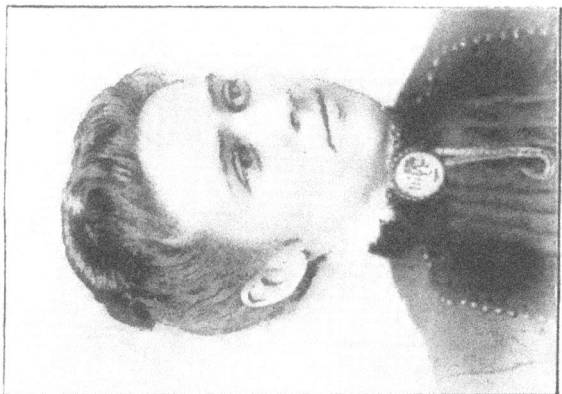

JENNIE LINDLY RIDGEWAY

CLARRIET LINDLY

In religion Mr. and Mrs. Lindly are Presbyterian. Mr. Lindly has served as an elder in the Presbyterian Church of Winfield, Iowa, for twenty-five years. He was a surveyor and farmer in early life; was admitted to the bar in Henry County, Iowa, in 1884, established the Bank of Winfield in 1885, which he still owns, and in addition has been in the drug business since 1879; is a member of the Iowa State Pharmaceutical Association, a member of the Iowa Bankers Association; served several terms as mayor of Winfield, Iowa.

JOHN MILTON LINDLY, born November 17, 1864; early education obtained in public schools; graduated from the State University of Iowa in 1889 with the degree of Ph. G.; from the National Institute of Pharmacy of Chicago in 1892; from the four years' course in the Chautauqua Literary and Scientific Circle in 1898 with admission to the order of the White Seal; elected without opposition mayor of Winfield, Iowa, in 1900, but declined the office; town clerk of Winfield, 1904–06; secretary of board of education of Winfield, 1898–; trustee and treasurer of Presbyterian Church of Winfield, 1898–; secretary of the Iowa State Pharmaceutical Association, 1905–11, and treasurer of same 1911–. He is a member of the Society of Colonial Wars, of the Sons of the American Revolution, of Colonial Governors, of the Old Northwest Genealogical Society, of the National Geographic Society, Iowa Academy of Science, State Historical Society of Iowa, Iowa Park and Forestry Association, Iowa State and American Pharmaceutical Association, Iowa Bankers' and American Bankers' Association. At a recent state druggists convention Mr. Lindly was re-elected treasurer. At the Democratic state election held in July, 1912, at Cedar Rapids, he had the honor of nominating the successful candidate, Mr. John E. Craig, for judge of the supreme court on the Democratic ticket. Mr. Lindly is a reliable genealogist. We are indebted to him for assistance in furnishing data for the Bryant Genealogy. He has compiled and published a genealogy of the Lindly family, from which the following is copied:

"The Lindly ancestry dates to two emigrants, John and Francis, brothers, who came to Connecticut in 1639. Francis married Susanna Culpepper, June 24, 1655. Their children were: Deborah, b. 1656; Ruth, b. 1658; Ebenezer, b. 1660; John, b. 1666 or 1667; Benjamin, Joseph, Jonathan. The first three were born in Bradford,

Connecticut, the last four in Newark, New Jersey. John and Jonathan lived at Morristown, New Jersey. John[1] had sons John[2] and Daniel. John[2] had following children: Stephen, Junia, Caleb (who served in Revolutionary War with New Jersey troops), John (captain in Revolutionary War), Levi, b. 1731 (d. 1801), Demas, Phillip (served in· Revolutionary War), Phoebe, and Hannah. Caleb, Levi, Demas, and Phillip went in an early day to Washington, Pennsylvania. The name has had various spellings; as, Linde, Lindsley, Lindsly, Linsly, Lindley, etc. Mr. Bayard B. Lindly descends from Levi, of 1731. Mr. John M. Lindly has a copy of the will of John, the father of Levi."

Mr. J. M. Lindly compiled an enumeration of the wild flowers of Story County, Iowa, from the herbarium of V. C. Gambell, which makes a valuable addition to the Iowa Academy of Science.

296

MARY ELLEN HANNA[8] (Jane[7] [108], Mary,[6] David,[5] Simeon,[4] Cornelius,[3] Pieter Cornelisse,[2] Cornelis[1]), b. Dec. 21 1843, Prosperity, Pa.; m. Sept. 24, 1868, DEMAS LINDLEY McVAY, who was b. Jan. 13, 1844; d. Sept. 2, 1911. He was the son of Franklin McVay and Priscilla Day. He was a liberal supporter of the Presbyterian Church of Prosperity, Pa., of which he was a member. Res., Prosperity, Pa.

Children:

666.   I.   Leanna Jane McVay, b. Dec. 10, 1869; m. Charles Donaldson+
667.   II.   Priscilla D. McVay, b. Dec. 8, 1871; m. John Calvin French+
668. III.   Thomas Franklin McVay, b. Apr. 3, 1874; m. Josephine Bell+
669.   IV.   John McVay, b. ......, 1880; d. Apr., 1885.

297

JOHN WALKER HANNA[8] (Jane[7] [108], Mary,[6] David,[5] Simeon,[4] Cornelius,[3] Pieter Cornelisse,[2] Cornelis[1]), b. Sept. 23, 1846, in Prosperity, Pa.; m. Oct. 26, 1882, CAROLINE ELIZABETH DUN-

JOHN WALKER HANNA AND FAMILY

CAN, who is a descendant of Governor Mayhew of Martha's Vineyard. She is graduate of the Council Bluffs High School; is a member of the order of the Eastern Star; is the leader of the church choir.

Children:

670.   I. John Thomas Hanna, b. Oct. 31, 1890, graduated from Winfield High School in 1908; graduated from College of Liberal Arts in state of Iowa in 1912 with degree of B. A.; is now a medical student at Iowa State University; is on the editorial staff of the College of Medicine of the University paper, the *Daily Iowan;* is a member of the Glee Club.

671.   II. Walker Duncan Hanna, b. Oct. 26, 1892; graduated from Winfield High School in 1910; is a junior student in Iowa State University. He is at times assistant cashier in the Bank of Winfield. He is first lieutenant of his company of the University Cadets.

Dr. Hanna graduated from the medical department of the State University of Iowa in 1873. He has taken post-graduate courses in St. Louis and in Chicago. He was in St. Louis, Missouri, at the time of the yellow fever epidemic in 1878, being in the city quarantine service. He has been located in Winfield, Iowa, since September, 1879. Held office of mayor of Winfield; president of Southwest Iowa Medical Association; for twenty-five years surgeon for Burlington and Western Railroad, and the Burlington and North Western Railroad; president of Winfield Board of Education; postmaster from 1885 to 1889; president of the Southeast Iowa Fair Association; was Democratic nominee for state senator. He is a Knight Templar of the Masonic Order, including membership in the Chapter, Commandery and Mystic Shrine. Mrs. Hanna is a leader in musical circles.

298

JANE HANNA[8] (Jane[7] [108], Mary,[6] David,[5] Simeon,[4] Cornelius,[3] Pieter Cornelisse,[2] Cornelis[1]), b. Dec. 15, 1848; m. Sept. 1, 1873, in Winfield, Iowa, FRANK D. KELLEY, who was b.

Sept. 22, 1843, at Carrollton, Ohio; retired farmer; in politics, a Democrat; in religion, Presbyterian.   Res., Phillipsburg, Kan.

Children:

672.   I.   Mary Frances Kelley, b. Oct. 8, 1875; m. Harry Roach+
673.   II.   Claude Kelley, b. Sept. 30, 1877.
674.   III.   Charles Kelley, b. Aug. 31, 1880.
675.   IV.   Frank Kelley, b. Mar. 22, 1885; d. Mar. 25, 1902.
676.   V.   Randolph Kelley, b. Mar. 23, 1888.
677.   VI.   Jennie D. Kelley, b. Feb. 7, 1894.

300

CHARLES COOPER ATKINSON[8] (Mary[7] [109], Mary,[6] David,[5] Simeon,[4] Cornelius,[3] Pieter Cornelisse,[2] Cornelis[1]), b. Feb. 18, 1841, at Hollidays Cove, Hancock Co., W. Va.; d. Apr. 10, 1905; m. Nov. 11, 1866, in the 1st Universalist ch. Pittsburgh, Pa., to AMELIA CHAPIN, who was b. Sept. 3, 1850, in Rochester, N. Y.; d. Jan. 5, 1881, at La Cygne, Kan.   She was dau. of Freeman Chapin.   Mr. Atkinson m. (2nd) MARGARET SELLERS, of Paola, Kan.   In politics he was a Democrat   He was a dentist and practiced in La Cygne, Kan., until the time of his death; buried in La Cygne.

Children, 1st m.:

678.   I.   Frank Atkinson, b. Aug. 21, 1868; d. May 10, 1899.
679.   II.   Nora Atkinson, b. Feb. 14, 1870; m. James O. Kelsey.   Res., 1218 Riverview Ave., Kansas City, Mo.
680.   III.   Mabel Atkinson, b. Sept. 25, 1871; m. Wilber Allen. Res., La Cygne, Kan.
Child: 994a.   Frank Allen.
681.   IV.   Ida Gertrude Atkinson, b. Dec. 16, 1874; m. ......
Reid.
682.   V.   Florence Josephine Atkinson, b. Oct. 25, 1876; m. Bruce Dennis.   Res., La Grande, Ore.
Child (994b): Claire Dennis.
2nd m.

683. VI. Cleda Atkinson, b. Sept. 15, 1885; m. William H. Blaker.

684. VII. Chester, b. ......; d. at age of two or three years.

303

CHARLES COOPER VANKIRK[8] (Sarah[7] [110], Mary,[6] David,[5] Simeon,[4] Cornelius,[3] Pieter Cornelisse,[2] Cornelis[1]), b. Oct. 10, 1842; m. ELIZABETH F. GAMBLE, b. June, 1848; d. Oct. 23, 1913. She was the dau. of Levi W. Gamble and Barbara Weygandt. Mr. Gamble followed farming and stock-raising. He d. Dec. 18, 1891. Mrs. Gamble d. Dec. 5, 1907.

Child:

685. I. Dora G. Vankirk, b. Jan. 22, 1869; d. Mar. 20, 1883.

Charles C. Vankirk was educated at Washington and Jefferson College and at State Normal College, California, Pennsylvania. He taught school three years. Later conducted a general merchandise store at Scenery Hill, Pennsylvania. In 1880 he removed to Washington, Pennsylvania. He was a commercial salesman for eighteen years. He is now living a retired life in Washington, Pennsylvania.

305

MARY JANE VANKIRK[8] (Sarah[7] [110], Mary,[6] David,[5] Simeon,[4] Cornelius,[3] Pieter Cornelisse,[2] Cornelis[1]), b. Oct. 10, 1846; m. GEORGE WASHINGTON MCELREE, Sept. 8, 1869, at the home of her parents in Washington, Pa. Mr. McElree was the son of James McElree and Martha Boyd Resided in Washington, Pa., and in Crafton, a suburb of Pittsburgh, Pa.

Children:

686. I. Hiram Winnett McElree, b. Mar. 11, 1873. He was graduated from Washington and Jefferson College in 1901. Since that time he has been engaged in educational work. He was principal of the Eighth Ward Schools, Washington, Pennsylvania, for eight years, principal of the Ingram Schools, in the suburbs of Pitts-

burgh, for four years.   He is now superin-
tendent-principal of three of the leading
schools of Pittsburgh — the Bane, Brashaer,
and Jefferson schools.

687.   II.   HELEN BROWN MCELREE, b. Nov. 13, 1885; was
graduated from the Washington Female Seminary in 1905.   She was a successful teacher
in the public schools of Washington, Pennsylvania, for six years, and is now a teacher
in the Pittsburgh schools.

698.   III.   RALPH ALEXANDER MCELREE, b. Nov. 13, 1888; d.
May 18, 1901.

307
MORRIS REVERDY DAY[8] (Elizabeth[7] [112], Mary,[6] David,
Simeon,[4] Cornelius,[3] Pieter Cornelisse,[2] Cornelis[1]), b. Aug. 11,
1846, in Morris Twp., Green Co., Pa.; m. 187-, DORA ELDER,
dau. of G. W. Elder and Emily Bonsell.   She was b. Aug. 11,
1852; d. Nov. 27, 1885, Klemme, Iowa.

Children:
689.   I.   Margaret Elizabeth Day, b. Nov. 26, 1871; m.
Frederick P. Skow+
690.   II.   Estella Dell Day, b. Feb. 5, 1875; m. Rev. Hans
Nissen+
691.   III.   Ida Alice Day, b. Apr. 30, 1877; m. John Baum-
gartner+
692.   IV.   John Nelson Day, b. Sept. 9, 1881; m. Anna Mildred
Smith, June 26, 1907.   Res., Buffalo Center, Iowa.
693.   V.   Stephen Hockley Day, b. Dec. 14, 1883; m. May 16,
1910, Esther Law.   Res., Hubbard, Ore.
Children: Iola Mary Day, b. Feb. 22, 1911. 693b.,
Wilma Lucille, b. June 19, 1913;
694.   VI.   Morris Reverdy Day, b. Dec. 15, 1885; m. Vivian
Kimball.   Res., Montpelier, Idaho.   Child:
M. Mildred Day, b. June 20, 1913.

Mr. Day was a large land owner and banker; in politics, a Democrat; in religion, a Methodist.   He enlisted in the Civil War, in
Company K, Third Illinois Cavalry, as a private in 1865, under

Lieutenant Danley (General Wilson, Division Commander) and was promoted to the office of Sergeant. He enlisted at Dixon, Illinois, and was honorably discharged October 10, 1865, at the age of eighteen years.

310

MARY ELIZABETH VAILE[8] (Caroline[7] [113], Mary,[6] David,[5] Simeon,[4] Cornelius,[3] Pieter Cornelisse,[2] Cornelis[1]), b. Apr. 28, 1849, near Washington, Pa., removing with her parents to Lane (now Rochelle), Ill., in the fall of 1853.

Mary, as she is called by a large and appreciative circle of friends, has led a quiet life of usefulness in deeds of kindness for others, living in quiet dignity in the parental home, an ever-ready assistant with loving care and sympathy. She is an extensive reader. Society has but little charm for her. Not an unkind word is ever spoken by her of anyone. She is an exemplification of a true Christian character; ever zealous in her Master's cause. She has been for several years treasurer of the Woman's Missionary Society of the First Presbyterian Church of Rochelle, Illinois, of which she is a member. She is a charter member of the Rochelle Chapter of the Daughters of the American Revolution.

311

CLARA E. VAILE[8] (Caroline[7] [113], Mary,[6] David,[5] Simeon,[4] Cornelius,[3] Pieter Cornelisse,[2] Cornelis[1]), b. Jan. 9, 1851, Washington, Pa.; m. Jan. 26, 1882, MILES JOSEPH BRAIDEN, who was b. Oct. 10, 1835, Castile, Wyoming Co., N. Y.; d. May 19, 1905; son of Roger Ascham Braiden, b. 1800, New York City, and Sophia Fletcher, dau. of Isaac Gardner Fletcher, b. Oct. 26, 1768, Westfield, Mass., and Ruth Pierce, b. Apr. 17, 1767, dau. of Jonathan Pierce. Res., Rochelle, Ill.

Children:

695.   I. Roscoe Vaile Braiden, b. May 7, 1888; m. Anna Geraldine Allen+

696.   II. Bryant Fletcher Braiden, b. Aug. 13, 1893; graduate of Rochelle High School; completed sophomore year at Monmouth College, Monmouth, Ill.

Entered Cornell Law School, at Ithaca, N. Y., 1913. He inherits the Bryant stature. He is six feet three inches in height; is a college athlete.

697.   III.   Marion Gillespie Braiden, b. May 10, 1896; student, sophomore year at Ferry Hall, Lake Forest, Ill.

Clara Vaile was educated in the public schools. Her father came from a long line of educators, and appreciated educational advantages. He was usually a member of the school board, and secured the best available instructors, sometimes supplementing personally the necessary funds to secure the best teachers. Clara was sent to Rockford College, Rockford, Illinois. In the fall of 1870, after leaving seminary, as it was then termed, she entered the Rochelle public school as a teacher, making a specialty of primary work "for which she was eminently fitted, receiving state recognition for best methods and best results." A specimen of this primary work was sent to the World's Centennial Exhibition held at Phildelphia, Pennsylvania, in 1876, and received third highest award in the United States. The Lakeland-Auburndale Herald of February, 1912, in a sketch written on the occasion of a visit of Mrs. Braiden to Lakeland, Florida, mentions in part as follows: "Mrs. Clara V. Braiden is one of the best known club women in the state of Illinois. She was instrumental in organizing the Woman's Club of Rochelle, Illinois, now consisting of one hundred and fifty members, and was its president for three terms. She was district president of the Federated Clubs of northern Illinois." In 1890 Mrs. C. V. Braiden organized a Chautauqua Reading Circle in Rochelle, which organization has since had a continuous flourishing existence, graduating students, which formed an alumni of sixty-three members. Mrs. Braiden has acted in the capacity of president of both organizations. She graduated from the Chautauqua Literary and Scientific Circle in class of 1904, with White Seal honors. She is a member of the Daughters of the American Revolution, having verified the military record of five Revolutionary ancestors. She is a charter member of the Rochelle Chapter of the Daughters of the American Revolution, of which chapter she served two terms as regent. She represented the Illinois chapters at the Conservation Congress held in Kansas City, Kansas, in 1911. and the American Peace Congress held in St. Louis, May, 1913, one of three Daughters of the American Revolution to represent

Clara Vaile Braiden

Illinois. If Mrs. Braiden were asked in what way she had best served the interests of the community in which she lives it would, we believe, be instruction in the Sabbath school. Always having had a fondness and fitness for teaching she began with a class in the Sunday school at the age of seventeen, and has been continously in that work for more than forty years, counting many scores who have received bible instruction from her.

She was thirteen years secretary of the Woman's Foreign Missionary Society of the First Presbyterian Church of Rochelle, and was twice president of the Ladies' Aid Society of that church. As a manager of business affairs, she deserves special mention. The Lakeland-Auburndale Herald says: "She ranks as one of the most successful business women of the State of Illinois." She has had the management of an estate for the past ten years, and owns a lumber and coal business established by her husband in 1871, which is conducted by a competent manager under her supervision. She has been equally successful in managing her real estate interests, which include more than eleven hundred acres of farming land. As busy as she has always been she has found time to search out Bryants in nearly every state in the Union and arrange their records in genealogical form. While traveling in America and in Europe she has ever been on the lookout for genealogical data. Mrs. Braiden is a member of the Salome Chapter of the order of the Eastern Star.

From Ogle County History: "Miles J. Braiden was for many years prominent among the energetic, far-seeing and successful business men of Rochelle. His life history most happily illustrates what may be attained by faithful and continued effort in carrying out an honest purpose. Integrity, activity, and energy have been the crowning points of his success, and his connection with various business enterprises and industries have been of decided advantage to his community, promoting its material welfare in no uncertain manner. He came from Wyoming County, New York, to Waukegan, Illinois, in 1850, where he attended the Waukegan Academy. He went to Rochelle, Illinois, in 1856, and embarked in the grocery and grain business. In 1860 he purchased six hundred and forty acres of land in Lee County, Illinois. For a term of years he devoted his time and attention to the occupation of farming. In 1868 he purchased two farms, upon which he platted additions to the city of Rochelle. In 1871 he began dealing in lumber, coal, ice and

building stone from the quarries on his own land within the limits
of the city, from which thousands of cords of excellent building
stone have been taken and an inexhaustable supply yet remains.
In this quarry abound exhaustless and never-failing springs of the
purest water from which each year the ice crop is taken for the city
supply.   Mr. Braiden has been instrumental in having built a large
number of houses in Rochelle by reason of his progressiveness and
by offering such inducements as would enable almost any one to
secure a home, thus adding to the welfare of the city.   No one has
had a higher place in the estimation of the people than he."   The
Chicago Evening Journal of February 9, 1877, gives as follows upon
the occasion of the completion of the branch of the Chicago, Burlington and Quincy Railroad through Rochelle: "Rochelle owes its
success and prosperity mainly to a few public-spirited individuals,
foremost among whom is M. J. Braiden, who has laid out four additions to the town, and built in all nearly one hundred dwellings,
which have either been sold or rented."

In political sentiment he was a stanch Republican, and took a
prominent and influential part in public affairs.   He was treasurer
of school funds of Reynolds Township, Lee County, for twelve
years during his entire residence there.   He was elected supervisor
of the township; held that office six years; the last two elections he
received every vote cast for the office.   He also served six years as
supervisor of Flagg Township, Ogle County.   In 1870 he was
elected to the General Assembly of Illinois, and most ably represented his district in that body.   He served in the city offices of
Rochelle.   He has been characterized as a man of enterprise, indomitable energy, liberal views, positive character, and very generally known for his kindness to those in need.   His father,
Roger Ascham Braiden, was of Scotch-English descent; born
in New York City.   Roger Braiden was the son of Joseph Braiden
and Nancy Gillespie, a descendant of the Campbell clan of
Scotland.   Miles J. Braiden[8] was the son of Sophia Fletcher Braiden,[7] who was the daughter of Isaac G. Fletcher,[6] who served in the
War of the Revolution; married Ruth Pierce.   Isaac G. Fletcher[6]
was the son of Joshua Fletcher[5] of Westford, Massachusetts; born
1731; married Elizabeth Raymond.   Joshua[5] was the son of
Joseph Fletcher,[4] born 1689, Chelmsford, Massachusetts; married
Sarah Adams of Concord, Massachusetts, a descendant of the
President John Adams and Samuel Adams family — ancestry: Ap.

MARION G. BRAIDEN

Adam of Early Scotland. Joseph Fletcher[4] was the son of Joshua Fletcher,[3] born 1648; married Sarah Willy. Joshua[3] was the son of William Fletcher,[2] born in England, 1622; came with his parents to Concord, Massachusetts, in 1630; married Lydia Bates. He was the son of Robert Fletcher,[1] who was born in England in 1592; emigrated to Concord, Massachusetts, in 1630. The name Fletcher is from the French *Fleche*, an arrow. Rev. W. G. Dymock Fletcher, of Oxford, England, who is well versed in the genealogy of the Fletcher family in England, remarks: "There can be no doubt but that the family is one of great antiquity, as is apparent from its ancient arms — sable, a cross flory between four scallop shells argent; this coat of arms would indicate that one or more of the members of the family took part in the crusades." Bentham, in his "Baronetage of England," says: "The Fletchers are supposed to be of Norman descent, and to have come over with William the Conqueror." He gave quotations to prove the assertion.

Mr. Braiden has the following Pierce ancestry: Ruth Pierce,[7] an aunt of President Franklin Pierce, was the daughter of Jonathan Pierce[6] of Groton, Massachusetts; born 1727; married 1750, Ruth Gilson, born 1728. Jonathan[6] was the son of Stephen Pierce,[5] born 1678; married Rachel Harrod. He was the son of Jacob Pierce,[4] who was the son of Steven Pierce,[3] born 1651; married Tabitha Parker. Steven[3] was the son of Thomas Pierce,[2] born 1608; married Elizabeth Cole. He was the son of the emigrant ancestor Thomas Pierce,[1] who came from England in 1633–4 with his wife Elizabeth, who was born in England in 1595. Thomas was born 1583. "The name Pierce is from Piercy or Percy. The renowned family of Percy of Northumberland, England, derived their name from the Percy forest in the provence of Maen, Normandy, from whence they came, which signifies a stony place, from Pierre, the ancient fief of the family who settled in Normandy before the cession of the province to Rollo (Wm. Arthur's Etymological Dictionary). The name de Perci is in the Doomsday Book, land owner. William de Perci and brother Serlo assisted in the Conquest of England, 1066.

312
SUSAN MARIA VAILE[8] (Caroline[7] [113], Mary,[6] David,[5] Simeon,[4] Cornelius,[3] Pieter Cornelisse,[2] Cornelis[1]), b. Aug. 8,

1852, Washington Co., Penna.; m. Feb 10, 1876, CHARLES EDWIN CORT, who was b. Mar. 1, 1841, in Monogahela City, Pa.; d. Aug. 3, 1903. He was the son of Jacob Cort and Jane Mary Carson, dau. of Andrew Carson and Ruth Clayton.

Children:

698.   I.   Belle Cort, b. Aug. 6, 1877; m. Abner Shirk+
699.   II.   Caroline Vaile Cort, b. Oct. 14, 1879; m. Mortimer Muraine. Graduate of Huron High School, Huron, S. D., and Huron College, S. D. Child, 955a, Thomas Edwin, b. July 7, 1913.
700.   III.   Jane Mary Cort, b. Mar. 14, 1883; m. Harry Lenhart+
701.   IV.   Edwin Gallatin Cort, b. Sept. 2, 1885; graduated from Huron High School, also graduated in 1911 from the State Agricultural College at Ames, Iowa. He is a professor in college at Browns Valley, Minn.
702.   V.   Joseph Clayton Cort, b. Dec. 3, 1887; graduated at Huron High School, is now (1913) a senior at Iowa State College at Ames, Iowa. He remained from college long enough to preëmpt a homestead near Caton, S. D.
703.   VI.   Ruth Helen Cort, b. June 10, 1892, in Huron, S. D.

Mrs. Cort was educated in the common schools. She is a person of much energy and decision of character. Having been left a widow while her children were still young, she used to the best possible advantage the means at her command to educate five of her six children through high school and college. She is very active and efficient in the duties of her church.

Charles Edwin Cort, fourth child and second son of Jacob and Jane M. Cort, was educated in the public schools of Monongahela City, Pennsylvania, and went to Illinois with the family and was one of the lads who made it possible to go on a farm, care for and provide for the family. He was on the farm until August of 1862, when, at the call of the President for 600,000 men, he went to the front and joined Company H, of the Ninety-second Illinois Volunteers, under Colonel Smith D. Atkins. They crossed the Ohio River at Covington, Kentucky, and came home by way of Baltimore, Maryland, having been through Kentucky, Tennessee,

CHARLES EDWIN CORT   MARIA VAILE CORT

Alabama, Georgia, South Carolina, North Carolina, and Virginia. The regiment was mounted when out eighteen months and they were "From Atlanta to the Sea" with General Kilpatrick. Charles Edwin was in constant and continuous service, having never been in the hospital or off duty. The regiment reached Chicago July 2, 1865, and the boys arrived at home for the Fourth. They were mustered out the latter part of July at Chicago, and Charles, like a large majority of the regiment, returned to the farm. The family, who had lived in Lee County, Illinois, from March, 1855, removed in 1867 to Ogle County, near Rochelle.

Captain Cort, besides his career as a soldier in the Civil War, had charge of Company F, Second Regiment, Illinois National Guards. He was an early settler in Dakota before it was a state, and was a member of the convention that framed its constitution. He was elected on the issue of a prohibitory clause, in the new constitution, helped to adopt it, and also to accept it at the polls. He was active in local affairs of the new state, especially in organizing churches and schools, being called the father of the first Presbyterian Church in St. Lawrence, South Dakota, and was one of its first elders. He was an able, fearless, and upright man, and died full of faith and hope.

313

ANNA ELIZA VAILE[8] (Caroline[7] [113], Mary,[6] David,[5] Simeon,[4] Cornelius,[3] Pieter Cornelisse,[2] Cornelis[1]), b. Apr. 13, 1854; d. May 23, 1911, of paralysis, living only two days; m. May 2, 1903, at Portland, Ore., DAVID BYRON HALL, who was b. May 28, 1852, at Bridgetown, Nova Scotia; son of Edward Fellows Hall and Hannah Tupper.

Mrs. Hall was for many years a successful primary teacher, holding a state certificate. She was also a teacher of physical culture. She lectured on Pschycology in several of the cities on the Pacific Coast, and is the author of several booklets on Physical Culture and kindred subjects. She was assistant editor of a magazine entitled "We." She traveled extensively. Residence, Los Angeles, California.

314

EMMA CAROLINE VAILE[8] (Caroline[7] [113], Mary,[6] David,[5] Simeon,[4] Cornelius,[3] Pieter Cornelisse,[2] Cornelis[1]), b. Mar. 13,

1864; m. Feb. 9, 1884, EUGENE L. COLE, son of Van Rensellaer Cole, who was the son of Abraham Cole. The mother of Eugene L. was Abigail Wilson, dau. of Kady Wilson, who was son of Peter Wilson of Horseneck, Conn., a soldier of the War of the Revolution.

Children:

704.   I.   Willard George Cole, b. Oct. 17, 1886; electrician.
705.   II.   Frederick Gallatin Cole, b. Aug. 26, 1890; in clothing house, Centralia, Ill.

Mrs. Emma Vaile Cole possesses more than ordinary artistic ability. She is not only an expert amateur with the brush, but this rare ability is shown in the industry of the home. Her needlework is of the finest, she having received an Illinois state diploma for fancy embroidery. The artistic quality of her literary talent is shown in her productions for the local clubs. Mrs. Cole is a member of the First Presbyterian Church of Rochelle and served as president of the Woman's Aid Society of the church. She is a member of the order of Eastern Star and, a charter member of the Rochelle Chapter of the society of the Daughters of the American Revolution. Residence, Rochelle, Illinois. Cole, also *Colle*, is an ancient family name — found in Doomsday Book as holding land in England in time of William the Conqueror.

315

EDWARD LEONARD VAILE[8] (Caroline[7] [113], Mary,[6] David,[5] Simeon,[4] Cornelius,[3] Pieter Cornelisse,[2] Cornelis[1]), b. Nov. 4, 1868, Rochelle, Ill.; m. June 5, 1899, at Ann Arbor, Mich., Maude Eggert, who was b. Feb. 28, 1877, dau. of Augustus Charles Eggert, son of Henry Eggert and Theresa Thomas, dau. of Anne Haine.

Child:

706.   I.   Edward Leonard Vaile, Jr., b. Oct. 23, 1900, in Kewanee, Ill.

Dr. Vaile graduated from the High School in 1887, and from the commercial department of Knox College in 1888. He attended the Northwestern University of Chicago, and graduated from the Ann

ANNA VAILE HALL

Arbor Dental College in 1897. He is a member of the First Presbyterian Church of Rochelle; served as trustee and as leader of choir. In politics Dr. Vaile was a Republican until the Third Party movement. He is now an ardent adherent of the Progressive policies. He is a member of the Masonic order (Horicon Lodge number 244), also a member of the Eastern Star (Salome Chapter). Practicing dentistry, Rochelle, Illinois.

Mrs. Maude E. Vaile graduated from the Jackson (Michigan) High School in 1894, and had completed the sophomore year at the University of Michigan at Ann Arbor when her marriage to Dr. Vaile occurred in 1899. She filled the office of state vice-president of Woman's Clubs for one term, was president of the Rochelle Woman's Club for two years. She is a member of Salome Chapter of Eastern Star. Has served as secretary of the chapter for eight years.

316

MARY DUYCKINCK COOPER[8] (Charles[7] [114], Mary,[6] David,[5] Simeon,[4] Cornelius,[3] Pieter Cornelisse,[2] Cornelis[1]), b. July 2, 1862; d. Mar. 20, 1894; m. Apr. 20, 1887, FRANK M. CUMMINGS, M. D., who d. Mar. ....., 1912. Mary D. Cooper was a graduate of Mt. Holyoke, Mass. Seminary.

Children:

707.   I. Caroline Seeley Cummings, b. 188–. She graduated from Vassar College with M. A. degree in 1911. She is now engaged in teaching in Cambridge, Mass.

708.   II. Margaret Duyckinck Cummings, b. .... She is a student at the Boston Medical College.

317

CHARLES BRYANT COOPER[8] (Charles[7] [114], Mary,[6] David,[5] Simeon,[4] Cornelius,[3] Pieter Cornelisse,[2] Cornelis[1]), b. Nov. 19, 1864, Babylon, N. Y.; m. KATHERINE CHRISTIE McGREW, who was b. Feb. 20, 1874, Honolulu, Island of Oahu, Hawaii. She was the dau. of JOHN STEYNOR McGREW and Pauline Gillette. Res., Honolulu, Hawaii.

Children:

709.　I.　Charles Bryant Cooper, Jr., b. Aug. 7, 1900.
710.　II.　John McGrew Cooper, b. Oct. 13, 1902.
711.　III.　Infant.

Dr. Charles Bryant Cooper was educated at Wallkill Academy, Middletown, New York, and Williston Seminary, Easthampton, Massachusetts; received his degree of Doctor of Medicine from the University of Missouri in 1889. Was president of the Hawaiian Territorial Medical Society and of the Hawaiian Territorial Board of Health; surgeon general of the Territory of Hawaii, U. G. H.; commissioner of public health, Territory of Hawaii. He was the first delegate in that capacity to attend the American Medical Association. He has also been attending physician to the Queen's Hospital, Honolulu, and chief surgeon of the Oahu Railroad. He was the first Exalted Ruler and District Deputy B. P. O. E. appointed in the new possessions in 1900. He belongs to the Masonic order, Blue Lodge, Royal Arch Masons, Commandery, Shrine, Sons of American Revolution. He is a great-great-grandson of General Andrew McMeyers, who was killed at the battle of Germantown. The following resolution adopted by the Territorial Board of Health in reference to Dr. Cooper's services will not be amiss in this place:

"We miss among our members to-day Dr. C. B. Cooper. I believe I state the unanimous sentiment of the board in expressing our regret that he decided to retire from a position where he has been for years an active and positive factor in public health matters. His record in quietly, economically, and effectively handling epidemic disease will stand to his lasting credit. His record in promoting the welfare of the lepers and effective work in enlisting the practical aid of the federal government in their behalf can not be forgotten. The support he has given the present president of the Board of Health is gratefully acknowledged.

"Dr. Mayo made the following statement concerning the work of Dr. C. B. Cooper, who resigned as a member of the Board of Health last week after being again confirmed in office by the Hawaiian Senate:

" 'We all agree, I am sure, with the remarks of the president appreciative of Dr. Cooper on his retirement from this board. Dr. Cooper has been so long identified with the conduct of the health affairs of the territory that the board cannot but suffer a distinct loss by the withdrawal of his ripe experience from our deliberations and counsels.

" 'A year and a half ago Dr. Cooper went East on a mission connected with the leprosy question which is already bearing fruit. He appeared before the American Medical Association, the great representative body of our profession, and enlisted their sympathies. He laid the matter before the United States public health authorities and gained their active co-operation. By his energy and personal force he made friends for the measure everywhere, who carried it forward in Congress until a substantial amount was secured for the endowment of a hospital on Molokai for the study of this disease, with especial reference to its prevention, melioration, and cure. Whatever benefits may accrue from this measure — and I am one of those who believe the benefits will be great and lasting, both to the unfortunates at the Settlement and to the American people at large — the credit belongs to Dr. Cooper.' "

319
ST. CLOUD COOPER[8] (John[7] [115], Mary,[6] David,[5] Simeon,[4] Cornelius,[3] Pieter Cornelisse,[2] Cornelis[1]), b. July 13, 1861, in Jefferson Tex.; m. DORA HUDSON.

Children:

712.   I.   Charles Hudson Cooper, b. Sept. 10, 1888; he is a scientific farmer.
713.   II.   Lucy Kathryn Cooper, b. Jan. 27, 1891; student.
714.   III.   Dora Cooper, b. Oct. 21, 1892; student.

320
MAUDE COOPER[8] (John[7] [115], Mary,[6] David,[5] Simeon,[4] Cornelius,[3] Pieter Cornelisse,[2] Cornelis[1]), b. Dec. 1, 1862, in Jefferson, Tex.; m. EUGENE W. BROWN.

Children:

715.   I.   William Cooper Brown, b. Nov. 8, 1888; d. Nov. 9, 1889.
716.   II.   Eugene Brown, b. Oct. 29, 1890; a student.

321

TEXANA G. COOPER[8] (John[7] [115], Mary,[6] David,[5] Simeon,[4] Cornelius,[3] Pieter Cornelisse,[2] Cornelis[1]), b. Sept. 25, 1868, in Carrollton, Mo.; m. W. STEWART WARREN Res., Poplar Bluff, Mo.

Children:

717.   I.   Eugene Cooper Warren, b. May 2, 1890; student.

322

HATTIE SCOTT COOPER[8] (John[7] [115], Mary,[6] David,[5] Simeon,[4] Cornelius,[3] Pieter Cornelisse,[2] Cornelis[1]), b. Oct. 5, 1873, in Carrollton, Mo.; m. in 1899; RUSSEL M. KNEISLEY.

Child:

718.   I.   John Russel Kneisley, b. Jan. 30, 1901; student.

323

HARRY BRYANT COOPER[8] (John[7] [115, Mary,[6] David,[5] Simeon,[4] Cornelius,[3] Pieter Cornelisse,[2] Cornelis[1]), b. Oct. 5, 1873, in Carrollton, Mo.; m. FLORENCE THOMAS.

Children:

719.   I.   John William Cooper, b. Dec. 4, 1905.
720.   II. Harry Bryant Cooper, Jr., b. ......, 1906.
720a. III. Elizabeth Cooper, b. ......, 1909.

Harry Bryant Cooper graduated from the Medical Department of Kansas City University, Kansas City, Missouri; practiced four years at Wakenda, Carroll County, Missouri; went to Honolulu, Hawaii, in December, 1904, where he held a government position as Inspector of Ships; now (1912), is physician on a sugar plantation at Aiea, Oaku, Hawaiian Islands, nine miles from Honolulu.

324

HARRIET BRYANT[8] (Joseph[7] [118], Simeon,[6] David,[5] Simeon,[4] Cornelius,[3] Pieter Cornelisse,[2] Cornelis[1]), b. Oct. 18, 1860; m. Jan. 1, 1884, E. S. IRWIN.   Harriet Bryant taught school for many years before her marriage.   After the birth of her oldest child the family removed to Los Angeles, Calif., where Mr. Irwin engaged in business, being one of the directors of the Los Angeles Can Company. Res., 1933 E. 2d St., Los Angeles, Calif.

Children:

721.   I. Samuel Bryant Irwin, b. Apr. 22, 1885; m. Waitie McDonald+

722. II. Ruth Harriett Irwin, b. Nov. 6, 1897.

330

WILLIAM BRYANT BLACKSTONE[8] (Margaret[7] [119], Simeon,[6] David,[5] Simeon,[4] Cornelius,[3] Pieter Cornelisse,[2] Cornelis[1]), b. Feb. 8, 1860; m. LOU SMITH, dau. of Rev. J. B. Smith and Rebecca Mercer. William graduated from Rush Medical College, Chicago, with degree of M. D. in 1884, with the highest grade in the class. He was an interne in St. Luke's Hospital the following year. Since then he has practiced medicine in Fort Wayne, Ind., and is now a leading specialist of that city. Res., 110 W. Wayne St., Fort Wayne, Ind.

Child:

723.   I. Lillian Belle Blackstone, b. Sept. 10, 1897; an earnest student, fine musician.

331

JOHN KING BLACKSTONE[8] (Margaret[7] [119], Simeon,[6] David,[5] Simeon,[4] Cornelius,[3] Pieter Cornelisse,[2] Cornelis[1]), b. May 29, 1862; m. Nov. 30, 1893, ELLA JUDSON HANKINS, dau. of Albert Hankins and Ella Thorpe. JOHN KING BLACKSTONE graduated from University of Louisville, Ky., taking the degree of M. D. in 1885. Since then he has taken post-graduate courses in Bellevue Medical College, New York; then Polytechnic, New York; Post-Graduate Medical School and Hospital of Chicago, and Medical College of Cincinnati. He has held the position of railroad surgeon for the Pennsylvania and Erie railroads. Res., Crown Point, Ind.

Child:

724   I. . Ella Anita Blackstone, b. Sept. 24, 1894. She is
        attending the Crown Point High School and
        is a student of music.

332
LILLIAN ELIZABETH BLACKSTONE[8] (Margaret[7] [119], Simeon,[6]
David,[5] Simeon,[4] Cornelius,[3] Pieter Cornelisse[2], Cornelis[1]), b.
July 1, 1870; m. Dec. 31, 1890, MURRAY TURNER, son of David
Turner and Caroline Bissel of Crown Point, Ind.; d. Nov. 21,
1900.   Lillian attended the Girl's Classical School in Indiana-
polis, Ind., for one year, after which she attended the Young
Ladies' College at Glendale, Ohio.   Graduated in June, 1890.
She was a devoted Christian of the Presbyterian faith.   Mr.
Turner is president of the First National Bank at Hammond,
Ind.

Child:

725.   I. Margaret Caroline Turner, b. Oct. 24, 1896. A
            student at the Girls' School, Kenosha, Wis.

340
JULIA BRYANT[8] (Elias[7] [122], Simeon,[6] David,[5] Simeon,[4]
Cornelius,[3] Pieter Cornelisse,[2] Cornelis[1]), b. Oct. 7, 1868; m.
Feb. .., 1901, HODSON MORROW, son of John Thomas Morrow
and Amy Green.   John T. Morrow was a native of Dundee,
Scotland, coming to America when a small boy.   He is a farm-
er, living a mile south of the old homestead near Hebron, Ind.
Mrs. Morrow is a graduate of the Hebron (Ind.) High School.

Children:

726.   I.   Merritt Blake Morrow.
727.   II. Wendell Bryant Morrow.
728.   III. Neil Morrow.
729.   IV. Carol Louise Morrow.

341
EMMA BRYANT[8] (Elias[7] [122], Simeon,[6] David,[5] Simeon,[4]
Cornelius,[3] Pieter Cornelisse,[2] Cornelis[1]), b. July 10, 1871; m.

LILLIAN E. TURNER

Aug. 24, 1894, JOHN MELVIN MORROW, son of John Morrow. She attended school at Valparaiso University; afterward taught 5 years.   Mr. Morrow was postmaster at Hebron, Ind., twenty-six years, his wife being assistant postmaster.   At the time of his marriage Mr. Morrow was teacher in high school, at Hebron, Ind.   During the World's Columbia Exposition in Chicago in 1893, Mr. Morrow was sergeant of Company 123 of the guards.

Children:

730.   I.   Helen May Morrow, b. Aug. 2, 1895.
731.   II.   Ruth Frances Morrow, b. Sept. 15, 1897.

343
EDMUND E. BRYANT[8] (Elias[7] [122], Simeon,[6] David,[5] Simeon,[4] Cornelius,[3] Pieter Cornelisse,[2] Cornelis[1]), b. May 12, 1877; m. June, 1904, EVA GILSON.

Children:

732.   I.   Bernice Bryant.
733.   II.   Margaret Bryant.
734.   III.   Lucile Bryant.

The mother died when Lucile was an infant.   The father returned to the home of his parents, who have the care of Bernice.   The other children are cared for by relatives.   Residence, Hebron, Indiana.

350
DAVID A. FISHER[8] (Nancy[7] [125], David,[6] David,[5] Simeon,[4] Cornelius,[3] Pieter Cornelisse,[2] Cornelis[1]), b. Mar. 13, 1855, in South East Grove, Lake Co., Ind.   He attended the public schools near his home, and also the high school at Hebron, Crown Point, and the Valparaiso Normal.   Politics, Republican; religion, Methodist; occupation, farming; m. June 7, 1876, near Hebron, Ind., ELIZABETH L. BLISS, who was b. Apr. 27, 1853, at Corning, Steuben Co., N. Y., dau. of William O. Bliss and Adelia A. French.   They lived a short time in Colorado Springs, Colo., then came back to Lake Co., Ind., where he has

followed farming for over 25 years. In 1912 he moved to Hebron, leaving his sons, Kenneth and Winfred, to manage the farm of 595 acres, which was the old Fisher homestead.

Children:

735. I. Gemm B. Fisher, b. Jan. 16, 1878; d. July 28, 1878.
736. II. Kenneth W. Fisher, b. Apr. 6, 1886; m. EDITH DONOHUE, Sept. 2, 1911. He attended the common schools near his home, also Valparaiso University, and Chicago Business College. He is occupied as a machinist and farmer. In religion, a Methodist. Res., near Hebron, Ind.
737. III. Winfred B. Fisher, b. June 11, 1887; m. Lillie Volkee+

351

ARABELLA FISHER[8] (Nancy[7] [125] David,[6] David,[5] Simeon,[4] Cornelius,[3] Pieter Cornelisse,[2] Cornelis[1]), b. Sept. 21, 1857, in South East Grove, Lake Co., Ind. Attended the public schools, also high school in Hebron, Crown Point, and Valparaiso Normal. Religion, Methodist; m. Nov. 29, 1876, at Hebron, Ind., CHARLES W. HAYWARD, who was b. Feb. 19, 1849, at Ross, Ind., the son of Alfred Hayward and Sarah Jane Pierce. For ten years they lived on a farm near Crown Point, Ind., and in January, 1887, moved to Santa Barbara, Calif., where they still reside. Mr. Hayward has a large furniture store in Santa Barbara, and is doing a good business. Religion, Methodist. Politics, Prohibition. Res., 331 Alisos St., Santa Barbara, Calif.

Children:

738. I. Alfred W. Hayward, b. Jan. 3, 1878; m. Kathryn Mullen+
739. II. Arthur Fisher Hayward, b. Oct. 6, 1881, on the farm near Ross, Lake Co., Ind., and resided there with his parents until he was 5 years of age, when they moved to Santa Barbara, Calif. He attended the public schools of Santa Barbara until the age of sixteen years, when after

Belle Fisher Hayward

only a few days of suffering, he was striken
with appendicitis and d. June 15, 1898. He
was a dutiful son, loved and respected by all
his friends and schoolmates. He was a member of the Methodist Episcopal Church at the
time of his death.

740. III. Ida May Hayward, b. July 25, 1883; m. Brooks B.
Brentner+

741. IV. Earl Grant Hayward, b. July 23, 1885; m. Fredrica
Dorothy Meyer+

742. V. Arabella Artha Hayward, b. May 14, 1898, in Santa
Barbara, Calif. She is at home with her parents, attending the public schools.

352

IDA E. FISHER[8] (Nancy[7] [125], David,[6] David,[5] Simeon,[4]
Cornelius,[3] Pieter Cornelisse,[2] Cornelis[1]), b. Mar. 7, 1860, near
Hebron, in Lake Co., Indiana.

Attended the common schools and high school in Hebron, and
Valparaiso College. She taught school for several years, and then
went into the Citizens' Bank, of which her father was president,
holding positions first as assistant cashier and bookkeeper for ten
years; and in 1907 became cashier, which position she still holds.
Religion, Congregational for many years, then when her father
went into the United Presbyterian Church, in 1910, she with her
mother went with him, where they still have membership. In
1902 Miss Fisher suggested and was chiefly instrumental in organizing the Bryant Reunions which have been held in Hebron for nine
years, to the great pleasure of the family. Through Miss Fisher's
efforts many of the records were collected for the Bryant Genealogy.
She remains with her venerable parents, to whom she accords the
deepest filial solicitude, and she is a loved factor in the religious
and social activities of her home village, even as she is efficient and
popular in its business circles. She has enjoyed the advantages of
somewhat extended travel, including two trips to California and
one through the eastern states, where she met with many pleasing
experiences. She is a member of the society of the Daughters of
the American Revolution. She is interested in the cause of missions. She has educated Fulda Butros, an Egyptian, in Luxor

Mission School in Egypt, and is now educating another girl in Cairo Mission College, at a cost of $95.00 a year.

361

JOSEPH ALLEN BRYANT, JR.[8] (Joseph[7] [128], David,[6] David,[5] Simeon,[4] Cornelius,[3] Pieter Cornelisse,[2] Cornelis[1]), b. June 6, 1882, in Neosho Co., Kan.; m. Aug. 21, 1903, at Los Angeles, Calif., MARGARET ANDERSON, b. Feb. 13, 1880, at Omaha, Neb.

Children:
743. I. Wilna Bryant, b. Sept. 4, 1905.
744. II. Orah Bryant, b. Feb. 21, 1907.
745. III. Elizabeth Bryant, b. Mar. 1, 1908.

Mr. Bryant when eighteen years old went with a lumber company to Port Elizabeth, Africa, thence crossing the Indian Ocean to Australia, and from there to San Francisco, California, thus making the circuit of the globe. He located in Los Angeles, where he is in an extensive laundry business.

368

MABEL ALBERTA DODDRIRGE[8] (Orah[7] [132], David,[6] David,[5] Simeon,[4] Cornelius,[3] Pieter Cornelisse,[2] Cornelis[1]), b. Sept. 13, 1877, in Hebron, Ind. Moved with her parents to Galva, Ill., and then to Mentone, Ind. She graduated from the Mentone High School, studied music in Indianapolis, and is a fine musician; m. Oct. 18, 1899, at Mentone, ADELBERT P. MEREDITH, who was b. June 15, 1877, at Mentone, Ind., son of Eli Meredith and Margaret Frost. Occupation, farmer; religion, Methodist. Res., Mentone, Ind.

Child:
746. I. Frank Doddridge Meredith, b. Oct. 14, 1911.

369

PHILLIP HARRISON DODDRIDGE[8] (Orah[7] [132], David,[6] David,[5] Simeon,[4] Cornelius,[3] Pieter Cornelisse,[2] Cornelis[1]), b. May 15,

Ida E. Fisher.

1888, in Mentone, Ind. He attended the home schools, graduated from the La Fayette (Ind.) High School, and was a student one year in the Purdue University, La Fayette, Ind., and Valparaiso University. At present he is assisting his father in the drug business in Mentone, Ind.

370
MATHEW MITCHELL[8] (David[7] [133], Hannah,[6] David,[5] Simeon,[4] Cornelius,[3] Pieter Cornelisse,[2] Cornelis[1]), b. Sept. 11, 1859, Spencerville, Ohio; m. Jan. 16, 1889, MARY J. IHIRIE, who was b. Mar. 19, 1860, in Lisbon, Ind.; dau. of Lake Ihirie and Marinda Bond. He was a farmer; was of the Baptist faith, and active in church affairs; in politics, a Democrat. d. June 30, 1901.

Children:
747.   I.   Robert Ihirie Mitchell, b. Dec. 14, 1890.
748.   II. Clarence M. Mitchell, b. Sept. 23, 1892; d. Aug. 27, 1893.
749.   III. Howard R. Mitchell, b. Nov. 20, 1894.
750.   IV. Charles Edwin Mitchell, b. Dec. 19, 1895.

371
LETTIE MITCHELL[8] (David[7] [133], Hannah,[6] David,[5] Simeon,[4] Cornelius,[3] Pieter Cornelisse,[2] Cornelis[1]). Received into the Amanda Church, Feb. 14, 1874; m. JASPER A. McMILLAN, Feb. 14, 1889. Res., Waynesfield, Ohio.

Children:
751.   I.   Mary McMillan.
752.   II. Charles McMillan.
753.   III. Ruth McMillan.
754.   IV. John McMillan.

373
WILLIAM TORRENCE MITCHELL[8] (Simeon[7] [138], Hannah,[6] David,[5] Simeon,[4] Cornelius,[3] Pieter Cornelisse,[2] Cornelis[1]),

b. July 15, 1852; m. ELLA JANE GIBSON of Carthage, Mo.; b. Mar. 20, 1856. Res., Dayton, Ohio.

Children:

755. I. Edna Gibson Mitchell, b. July 10, 1879.
756. II. Edwin Gibson Mitchell, b. Aug. 24, 1880.
757. III. George Ashley Mitchell, b. Sept. 3, 1882.
758. IV. Kathryn Mitchell, b. July 17, 1884.

376
MATHEW F. MITCHELL[8] (Simeon[7] [138], Hannah,[6] David,[5] Simeon,[4] Cornelius,[3] Pieter Cornelisse,[2] Cornelis[1]), b. Nov. 17, 1858; m. NETTIE AMANDA WHITE of Carthage, Mo. Business, clothing establishment.

Children:

759. I. Mathew White Mitchell.
760. II. Robert Baxter Mitchell.
761. III. William Deane Mitchell.

377
MARY BRYANT MITCHELL[8] (Simeon[7] [138], Hannah,[6] David,[5] Simeon,[4] Cornelius,[3] Pieter Cornelisse,[2] Cornelis[1]), b. Sept. 10, 1864; m. June 26, 1888, RICHARD ALSTON METCALF of Damariscotta, Me.

Children:

762. I. Marjory Metcalf.
763. II. Alston Metcalf.
763a. III. Mitchell Metcalf.
763b. IV. Isabeth Metcalf.

380
FRANCES LETTIE MITCHELL[8] (Joseph[7] [139], Hannah,[6] David,[5] Simeon,[4] Cornelius,[3] Pieter Cornelisse,[2] Cornelis[1]), b. July 15, 1858, at Bloomington, Ill.; m. Sept. 19, 1877, at Altona, Ill., to MILLARD ALBERT BURRELL, who was b. June 16, 1849, in

Bessie E. Bryant

Rock Run Twp., Stevenson Co., Ill.; son of Daniel Burrell and Martha Getterny; occupation, tinner; politics, Republican. Mrs. Burrell is a member of the United Presbyterian church.

381

NANCY KATE MITCHELL[8] (Joseph R.[7] [139], Hannah,[6] David,[5] Simeon,[4] Cornelius,[3] Pieter Cornelisse,[2] Cornelis[1]), b. Sept. 27, 1859, in Altona, Ill.; m. Feb. 26, 1880, at Altona, WILLIAM EDWARD JOHNSON, who was b. Oct. 18, 1851, son of Zopher Johnson and Elizabeth Janes. In religious faith, Presbyterian. Res., in Monmouth, Ill., 723 E. First Ave.

Children:

764.   I.   Myron Clyde Johnson, b. Jan. 6, 1881; m. Nellie Edom. They reside at Englewood, Colo.

Child: 868a. I. Melvin Clyde Johnson, b. Sept. 15, 1911.

765.   II. Joseph Roland Johnson, b. Feb. 9, 1883; employed with the McCullough Hardware Co., Monmouth, Ill.

766. III. Gertrude C. Johnson, b. Apr. 26, 1885; employed in office of Monmouth Plow Factory.

767. IV. Frances Lettie Johnson, b. Jan. 23, 1890; employed in office of E. B. Colwell Co., Monmouth, Ill.

768.   V. Carrie Ellen Johnson, b. Mar. 10, 1892; a student in Monmouth College.

769. VI. Anna Catharine Johnson, b. Sept. 15, 1894; student in Monmouth High School.

385

JOHN FRANKLIN MITCHELL[8] (John[7] [140], Hannah,[6] David,[5] Simeon,[4] Cornelius,[3] Pieter Cornelisse,[2] Cornelis[1]), b. Dec. 23, 1866; m. July 10, 1878, ESTELLA McCLANDISH.

Children:

     I. Son, 770a, d. in infancy.

770.   II. Charlotte 770b, Mitchell, b. 1892.

770a. III. Bryant 770c, Mitchell, b. 1894.

389

CAROLINE ELIZABETH HOVER[8] (Martha[7] [146], Elizabeth,[6] David,[5] Simeon,[4] Cornelius,[3] Pieter Cornelisse,[2] Cornelis[1]), b. June 27, 1848, at Lima, Ohio; m. Sept. 1, 1870, at Spencerville, Ohio, PHILIP LE MASTERS, who was b. June 10, 1836, in Port Jefferson, Ohio, son of Luman Walker Le Masters and Nancy Young. Rev. Philip Le Masters is a clergyman of the Methodist ch. of Spencerville, Ohio; in politics, a Republican.

392

MARY ELIZA HOVER[8] (Martha[7] [146], Elizabeth,[6] David,[5] Simeon,[4] Cornelius,[3] Pieter Cornelisse,[2] Cornelis[1]), b. Mar. 26, 1854, at Delphos, Ohio; m. Apr. 6, 1875, at Lima, Ohio, ROBERT H. GAMBLE, who was b. Apr. 6, 1849, at Winchester, Va., son of William Gamble and Ruth A. Montgomery. Mr. Gamble is a civil engineer; in politics, a Republican; in religion, a Congregationalist; Res., Lima, Ohio.

Children:

771   I.   Agnes L. Gamble, b. May 22, 1876.
772. II. Carrie L. Gamble, b. Dec. 9, 1878; m. Hoyt Partch+
773. III. Ruth Gamble, b. Jan. 7, 1881.
774. IV. Martha Gamble, b. Jan. 25, 1883.
775. V.   John Gamble, b. July 20, 1887.

393

CHARLES ALFRED HOVER[8] (Martha[7] [146], Elizabeth,[6] David,[5] Simeon,[4] Cornelius,[3] Pieter Cornelisse,[2] Cornelis[1]), b. Oct. 25, 1856, in Delphos, Ohio; m. ...... 1881, MERCY ELLEN SUNDERLAND, dau. of James Sunderland and Jemima Baker. She was b. Mar. 28, 1855. Mr. Hover is a Methodist, and a Republican. Res., Lima, Ohio.

Child:

393a.   I.   Mercy Winifred Hover, b. Mar. 1, 1884; m. June 14, 1911, William Brown.

394

KATE PAULINE HOVER[8] (Martha[7] [146], Elizabeth,[6] David,[5] Simeon,[4] Cornelius,[3] Pieter Cornelisse,[2] Cornelis[1]), b. Apr. 13, 1859, in Delphos, Ohio; m. Nov. 15, 1882, DANIEL H. CRITES, son of Jacob Crites and Emeline C. Crimean. In religion, Methodists; in politics they are Republicans. Res., Elida, Ohio.

Children:

776.   I.   Harold H. Crites, b. Aug. 7, 1883; m. Apr. 1906, HAZEL JAMISON; in politics, a Democrat; in religion, a Presbyterian.

777.   II.   Carl Deane Crites, b. Jan. 27, 1887; m. Feb. 1, 1907, NELLIE VERNON WILLIAMS, who was b. Mar. 13, 1886; d. May 1, 1909.

395

BRYANT GRAHAM HOVER[8] (Martha[7] [146], Elizabeth,[6] David,[5] Simeon,[4] Cornelius,[3] Pieter Cornelisse,[2] Cornelis[1]), b. Dec. 1, 1861, in Delphos, Ohio; m. Nov. 15, 1882, MERCY NAOMI BICE, dau. of William Bice and Tabitha Sunderland. In politics Mr. Hover is a Republican; in religion, a Methodist. Res., Spencerville, Ohio.

399

MARTHA JANE HOVER[8] (Martha[7] [146], Elizabeth,[6] David,[5] Simeon,[4] Cornelius,[3] Pieter Cornelisse,[2] Cornelis[1]), b. July 14, 1872; m. Dec. 20, 1894, FRANK AUSTIN HITCHCOCK, son of Dr. S. A. Hitchcock and Ellen Beck. Res., Hammond, Ind.

Children:

778.   I.   John Vance Hitchcock, b. Mar. 22, 1897.

779.   II.   Helen Frances Hitchcock, b. Oct. 27, 1899; burned to death May 17, 1902.

780.   III.   Adaline Flora Hitchcock, b. June, 1901.

781.   IV.   Bryan H. Hitchcock, b. Oct. 12, 1902; d. Feb., 1903.

782.   V.   Frank Hitchcock, b. Oct. 12, 1902.

783. VI. Robert Marshall Hitchcock, b. Nov. 4, 1903.
784. VII. Pearl Hitchcock, b. June 23, 1906.
785. VIII. Donald Edwin Hitchcock, b. ......; d. Mar. 20,
            1909.
786. IX. Ruth Hitchcock, b. Dec. 17, 1909.

401

SAMUEL ALVEN POST[8] (Leonidas[7] [148], Elizabeth,[6] David,[5]
Simeon,[4] Cornelius,[3] Pieter Cornelisse,[2] Cornelis[1]), b. Nov. 22,
1856; d. Mar. 24, 1899; m. Aug. 19, 1880, SARAH ALICE CRITES,
dau. of Jacob Crites and Emily .... She was b. in German
Twp., Allen Co., Ohio.   Res., near Allentown, Ohio.

Children:

787.   I. William Stewart Post, b. Oct. 19, 1881; m. Clara
           Etta Carey+
788.   II. Cora Ethel Post, b. Nov. 22, 1882; m. Alva Bene-
           dum+
789. III. Louie Crites Post, b. Dec. 10, 1884.
790.   IV. Charles Bryant Post, b. Dec. 8, 1888; m. Nona
           Endora Weyer.
791.   V. Clarence Minor Post, b. Dec. 7, 1892.

Samuel A. Post was a leading citizen of German Township for
many years, a substantial farmer and a representative man.   He
was reared on his father's farm and attended the local schools,
where he prepared for college, subsequently entering the Ohio
Normal University at Ada.   He spent but one term there on
account of delicate health, returning to farm work, the outdoor
life suiting him better than the confinement of the schoolroom.
The passing away of Mr. Post in early middle life occurred very
suddenly.   He was striken with spinal meningitis and survived the
attack only four days.   He was buried in the Allentown Cemetery.
He was the kind of a man to be much missed, both in his household
and in his neighborhood.   Honest and upright in all his dealings
with others, he secured friendships and esteem.   He was intel-
ligently interested in all public matters in his township and served
for a long time as school director.   In politics he was a Republican,
and at the time of his death was his party's candidate for township
treasurer.

Charles C. Post

402
CHARLES CYRUS POST[8] (Leonidas[7] [148], Elizabeth,[6] David,[5] Simeon,[4] Cornelius,[3] Pieter Cornelisse,[2] Cornelis[1]), b. Oct. 8, 1858, in Allen Co., Ohio; m. Nov. 19, 1884, at Urbana, Ohio, IDA E. CRITES, who was b. Feb. 22, 1862, at Kempton, Ohio; d. Mar. 22, 1889. She was the dau. of Isaac Crites and Elizabeth Ireland. Mr. Post m. (2nd) June 21, 1905, ETTE MARTHA POST, dau. of Clark C. Post, and Nancy McVay of Washington, Pa. Res., Spencerville, Ohio.

Children: 1st m.

792. I.   Claire Bryant Post, b. Aug. 18, 1885; m. Jessie Carr+
793. II. Ida Gertrude Post, b. Mar. 8, 1889; m. Edward L. Baxter+

2nd m.

794. III. Helen Rebecca Post, b. May 26, 1906.
795. IV. Leonidas Charles Clark Post, b. July 28, 1908.

Charles C. Post was educated in the public school and at the University of Ada, Ohio. He has always followed farming and stock-raising, in both of which he has been successful, for now he resides on a well-kept and well-improved farm of two hundred and fifty-one acres. He is held in high esteem in the community in which he has always lived, having held several offices of trust.

Etta Martha Post was educated in the Normal School at Warrensburg, Missouri, and at the State Normal of California, Pennsylvania. She taught school five years in Missouri and ten in Pennsylvania. She was assistant principal of the Carnegie (Pennsylvania) School just prior to her marriage.

403
EDWARD GRANT POST[8] (Leonidas[7] [148], Elizabeth,[6] David,[5] Simeon,[4] Cornelius,[3] Pieter Cornelisse,[2] Cornelis,[1]), b. Sept. 11, 1867, in Allen Co., Ohio; m. Dec. 27, 1886, JENNIE FLORENCE WHETSTONE. Res., Urbana, Ohio.

Children:

796. I.   Edna Jane Post, b. Feb. 23, 1888; m. Mar. 20, 1912, Evert Russel McClain.

797.   II.   Adelaide Elizabeth Post, b. Jan. 6, 1890.
798.   III. Ruth Post, b. Apr. 8, 1893; m. Nov. 18, 1912, Samuel
             Clay Hunt.
799.   IV.   Martha Helen Post, b. Sept. 29, 1895; d. Oct. 26,
             1896.
800.   V.   Florence Naomi Post, b. Oct. 9, 1897.

The oldest of these children was born in Allen County, Ohio;
the four younger ones were born in Champaign County.

406

LEONIDAS HAMLINE POST, JR.[8] (Leonidas[7] [148], Elizabeth,[6]
David,[5] Simeon,[4] Cornelius,[3] Pieter Cornelisse,[2] Cornelis[1]), b.
Sept. 11, 1875; m. Feb. 20, 1901, ALTHA MOORMAN, who was
b. Feb. 28, 1876, at Spencerville, Ohio.

Children:

801.   I.   Martha Louise Post, b. Oct. 20, 1903.
802.   II.   Mildred Aleen Post, b. July 16, 1905.
803.   III. Sarah Jane Post, b. Feb. 1, 1907.
804.   IV.   Alice Lenora Post, b. Oct. 29, 1908.
805.   V.   Katherine Altha Post, b. Sept. 29, 1910.

407

MARTHA POST[8] (Adam[7] [149], Elizabeth,[6] David,[5] Simeon,[4]
Cornelius,[3] Pieter Cornelisse,[2] Cornelis[1]), b. Aug. 14, 1856, at
Spencerville, Ohio; m. Oct. 24, 1883, at Carthage, Mo., ANDREW
CLARK ALE, who was b. Nov. 27, 1855, at Bloomsburgh, Pa.,
son of Samuel Ale and Margaret Dildine.   Mr. Ale is a farmer.
Res., near Carthage, Mo.

Children:

806.   I.   Grace Ale, b. Dec. 15, 1884.
807.   II.   Minnie Naomi Ale, b. Sept. 25, 1886.
808.   III. Ruth Marguerite Ale, b. Sept. 10, 1891.

408

CHARLES ARCHELAUS POST[8] (Adam[7] [149], Elizabeth,[6] David,[5]
Simeon,[4] Cornelius,[3] Pieter Cornelisse,[2] Cornelis[1]), b. Oct. 20,

1857, at Spencerville, Ohio; m. Mar. 4, 1885, CORA ANNETTA BOWMAN, who was b. Aug. 16, 1860, at Bloomburgh, Pa. Politics, Republican.

Children:

809. I. Raymond Archelaus Post, b. Aug. 26, 1893.
810. II. Albert Laurance Post, b. Aug. 18, 1899.
811. III. Cyrus Vernon Post, b. June 28, 1902.

410
WINFRED BRYANT POST[8] (Adam[7] [149], Elizabeth,[6] David,[5] Simeon,[4] Cornelius,[3] Pieter Cornelisse,[2] Cornelis[1]), b. Oct. 19, 1871, Carthage, Mo.; m. Dec. 30, 1896, ELIZABETH ELEANOR LUSCOMBE, who was b. Nov. 20, 1874, at Carrollton, Mo.; dau. of Thomas Tennyson Luscombe and Christiana Walker Orchard. Mr. Post is a practicing physician at Carthage, Mo. He is a Republican, and an adherent of the Presbyterian faith.

Child:

812. I. Winfred Luscombe Post, b. Nov. 21, 1897.

415
IRA B. POST[8] (Isaac B.[7] [150], Elizabeth,[6] David,[5] Simeon,[4] Cornelius,[3] Pieter Cornelisse,[2] Cornelis[1]), b. Oct. 14, 1875; m. July 23, 1899, IDA M. ROBBINS Res., Spencerville, Ohio.

Children:

813. I. Stanley Bryant Post, b. Sept. . . . . . . , 1903.
814. II. Howard Post, b. May, 1907.

417
HAROLD R. POST[8] (Charles G.[7] [151], Elizabeth,[6] David,[5] Simeon,[4] Cornelius,[3] Pieter Cornelisse,[2] Cornelis[1]), b. Nov. 7, 1870, Spencerville, Ohio; m. Nov. 22, 1892, LILLIAN KEITH, who was b. June 10, 1872, at Spencerville, Ohio; dau. of John Keith and Mary E. Partelle. In politics Mr. Post is a Republican; in religion a Methodist. Res., Haskell, N. J.

Children:

815.   I.   Jerome Keith Post, b. Nov. 30, 1893.
816.   II.   John Charles Post, b. Jan. 20, 1896.
817. III.   Winfred Hixson Post, b. Jan. 11, 1897; d. Mar. 29,
             1897.
818.   IV.   Frank Partelle Post, b. July 12, 1900.

418

VERNON BRYANT POST[8] (Charles Graham[7] [151], Elizabeth,[6]
David,[5] Simeon,[4] Cornelius,[3] Pieter Cornelisse,[2] Cornelis[1]), b.
Dec. 23, 1873, Spencerville, Ohio; m. Feb. 4, 1895, at Lima,
Ohio, ALICE HANLEY, who was b. Jan. 24, 1875, at Delphos,
Ohio; dau. of James Hanley and Hester Martin.   Occupation,
dairyman; politics Republican; religion Methodist.   Res.,
Parma, Mo.

Children:

819.   I.   Laurence Post, b. Dec. 15, 1896; d. Dec. 20, 1896.
820.   II.   Robert Rockwell Post, b. Jan. 4, 1897.
821. III.   Arthur Corwin Post, b. Jan. 27, 1898; d. Aug. 17,
             1898.
822.   IV.   Helen Martin Post, b. June 13, 1899.
823.   V.   Marion Post, b. June 4, 1901.

423

EDMUND RANDOLPH BRYANT, JR.[8] (Edmund R.[7] [153], Jacob,[6]
David,[5] Simeon,[4] Cornelius,[3] Pieter Cornelisse,[2] Cornelis[1]), b.
Feb. 9, 1855, near Bucyrus, Ohio; m. June 27, 1883, EMILY
ELIZABETH SWEENY, of Hebron, Ind.; a dau. of David Lyell
Sweeny and Hannah J. . . . . Edmund Randolph, Jr., moved
with his parents to Bucyrus, Ohio, in 1875, where he went into
business for himself.   He remained at this place until the fall
of 1877 when he with his father's family removed to Hebron.

Children:

824.   I.   Lyell S. Bryant, b. Dec. 13, 1884.
825.   II.   Avis B. Bryant, b. Sept. 24, 1888.

Both children attended the grades and high school of Hebron. In 1902 Lyell began working in the printing office of the Hebron News. In 1903 he went into partnership with his father in the retail meat business. Since January, 1905, he has been with Bryant, Dowd & Company in general merchandise business. He was elected town clerk of Hebron, Indiana, September, 1910, and November 7, 1911.

Avis graduated from the Hebron High School, May, 1907. In 1908 she entered the North Western University at Evanston, Illinois. She is a teacher in the high school of Cass City, Michigan.

425

WILLIAM CULLEN BRYANT[8] (Edmund R.[7] [153], Jacob,[6] David,[5] Simeon,[4] Cornelius,[3] Pieter Cornelisse,[2] Cornelis[1]), b. June 11, 1858; m. LULU STANSELL, who was b. Nevada, Ohio. Res., Bucyrus, Ohio.

Child:

826.   I.   Beth Bryant, b. May 19, 1889.

Mr. Bryant has followed photography for twenty-five years in Nevada and Bucyrus, Ohio.

426

LULU BRYANT[8] (Edmund R.[7] [153], Jacob,[6] David,[5] Simeon,[4] Cornelius,[3] Pieter Cornelisse,[2] Cornelis[1]), b. Dec. 3, 1859, at Bucyrus, Ohio, and moved with her parents to Hebron, Ind., 1878; m. June 15, 1881, HARRY J. SHELDON, of Hebron, Ind., who was engaged in the lumber business for several years; now is a builder and contractor.

Children:

827.   I.   Ruby Sheldon, b. Mar. 15, 1882; m. Hal O. Binyon+
828.   II.   Berta Sheldon, b. May 30, 1883; m. Jay Baldwin+
828a. III.   Walter Bryant Sheldon, b. Feb. 27, 1892; graduated from high school in class of 1909, Hebron, Ind. He is employed as bookkeeper in Marshall Field & Co.'s wholesale house.

430

AGNEW WELSH[8] (Margaret J.[7] [159], Nancy,[6] David,[5] Simeon,[4] Cornelius,[3] Pieter Cornelisse,[2] Cornelis[1]), b. Apr. 11, 1856; m. July, 1880, CORA E. HOUFSTATER, of Huron Co., Ohio. Res., Ada, Ohio.

Children:

829.   I. Earl Basil Welsh, b. May 12, 1881; m. Garnet Varner.

830. II. Dana Eugene Welsh, b. Aug. 15, 1882, owner of a drug-store in Ada, Ohio.

831. III. Rhea Madonna Welsh, b. Nov. 17, 1885; for five years a teacher in Ada public school.

832. IV. Opal Muriel Welsh, b. Oct. 1, 1889; m. Dec. 27, 1911, A. Frank Hixon of Columbus, Ohio; teacher.

833. V. Margaret Agnew Welsh, b. Feb. 9, 1895; graduated class of 1912, from Ada, Ohio, High School, with honors of highest grade of her class.

Mr. Welsh received his early education in the country schools of his vicinity, and in May, 1875, he went to Mount Union College, Ohio. He spent the following two years in the normal school of Ada, Ohio. He taught during the summer vacation one term. In 1877 he spent nine months as clerk in a clothing house. Early in 1878 he purchased a bookstore in Ada, Ohio, which he conducted until July, 1881, when he sold it, and purchased the Ada Record, a local newspaper, which enterprise he has conducted for more than thirty years. Since early manhood he has been a member of the Disciple Church, in which faith his mother was baptized on July 7, 1850. That rite was performed by her uncle, Joseph Bryant, who married Dorothy Campbell, sister of Alexander Campbell, founder of the Disciple Church or Church of Christ. Mr. Welsh has been solicited a number of times to run for a county office but never cared to jeopardize his newspaper, which represents his life-work, by neglecting it for outside work. He has, however, served as a member and clerk of the board of education of Ada for twenty years.

In politics he is a Republican and a "Standpatter" at that; in religion himself and all his family save one are members of the Disciple Church. He is a member of the Masonic, Eastern Star, and Maccabee orders and enjoys life to the fullest. He has a good

AGNEW WELSH

home, has traveled from ocean to ocean and from the lakes to the gulf, and has visited every exposition of note from and including that at Chicago and ending at Seattle, his family accompanying him to a majority of them.

The compiler of this Bryant Family History finds the following compliments upon the Ada Record on the occasion of its thirty-ninth birthday:

Nevada News: With its last issue the Ada Record celebrated its thirty-ninth anniversary. During the greater portion of its existence the Record has been under the efficient management of that veteran publisher, Mr. Agnew Welsh, recognized as one of the ablest editors in this part of Ohio. Mr. Welsh publishes a splendid paper — a journal of both literary and news merit — and by token of many evidences of success we are led to infer that the good people of Ada appreciate Bro. Welsh's honest efforts to give them a paper of which they may well be proud.

Findlay Courier: The Ada Record has entered upon the 39th year of its existence. It is and always has been an exceptionally good weekly paper. The editor of the Record, Agnew Welsh, is a good newspaper man, enterprising and progressive, and he gives his patrons a clean and wholesome paper.

The Arlingtonian: Last week the Ada Record began its 39th year of publication, having been under its present management nearly 29 years. To those who know the Record words of praise are superfluous. No journal in the state shows more painstaking care both in its literary and mechanical features than the Record. Mr. Welsh has already reared a worthy monument to his memory when the time shall come to him to be gathered to his fathers, which time we hope is far in the future.

Bucyrus News-Forum: The Ada Record is bright and lively as a youngster in its earlier years, together with the wisdom and judgment born of experience. For nearly twenty-nine years the paper has been under the management of the present proprietor, Agnew Welsh, who has been the right man in the right place and has achieved well deserved success in his venture.

439

MARGARET JANE WELLMAN[8] (Elizabeth[7] [161], Nancy,[6] David,[5] Simeon,[4] Cornelius,[3] Pieter Cornelisse,[2] Cornelis[1]), b.

Sept. 2, 1856, Independence, Iowa; m. JAMES O. VINCENT.
Res., Wood Lake, Neb.

>   *Children:*
834.   I.   Fred M. Vincent, b. Dec. 2, 1878.
835.   II.   Earl B. Vincent, b. May 21, 1885.
836.   III. Hugh Ross Vincent, b. Dec. 7, 1893.
837.   IV.   Rex Rosemond Vincent, b. Oct. 23, 1900.

441
FAY D. AGNEW[8] (David[7] [162], Nancy,[6] David,[5] Simeon,[4]
Cornelius,[3] Pieter Cornelisse,[2] Cornelis[1]), b. Dec. 24, 1866; m.
July, 1892, MINNIE B. GREENWOOD. Res., Fairbanks, Iowa.

>   *Children:*
838.   I.   Belle M. Agnew.
839.   II.   Genevieve Agnew.

442
JESSE WINFIELD AGNEW[8] (David,[7] [162], Nancy,[6] David,[5]
Simeon,[4] Cornelius,[3] Pieter Cornelisse,[2] Cornelis[1]), b. Sept. 9,
1868; m. 1890, KITTY M. NALBERT. He was educated in
Dixon, Ill. Res. in Rowley, Ill.

>   *Children:*
840.   I.   Adah M. Agnew, b. . . . .
841.   II.   Park David Agnew, b. 190–.
841a.   III. Jesse M. Agnew, b. 190–.

457
ALICE ELMIRA WELSH[8] (Bryant[7] [169], Jane,[6] David,[5] Simeon,[4]
Cornelius,[3] Pieter Cornelisse,[2] Cornelis[1]), b. Jan. 1, 1854,
Wyandot, Ohio; m. Oct. 17, 1878, AARON MOSES HOLLER, who
was b. Aug. 3, 1853, in St. Thomas, Franklin Co., Pa. In
religious faith they are Presbyterian. Mr. Holler is Republican
in politics Res., Apache, Okla.

Children:

842.   I.   Ida Bryant Holler, b. Sept. 3, 1879; m. Haldine Roland Stealy+

843.   II.   Edna E. Holler, b. June 18, 1882; m. 1910, Joseph McLean+

844.   III.   Avis Margaret Holler, b. Sept. 19, 1893. Nature endowed her with an unusually fine contralto voice, which is under training.

458

JANE WELSH[8] (Bryant[7] [169], Jane,[6] David,[5] Simeon,[4] Cornelius,[3] Pieter Cornelisse,[2] Cornelis[1]), b. Dec. 25, 1855, in Altona, Ill.; m. Sept. 21, 1875, in Lathrop, Mo., WILLIAM Z. THOMPSON, b. Nov. 7, 1846. In industry he follows agriculture and stockraising. Resided at Granite, Okla. Present res., Hagerman, N. M.

Children:

845.   I.   Ada Ellen Thompson, b. Apr. 16, 1881; m. Oct. 21, 1903, Thomas Laws. Res., Blanchard, Okla.

846.   II.   Elizabeth Avis Thompson, b. Apr. 16, 1881; m. Lee West. Res., Alva, Okla; child: 846a. I. Frances West.

847.   III.   Charles Bryant Thompson, b. July 19, 1883. Res., Hagerman, N. M. Children: 847a. William Thompson; 847b. Jay Thompson.

460

ANNA WELSH[8] (Bryant[7] [169], Jane,[6] David,[5] Simeon,[4] Cornelius,[3] Pieter Cornelisse,[2] Cornelis[1]), b. Sept. 23, 1861, in Altona, Ill.; m. Apr. 25, 1894, CECIL WOODWARD BROWNE, who was b. Dec. 21, 1859. He was a merchant in Las Vegas, New Mex. Res., Kansas City, Mo. In politics a Republican; in religion, a Presbyterian.

Children:

848.   I.   Bryant Welsh Brown, b. June 25, 1896; d. June 27, 1896.

849.   II.   Cecil Bryant Brown, b. Jan. 25, 1898.
850.   III. Allen Roland Brown, b. Nov. 18, 1900.
460a. IV.   Margaret Constance Brown.

462

HARRY MADISON WELSH[8] (Bryant[7] [169], Jane,[6] David,[5] Simeon,[4] Cornelius,[3] Pieter Cornelisse,[2] Cornelis[1]), b. Sept. 7, 1866; m. June 1, 1892, LILIAN MARY BOHART of Purcell, Okla., dau. of J. C. Bohart of Chickasaw, Okla. She d. Dec. 28, 1901, in St. Joseph Hospital, Kansas City.

Children:

851.   I.   Mary Alice Welsh, b. Jan. 11, 1898.
852.   II. Bryant Madison Welsh, Jr., b. Feb. 7, 1900.

Mrs. Lilian Welsh united with the Christian Church at the age of thirteen. After their marriage, during their residence in Chickasaw, Oklahoma, she was instrumental in organizing the first Christian Church in the village. Her voice, her presence, and her money always spoke forth her devotion in no uncertain tones — her eager faithfulness to her Master's cause. About two months before her passing away they removed to Apache, Oklahoma, where Mr. Welsh embarked in the banking business. Mr. Welsh is a member of the Christian Church. Residence, Lawton, Oklahoma.

463

ALBERT CLAY WELSH[8] (Bryant[7] [169], Jane,[6] David,[5] Simeon,[4] Cornelius,[3] Pieter Cornelisse,[2] Cornelis[1]), b. Nov. 6, 1869; m. Dec. 14, 1892, IDA LENA PERRY of Lathrop, Mo. He is a merchant in Lathrop, Mo., where they have lived for more than forty years.

Children:

853.   I.   Helen Clay Welsh, b. Oct. 31, 1893; graduated from Lathrop High School as valedictorian.
854.   II. Emma Margaret Welsh, b. Dec. 7, 1896.

464

MARGARET BRYANT WELSH[8] (Bryant[7] [169], Jane,[6] David,[5] Simeon,[4] Cornelius,[3] Pieter Cornelisse,[2] Cornelis[1]), b. July 13,

ANNA WELSH BROWN

1874, Lathrop, Mo.; m. Oct. 21, 1903, SETH CARSON GEORGE of Apache, Okla. Res., Medford, Ore.

Children:
855.   I.   Virginia Varda George, b. July 24, 1904.
856.   II.   Seth Carson George, Jr., b. Feb. 8, 1906.
857.   III.   Cecil Maurice George, b. Aug. 6, 1908.
464a.   IV.   Edward George.
464b.   V.   Margaret George.

469
EMMA EUGENE WELSH[8] (George[7] [171], Jane,[6] David,[5] Simeon,[4] Cornelius,[3] Pieter Cornelisse,[2] Cornelis[1]), b. Sept. 2, 1877; d. 1911; m., in 1897, THOMAS GADDES, M. D., a Canadian. In January, 1901, they removed to Didsbury, Alta., Can., where they, with her mother, now reside.

Children:
858.   I.   George William Gaddes, b. July 2, 1902.
859.   II.   Thomas Bryant Gaddes, b. ......, 1904.

470
BRYANT WELSH GILLESPIE[8] (Hannah[7] [172], Jane,[6] David,[5] Simeon,[4] Cornelius,[3] Pieter Cornelisse,[2] Cornelis[1]), b. Jan. 26, 1863, in Newman, Ill.; m. LAURA A. MILAN. Occupation, stock salesman; one of the firm of Stockton, Gillespie, and Clay of Indianapolis, Ind. Mr. Gillespie is the possessor of a fine residence in a suburb of Indianapolis, where the family resides.

Children:
860.   I.   Boyd Milan Gillespie, b. May 21, 1895.
861.   II.   Bryant Welsh Gillespie, b. Nov. 17, 1897.

472
LUELLA JANE GILLESPIE[8] (Hannah[7] [172], Jane,[6] David,[5] Simeon,[4] Cornelius,[3] Pieter Cornelisse,[2] Cornelis[1]), b. Oct. 16,

1866; m. OLIVER O. HOCKETT, July 23, 1895, at Montezuma, Ind. Dr. Hockett was a physician and surgeon. He d. Feb. 3, 1901. Mrs. Hockett, with her father and son, resides at Newman, Ill.

Child:

862.   I.   J. Maxwell Hockett, b. Nov. 5, 1898.

475

PAULINE W. GILLESPIE[8] (Hannah[7] [172], Jane,[6] David,[5] Simeon,[4] Cornelius,[3] Pieter Cornelisse,[2] Cornelis[1]), b. Aug. 25, 1871; m. CLARENCE W. FUNK.

Child:

863.   I.   Bernadine Funk.

479

MADISON WELSH STUCKEY[8] (Pauline[7] [174], Jane,[6] David,[5] Simeon,[4] Cornelius,[3] Pieter Cornelisse,[2] Cornelis[1]), b. Jan. 24, 1869; m. June 22, 1890, KATE RAY DANIELS.

Child:

864.   I.   Julia Pauline Stuckey, b. Apr. 7, 1896.

Mr. Stuckey at an early age commenced business in his father's bank at Lexington, Nebraska, and soon became assistant cashier. He afterwards was cashier of the bank at Eddyville, in the same state, and later was appointed administrator to settle his father's estate, assuming the entire management of the bank at Eddyville. The cares of business weighed heavily upon him. While on a trip to Denver, Colorado, where he had gone with others on business, he was taken ill. An operation was performed; he rallied, smiled, then sank into unconsciousness and died, July 29, 1898.

The Lexington paper said in part: "Madison Stuckey was a good husband, a kind father, and one of our best citizens. He had a bright future before him. He had the training and ability which made him a successful man in business. Warm-hearted and generous and genial qualities which made him friends wherever he went."

RUBY STUCKEY EVES

480

ANNA STUCKEY[8] Pauline[7] [174], Jane,[6] David,[5] Simeon,[4] Cornelius,[3] Pieter Cornelisse,[2] Cornelis[1]), b. Jan. 28, 1872; m. Jan. 24, 1891, BENTON MARET. Res., 418 15th Ave., Spokane, Wash.

Child:

865. I. Norma Stuckey Maret, b. Sept. 16, 1894, at Eddyville, Neb.

Anna Stuckey attended school at Lexington and Clinton colleges in Missouri, also at Hastings, Nebraska. Her education included music and painting, and was completed at Clinton. Her husband was reporter for the Kansas City Times, later assistant cashier in a bank at Eddyville, Nebraska. He was also private secretary for Governor Silas A. Holcomb of Nebraska, and held the office for two terms with Governor Holcomb. He is now manager of the Automatic Telephone Company at Lincoln, Nebraska.

482

RUBY STUCKEY[8] (Pauline[7] [174], Jane,[6] David,[5] Simeon,[4] Cornelius,[3] Pieter Cornelisse,[2] Cornelis[1]), b. Sept. 15, 1876, at Lexington, Neb.; m. EDWIN S. EVES. Mr. Eves is a publisher. Res., Spokane, Wash.

Mrs. Eves graduated at Lathrop, Missouri, afterwards attending a private school where she took up the higher studies with a view to graduating at Lexington, Missouri. Her art studies included music and painting. In 1896 and 1897 she assisted as cashier in her father's bank at Eddyville, Nebraska. After her marriage she continued the study of music at Lincoln, Nebraska, where she graduated at the Conservatory of Music. In 1903 she was a student of William H. Sherwood, pianist, of Chicago, taking post-graduate work.

483

GEORGIA WELSH[8] (John B.[7] [175], Jane,[6] David,[5] Simeon,[4] Cornelius,[3] Pieter Cornelisse,[2] Cornelis[1]), b. Nov. 22, 1874, near Upper Sandusky, Ohio; m. WALTER B. THOMPSON.

Children:

866.   I.   Christine B. Thompson, b. Nov. 13, 1895.
867.   II.   John B. Thompson, b. Oct. 26, 1899.
868. III.   Wilma C. Thompson, b. Dec. 6, 1903.

After their marriage they resided in Kirksville, Missouri; later on a farm near Milan, Missouri. In 1900 they entered a claim upon one hundred and eighty acres of land fifteen miles from Woodward, Oklahoma. They now reside at Shattuck, Oklahoma.

494   NINTH GENERATION

OTTO DEFOREST BRYANT[9] (Daniel[8] [185], Robert,[7] Elias,[6] David,[5] Simeon,[4] Cornelius,[3] Pieter Cornelisse,[2] Cornelis[1]), b. July 7, 1881; m. July 3, 1904, GRACE STEWART, b. Aug. 7, 1883.

Children:

869.   I.   Donald Keith Bryant, b. Apr. 4, 1905.
869a.   II.   Lois Anna Bryant, b. Dec. 7, 1906.
869b. III.   Darwin Dean Bryant, b. Apr. 6, 1909.
869c. IV.   Robert Maxwell Bryant, b. June 21, 1886.

498
RAY BRYANT[9] (Charles[8] [186], Robert,[7] Elias,[6] David,[5] Simeon,[4] Cornelius,[3] Pieter Cornelisse,[2] Cornelis[1]), b. Mar. 8, 1883; m. Dec. 31, 1908, GLADYS STEWART.   Res., Hebron, Ind.

Child:

869d.   I.   Darl Olga Bryant, b. July 13, 1909.

502
BERTHA M. SPITTAL[9] (Luella C.[8] [188], John,[7] Elias,[6] David,[5] Simeon,[4] Cornelius,[3] Pieter Cornelisse,[2] Cornelis[1]), b. .... in Chicago, Ill.; m. FRANK M. PIERSON, who was b. in Chicago. Res., 200 E. 74th St., Chicago, Ill.

Child:

870.   I.   Frank M. Pierson, Jr.

523

VIOLETTA PEARL SANGER[9] (L. W. Sanger[8] [223], Sarah Ann,[7] Samuel,[6] David,[5] Simeon,[4] Cornelius,[3] Pieter Cornelisse,[2] Cornelis[1]), b. Nov. 2, 1875, near Lowell, Ind.; m. June 29, 1899, to WILLIAM BUCKLEY, son of Patrick Buckley.

Children:

872.   I.   Itha Ileen Buckley, b. Mar. 30, 1900.
873.   II.   Marguerite Buckley, b. July 29, 1902.
874.   III.   Tracy May Buckley, b. Mar. 12, 1904.
875.   IV.   Clara Pearl Buckley, b. Mar. 11, 1907.
876.   V.   Olive Buckley, b. May 23, 1909.

527

BENJAMIN HARRY SANGER[9] (Ross[8] [224], Sarah Ann,[7] Samuel,[6] David,[5] Simeon,[4] Cornelius,[3] Pieter Cornelisse,[2] Cornelis[1]), b. Jan. 11, 1867; m. Sept., 1893, JULIA A. WALL. Res., South Omaha, Neb.

Children:

877.   I.   Harvey Colvan Sanger, b. Mar. 4, 1896.
878.   II.   Julia Sanger, b. Oct. 9, 1898.
879.   III.   Ross Sanger, b. Feb. 4, 1900.

529

EDITH MAY SANGER[9] (Ross[8] [224], Sarah Ann,[7] Samuel,[6] David,[5] Simeon,[4] Cornelius,[3] Pieter Cornelisse,[2] Cornelis[1]), b. Mar. 21, 1877; m. June 4, 1902, to CHARLES SIDNEY FULLMER. Res., St. Joseph, Mo., Station D.

Children:

880.   I.   Charles Sidney Fulmer, b. Sept. 18, 1904.
881.   II.   Regina Bernice Fulmer, b. Dec. 3, 1908.

533

DELLA ADELIA ROGERS[9] (Martha[8] [233], Jacob,[7] Samuel,[6] David,[5] Simeon,[4] Cornelius,[3] Pieter Cornelisse,[2] Cornelis[1]), b.

Oct. 9, 1873, in Chickasaw Co., Iowa; m. Jan. 25, 1895, ALBERT A. LINDLEY; b. Oct. 2, 1873, at Lebanon, Ind., son of Samuel L. Lindley, b. Jan. 18, 1852, and Martha Frances Peters, and grandson of Albert Lindley, who was b. Jan. 16, 1819, and m. Emiline ...... Oct. 26, 1843. Present res., Wichita, Kan.

Child:

882   I. Albert Greer Lindley, b. Feb. 2, 1897.

534
ELEA MAY ROGERS[9] (Martha[8] [233], Jacob,[7] Samuel,[6] David,[5] Simeon,[4] Cornelius,[3] Pieter Cornelisse,[2] Cornelis[1]), b. Dec. 25, 1875, in Chickasaw Co., Iowa; m. Mar. 18, 1896, LOREN H. BUMP, son of Loren Romain Bump and Mary E. ...., Douglas, Kan. He was b. Oct. 6, 1871, at Stevenville, Pa. Present home, Wichita, Kan.

Children:

883.   I. Frances Lorena Bump, b. Feb. 4, 1897.
884.   II. Infant son, b. Jan. 24, 1902.

537
GRACE MILDRED TUCKER[8] (Mary[7] [236], Jacob,[6] Samuel,[5] David,[4] Cornelius,[3] Pieter Cornelisse,[2] Cornelis[1]), b. July 26, 1878; m. FRANK CAGLEY, Jan. 24, 1895. He is the son of Frank Cagley. Res., near Nashua, Iowa.

Child:

885.   I. Gladys Mildred Cagley, b. Jan. 7, 1897.

538
MARTHA FRANCES TUCKER[9] (Mary[8] [236], Jacob,[7] Samuel,[6] David,[5] Simeon,[4] Cornelius,[3] Pieter Cornelisse,[2] Cornelis[1]), b. Apr. 25, 1883; m. Feb. 11, 1907, JOHN PARSONS, son of Hiram . Olson Parsons and Eliza Mildred ....

Children:

886.   I.   Truman Parsons, b. Dec. 23, 1907.
887.   II. Dorothy Theodosia Parsons, b. May 2, 1909.
888.   III. John Henry Parsons, b. Apr. 28, 1911.
889.   IV. Ella Parsons, b. Sept. 12, 1912.

542
MARION ELMER DINWIDDIE[9] (Mary J.[8] [237], Hannah,[7]
Samuel,[6] David,[5] Simeon,[4] Cornelius,[3] Pieter Cornelisse,[2]
Cornelis[1]), b. Nov. 18, 1874, at Plum Grove, Lake Co., Ind.;
m. Apr. 20, 1898, EDNA IRENE GROMANN at Crown Point, Ind.,
dau. of Henry Gromann and Henretta C. Sasse and great granddaughter of Dr. Charles Gromann of Brunswick, one of the
early settlers of Lake Co., Ind.   She was b. Dec. 14, 1876.

Child:
891.   I.   Eleanor Dinwiddie, b. Aug. 10, 1899.

Marion E. Dinwiddie received a good common school education, which was supplemented by a commercial course at the
Northern Indiana Business College at Valparaiso.   In February,
1895, he obtained a position as clerk in the State Bank of Lowell;
in November of the same year he accepted a position with Amos
Allman & Sons, abstractors, at Crown Point, which position he held
until August, 1900.   He then formed a partnership with Herman
E. Sasse, and purchased the abstract business of Morton and
Griggs.   He is now engaged in the abstract, real estate and insurance business in Crown Point, Indiana.   He united with the First
Presbyterian Church of Crown Point in 1897, and for over five
years has been superintendent of the Sunday school, and for two
years an elder in the church.

543
JOSEPH PERKINS DINWIDDIE[9] (Mary J.[8] [237], Hannah,[7]
Samuel,[6] David,[5] Simeon,[4] Cornelius,[3] Pieter Cornelisse,[2]
Cornelis[1]), b. Feb. 3, 1876, at Plum Grove, Lake Co., Ind.;
m. Feb. 3, 1897, at Lowell, Ind., ALICE ERMINA SHURTE, b.

Sept. 12, 18—, at Lowell, Ind., dau. of John Shurte and Helen Marion Drury. Occupation, farming; politics Republican. Res., Lowell, Lake Co., Ind.

> *Children:*
>
> 892.   I.   Lawrence Keith Dinwiddie, b. Aug. 3, 1897.
> 893.   II.   Maxine Drury Dinwiddie, b. May 19, 1911.

578

MAUDE SNYDER[9] (Elura[8] [258], Jane,[7] Samuel D.,[6] David,[5] Simeon,[4] Cornelius,[3] Pieter Cornelisse,[2] Cornelis[1]), b. Aug. 9, 1880, in Kansas; m. Jan. 31, 1897, at Chandler, Okla., F T. WISLEY.

> *Children:*
>
> 894.   I.   Mary Eunice Wisley, b. Sept. 28, 1897.
> 895.   II.   Everett T. Wisley, b. Nov. 16, 1898.
> 896.   III.   Roy Oscar Wisley, b. Sept. 12, 1903.

627

SYLVANUS COOPER GAMBELL[9] (John,[8] [280], Catherine,[7] Mary,[6] David,[5] Simeon,[4] Cornelius,[3] Pieter Cornelisse,[2] Cornelis[1]), b. Mar. 8, 1863, near Winfield, Iowa; d. May 22, 1898; m. NELLIE WEBSTER of Rhodes, Iowa.

> *Child:*
>
> 897.   I.   Margaret Gambell, b. Apr. 13, 1897, on St. Lawrence Island; d. May 22, 1898.

Sylvanus Gambell was a student at Ames, Iowa, during the early part of the decade of 1880–1890. He received his B. S. degree in 1886 from Iowa Agricultural College. R. L. Kirkpatrick, of the faculty, stated that he was considered one of the best bontanists in the state. He took an active part in the religious activities of the college; was also interested in military drill, having taken extra work in that line, and at the time of graduation was captain of cadets.

Mr. Gambell was sent out accompanied by his wife in 1894 as a missionary to the native Eskimos at St. Lawrence Island, Alaska. This school was then the farthest west of any over which the

NELLIE WEBSTER GAMBELL   MARGARET GAMBELL   SYLVANUS COOPER GAMBELL.

American flag floated. The island lies almost within the Arctic Circle, and is nearly destitute of vegetation. In the fall of 1897 they returned to their home in Iowa. In January of 1898 Mr. Gambell was sent by the United States government to take charge of the school for white children at Juneau. Two months later came back to Iowa for his wife and child. They took passage on the *Jane Grey*, and sailed from Seattle, ninety miles off Cape Flattery, a heavy gale was encountered during which the schooner sprung aleak and sank early Sabbath morning May 22, 1898. Thirty-two of the passengers including Mr. and Mrs. Gambell and child were lost. The crew offered an opportunity to Mrs. Gambell to be rescued, but she preferred to share her husband's fate. The Youth's Companion published a series of articles in 1900 relating the adventures of these missionaries who were the first to carry the gospel to these far-away people.

628

ANNA GAMBLE[9] (John[8] [280], Catherine,[7] Mary,[6] David,[5] Simeon,[4] Cornelius,[3] Pieter Cornelisse,[2] Cornelis[1]), b. Mar. 19, 1865; m. July 1, 1885, Rev. JAMES BUTTER, a native of Scotland and a graduate of Aberdeen, Scotland. He was pastor of Presbyterian ch. at Winfield, Iowa, from 1884 to 1888; for several years has been located at Phillipsburg and Culberton, Mont. Now located at Florence, Neb. Mrs. Butter was president of the Synodical Society of the Presbyterian ch. of Iowa. Res., Phillipsburg, Mont.

Children:

898.   I.   Donald Butter, b. July, 1886.
899.   II. Margaret Jean Butter, b. July, 1887. She was a graduate of Montana State Normal. She sailed Aug., 1908, for Germany for a year's study. Afterward taught in Nebraska.
900.   III. Marion Butter, b. Oct., 1889; d. Dec., 1890.
901.   IV. John Gamble Butter, b. Jan., 1895.

629

HERBERT FULTON GAMBELL[9] (John[8] [280], Catherine,[7] Mary,[6] David,[5] Simeon,[4] Cornelius,[3] Pieter Cornelisse,[2] Cornelis[1]), b.

June 10, 1868; m. BERDEAN FRAKER of Arkansas; m. (2nd)
HELEN SWAIN of Osage, Iowa. He was assistant postmaster
at Winfield, Iowa, 1889. He was for several years in the U. S.
postal service at Tacoma, Wash., and held such position at
Manila, P. I., for several years; now (1912) has position in
postal department at Washington, D. C. Res. Winfield,
Iowa.

630

FRANCIS HARVEY GAMBELL[9] (John[8] [280], Catherine,[7] Mary,[6]
David,[5] Simeon,[4] Cornelius,[3] Pieter Cornelisse,[2] Cornelis[1]), b.
Apr. 3, 1870; m. Oct. 15, 1902, HELEN MABELLE FERNSTROM,
who was b. Oct. 15, 1875, dau. of Charles Fernstrom and Mabelle Evans of Lone Tree, Iowa.

> *Children:*
>
> 902.   I.   Francis Fernstrom Gambell, b. July 20, 1903.
> 903.   II. John C. Gambell, b. Mar. 19, 1906.
> 904.   III. George Fernstrom Gambell, b. July 14, 1909.
> 905.   IV. William Bryant Gambell, b. Jan. 29, 1911.

Mr. Gambell is a graduate of the Keokuk (Iowa) Medical
College. He made a trip to Europe in 1895. He was United
States government physician and teacher to the Eskimos at
Unilaklik, west coast of Alaska, and had charge of the government
reindeer station at Eaton from 1895 to 1901. He is at present
practicing medicine at Thief River Falls, Minn.

631

CATHARINE GAMBLE[9] (John[8] [280], Catherine,[7] Mary,[6]
David,[5] Simeon,[4] Cornelius,[3] Pieter Cornelisse,[2] Cornelis[1]), b.
Sept. 9, 1872; m. JEROME L. RAWHOUSER, who was at one
time a druggist of Lone Tree, Iowa; later studied medicine
at the Keokuk (Iowa) Medical College from which he graduated. Now (1910) located in Cassville, Mo.

> *Children:*
>
> 906.   I.   Anna Rawhouser, b. June ......, 1896.
> 907.   II. John Gambell Rawhouser, b. Sept. ......, 1899.
> 908.   III. Jerome Leon Rawhouser, b. Aug. 15, 1908.

632

ELIZABETH GAMBLE[9] (John[8] [280], Catharine,[7] Mary,[6] David,[5] Simeon,[4] Cornelius,[3] Pieter Cornelisse,[2] Cornelis[1]), b. Oct. 25, 1876; m. FRED C. BERKS at Phillipsburg, Mont., where they reside. She is a soprano singer of more than ordinary merit.

Children:

909. I. George Edwin Berks, b. Apr., 1901.
910. II. Margaret Elizabeth Berks, b. July 29, 1902.
911. III. Carlisle Berks, b. Dec. 4, 1903.
912. IV. Oscar Berks.
913. V. John Berks.
914. VI. James Berks.

633

HARVEY C. GAMBLE[9] (Leroy[8] [282], Catherine,[7] Mary,[6] David,[5] Simeon,[4] Cornelius,[3] Pieter Cornelisse,[2] Cornelis[1]), b. Feb. 15, 1870; m. Oct. 2, 1900, MINNIE FOSTER of Bay Saint Louis, Miss., dau. of Rev. William Foster. Mr. Gamble is a railway lineman.

Children:

915. I. Cecil Gamble, b. Feb. 15, 1903.
916. II. Russell Gamble, b. Jan. 6, 1906.
917. III. Harvey Gamble, b. Feb. 29, 1908.

635

EDWIN R. GAMBLE[9] (Leroy[8] [282], Catherine,[7] Mary,[6] David,[5] Simeon,[4] Cornelius,[3] Pieter Cornelisse,[2] Cornelis[1]), b. Aug. 11, 1876; m. Jan. 2, 1902, in Salt Lake City, Utah, MAY VIGLENNY, dau. of ...... Viglenny and ...... Simpkins. Res., Indianola, Iowa. Occupation, electrician and carpenter.

Children:

918. I. Raymond Gamble, b. Nov. 11, 1902.
919. II. Walter Gamble, b. Mar. 4, 1904.
920. III. Edwin Gamble, Jr., b. Jan. 13, 1906.
921. IV. Mildred Gamble, b. Jan. 17, 1908.

636

CAROLINE GAMBLE[9] (Leroy[8] [282], Catharine,[7] Mary,[6] David,[5] Simeon,[4] Cornelius,[3] Pieter Cornelisse,[2] Cornelis[1]), b. Aug. 28, 1879; m. LEWIS E. HAWES, Sept. 17, 1905, in El Paso, Tex. She was formerly a teacher in the public schools of Indianola. Res., Bisbee, Ariz.

637

CHARLES OSCAR GAMBLE[9] (Charles White[8] [283], Catharine,[7] Mary,[6] David,[5] Simeon,[4] Cornelius,[3] Pieter Cornelisse,[2] Cornelis[1]), b. Jan. 1, 1875; m. MARY ALMA HEWETT, Jan. 8, 1902. He is a graduate of the Winfield (Iowa) High School. Attended Parsons College; served as bugler in the First Regt., Colorado Volunteers in the late Spanish War; was present at the siege of Manila, and claims the honor of being the first man who entered the fort. He later took part in the campaigns against the Filippinos. He and his family live on the Harvey Gamble homestead near Winfield, Iowa.

Children:

922.   I.   Raymond Leroy Gamble, b. Oct. 2, 1904.
923.   II. Janet Lavinia Gamble, b. July 14, 1909.

661

MARTHA JANE SMITH[9] (Adaline[8] [294], Jane,[7] Mary,[6] David,[5] Simeon,[4] Cornelius,[3] Pieter Cornelisse,[2] Cornelis[1]), b. Apr. 29, 1867; m. FRANK WHITE of East Liverpool, Ohio.

Children:

924.   I.   John Vance White, b. Mar. 22, 1897.
925.   II.   Helen Frances White, b. Oct. 27, 1899; burned to death May 17, 1902.
926.   III.   Adaline Flora White, b. June .., 1901.
927.   IV.   Bryan H. White, b. Oct. 12, 1902.
928.   V.   Frank White, twins, b. Oct. 12, 1902; d. Feb., 1903.
929.   VI.   Robert Marshall White, b. Nov. 4, 1903.
930.   VII.   Pearl White, b. June 23, 1906.
931.   VIII.   Donald Edwin White, b. ......; d. Mar. 20, 1909.
932.   IX.   Ruth White, b. Dec. 17, 1909.

CLARRIET A. RIDGEWAY

663

LULU N. SMITH[9] (Adeline[8] [294], Jane,[7] Mary,[6] David,[5] Simeon,[4] Cornelius,[3] Pieter Cornelisse,[2] Cornelis[1]), b. Dec. 1, 1873; m. GEORGE KURFISS, Nov. .., 1900.

Children:

933.   I. John Earl Kurfiss, b. Oct. 26, 1903.
933a. II. Hattie Odessa Kurfiss, b. July 11, 1906.

665

JENNIE FRANC LINDLY[9] (Clarriet[8] [295], Jane,[7] Mary,[6] David,[5] Simeon,[4] Cornelius,[3] Pieter Cornelisse,[2] Cornelis[1]), b. Oct. 27, 1867; m. WILLIAM BAILEY RIDGEWAY, Jan. 25, 1899. He was the son of James Lindsay Ridgeway and Mary Adaline Bailey and was born at Eldora, Iowa, Dec. 8, 1872; d. Oct. 23, 1907, at Little Rock, Ark., while on a business trip in that state. He was a graduate in law from the State University of Iowa. Res., Winfield, Iowa.

Children:

934.   I.   Philip Lindly Ridgeway, b. Dec. 30, 1899; d. Aug.
             21, 1900.
934a. II. Clarriet Adaline Ridgeway, b. Oct. 16, 1907.
934b. III. Wilma Jenevieve Ridgeway, b. Oct. 16, 1907.

666

LEANNA JANE McVAY[9] (Mary[8] [296], Jane,[7] Mary,[6] David,[5] Simeon,[4] Cornelius,[3] Pieter Cornelisse,[2] Cornelis[1]), b. Dec. 10, 1869, in Prosperity, Pa.; d. Apr. 11, 1909; m. Oct. 12, 1893, CHARLES DONALDSON, son of Robert Donaldson and Rachel Walker. In politics Mr. Donaldson is a Democrat; in religion a Presbyterian. Res., Buffalo, Pa.

Child:

935.   I. Mary Ethel Donaldson, b. Sept. 13, 1894.

667

PRISCILLA D. McVAY[9] (Mary[8] [296], Jane,[7] Mary,[6] David,[5] Simeon,[4] Cornelius,[3] Pieter Cornelisse,[2] Cornelis[1]), b. Dec. 8,

1871; d. Jan. 25, 1911; m. Sept. 15, 1896, JOHN CALVIN FRENCH, b. July 14, 1874, son of John Calvin French and Savilla Vaile. Rev. J. C. French is pastor of the First Presbyterian ch. of Frenchtown, N. J He is a graduate of Washington and Jefferson College and of the Theological Department of Princeton University, New Jersey.

Child:

936. I. Leanna May French, b. May 9, 1902.

668

THOMAS FRANKLIN McVAY[9] (Mary[8] [296], Jane,[7] Mary,[6] David,[5] Simeon,[4] Cornelius,[3] Pieter Cornelisse,[2] Cornelis[1]), b. Apr. 3, 1874; m. Mar. 28, 1900, JOSEPHINE BELL, dau. of Robert Bell and Mary Jane McLeary. In politics a Republican; religion, Presbyterian; occupation, farming. Res., Prosperity, Pa.

Children:

937. I. Robert McVay, b. July 29, 1902.
938. II. Demas Lindly McVay, b. Apr. 5, 1905.

672

MARY FRANCES KELLEY[9] (Jane[8] [398], Jane,[7] Mary,[6] David,[5] Simeon,[4] Cornelius,[3] Pieter Cornelisse,[2] Cornelis[1]), b. Oct. 8, 1875; m. Feb. 19, 1902, HENRY ROACH. Res., Phillipsburg, Kan.

Children:

939. I. Raymond Roach, b. ......, 1902.
940. II. Harold Vivian Roach, b. Oct. 25, 1904.

689

MARGARET ELIZABETH DAY[9] (Morris,[8] [307], Elizabeth,[7] Mary,[6] David,[5] Simeon,[4] Cornelius,[3] Pieter Cornelisse,[2] Cornelis[1]), b. Nov. 26, 1871, in Goodell, Iowa; m. Feb. 21, 1894, FREDERICK P. SKOW, b. Apr. 24, 1868, in Hadersleben, Sleswick-Holstein, Germany; son of Mads Skow and Caroline

Freese. Religion, Lutheran; politics, Democratic. Res., Watertown, S. Dak.

Children:

941. I. Dora Lavinia Skow, b. Nov. 27, 1894.
942. II. Margaret Daisy Skow, b. Oct. 19, 1905.

690

ESTELLA DELL DAY[9] (Morris[8] [307], Elizabeth, Mary,[6] David,[5] Simeon,[4] Cornelius,[3] Pieter Cornelisse,[2] Cornelis[1]), b. Feb. 5, 1875; m. July 15, 1896, at Klemme, Iowa, HANS NISSEN, b. Apr. 12, 1873, son of Nis Nissen and Catherine Elizabeth Ell. Rev. Nissen is pastor of the Methodist Church of Haywarden, S. Dak. In politics he is a Prohibitionist. Mrs. Nissen is a member of the Daughters of the American Revolution.

Children:

943. I. Mary Ethel Nissen, b. May 19, 1897; d. July 5, 1897.
944. II. Harold Sebastine Nissen, b. Apr. 19, 1898.
945. III. Charles Donald Nissen, b. Aug. 27, 1899.
946. IV. Catherine Alice Nissen, b. Nov. 28, 1900.
947. V. Walter Raymond Nissen, b. Feb. 11, 1902.

691

IDA ALICE DAY[9] (Morris[8] [307], Elizabeth,[7] Mary,[6] David,[5] Simeon,[4] Cornelius,[3] Pieter Cornelisse,[2] Cornelis[1]), b. Apr. 30, 1877, at Klemme, Iowa; m. Dec. 28, 1898, JOHN BAUMGAERTNER, b. Dec. 27, 1872, son of John Baumgaertner and Justine Grau. Occupation, hotel proprietor; in politics a Republican; in religion, Methodists. Res., Garner, Iowa.

Children:

948. I. Daughter, b. Oct. 29, 1899; d. in infancy.
949. II. Donna Estella Baumgaertner, b. July 6, 1901.
950. III. John Morris Baumgaertner, b. Sept. 24, 1907.

695

ROSCOE VAILE BRAIDEN[9] (Clara[8] [311], Caroline,[7] Mary,[6] David,[5] Simeon,[4] Cornelius,[3] Pieter Cornelisse,[2] Cornelis[1]), b.

May 7, 1888; in Rochelle, Ill.; m. ANNA GERALDINE ALLEN, who was b. Jan. 3, 1888; dau. of Ira W. Allen and Mary Denry.

Children:

951.   I.   Miles Joseph Braiden, b. Oct. 10, 1908.
952.   II.   Robert James Braiden, b. Oct. 13, 1909.
953.   III. Ruth Marion Braiden, b. Oct. 12, 1910.

Roscoe was educated in the Rochelle Public School, attended Gambier Military Academy, was within a few months of graduating when the buildings were burned and the academy closed. He then attended the University of Chicago. He is now conducting the ice business of Rochelle. He is a member of the First Presbyterian Church of Rochelle, Illinois. In politics a Progressive Republican.

698

BELLE CORT[9] (Susan[8] [312], Caroline,[7] Mary,[6] David,[5] Simeon,[4] Cornelius,[3] Pieter Cornelisse,[2] Cornelis[1]), b. Aug. 6, 1877, at Rochelle, Ill.; m. Oct. 24, 1900, in Huron, S. Dak., ABNER SHIRK, son of Michael Shirk (name originally Scherrick) and Fianna Burge. He was b. Aug. 19, 1866, at McAllisterville, Pa.

Children:

954.   I.   Edwin Cort Shirk, b. Dec. 29, 1903, at Atlantic, Mich.
955.   II.   Richard Alvin Shirk, b. Feb. 20, 1906, at Canton, Ill.

Mrs. Shirk graduated from Huron High School in 1896, and from Huron College in 1899. Mr. Shirk graduated from Dana's Musical Institute of Warren, Ohio, in 1898, and completed a business course at McAllister, Pennsylvania. He is a musician. Mr. and Mrs. Shirk are members of the Presybterian Church. Mrs. Shirk is a member of the Daughters of the American Revolution. Residence, De Kalb, Illinois.

700

JANE MARY CORT[9] (Susan[8] [312], Caroline,[7] Mary,[6] David,[5] Simeon,[4] Cornelius,[3] Pieter Cornelisse,[2] Cornelis[1]), b. Mar. 14,

1883, in Rochelle, Ill.; m. HARRY LENHART, Oct., 1905. Jane Mary is a graduate of Huron (S. Dak.) High School and of Huron College.

Child:

956. I. John Henry Lenhart, b. Oct. 22, 1908.

721

SAMUEL BRYANT IRWIN[9] (Harriett[8] [324], Joseph,[7] Simeon,[6] David,[5] Simeon,[4] Cornelius,[3] Pieter Cornelisse,[2] Cornelis[1]), b. Apr. 27, 1885; m. June 26, 1907, WAITIE MCDONALD. Samuel is in the employ of the Home Telephone Company of Los Angeles.

Chi[3]d:

957. I. Helen Waitie Irwin, b. Feb. 19, 1909.

737

WINFRED B. FISHER[9] (Davis A.[8] [350], Nancy,[7] David,[6] David,[5] Simeon,[4] Cornelius,[3] Pieter Cornelisse,[2] Cornelis[1]), b. June 11, 1887. On his seventeenth birthday, June 11, 1904, he m. LILLIE VOLKEE, dau. of William Volkee and Corrilla Rich. Res., near Hebron, Ind. Occupation, farmer; religion, Methodist.

Children:

958. I. David W. Fisher, b. May 5, 1905.
959. II. Charlotte Fisher, b. June 20, 1907.
960. III. Gilbert Fisher, b. Nov. 25, 1908.

738

ALFRED W. HAYWARD[9] (Arabella[8] [351], Nancy,[7] David,[6] David,[5] Simeon,[4] Cornelius,[3] Pieter Cornelisse,[2] Cornelis[1]), b. Jan. 3, 1878, near Merrillville, Lake Co., Ind.; m. Feb. 7, 1905, KATHRYN ISABELLA MULLEN. His parents when he was one year and a half old moved to the farm where his father was born near Ross, Lake Co., Ind., and resided there until he was nine years old, when he with his parents moved to Santa Barbara,

Calif., where he has lived 25 years   He attended high school and business college at Santa Barbara, Calif.   He is in business with his father — furniture and upholstery.   Religion, Methodist; politics, Republican.   Res., 1414 Laguna St., Santa Barbara, Calif.

Children:

961.   I.   Alfreda Isabella Hayward, b. Apr. 1, 1906.
962.   II.   Roland Fisher Hayward, b. Jan. 9, 1908.
963.   III.   Earl Bryant Hayward, b. Oct. 14, 1909.

740

IDA MAY HAYWARD[9] (Arabella[8] [351], Nancy,[7] David,[6] David,[5] Simeon,[4] Cornelius,[3] Pieter Cornelisse,[2] Cornelis[1]), b. July 25, 1883, on the farm near Ross, Lake Co., Ind., and resided there with her parents until she was three years of age, when she with them went to Santa Barbara, Calif.   She graduated from the Santa Barbara High School in 1902; m. BROOKS B. BRENTNER, Dec. 29, 1903, who was the son of L. L. Brentner.

Child:

964.   I.   Charles Wilfred Brentner, b. Jan. 9, 1907.
They were living in Oakland, California, at the time of the earthquake in San Francisco in 1906.   Shortly afterwards they went back to Santa Barbara where they lived for two years, moving to Los Angeles, where they bought a home and now reside.   Religion, Methodist.

Mr. Brentner is in the automobile business; politics, Republican. Residence, 148 West 48 Street, Los Angeles, California.

741

EARL GRANT HAYWARD[9] (Arabella[8] [351], Nancy,[7] David,[6] David,[5] Simeon,[4] Cornelius,[3] Pieter Cornelisse,[2] Cornelis[1]), b. July 23, 1885, on the farm near Ross, Lake Co., Ind., and resided there with his parents until he was a year and a half old, when he moved to Santa Barbara, Calif., with his parents where he still resides.   He attended the Santa Barbara High

School and helped his father in the furniture business. Religion, Methodist; politics, Republican; m. FREDRICA DOROTHY MEYER, Sept. 11, 1907, dau. of Mr. and Mrs. Wm. Meyer, of Denver, Colo. Mr. Meyer is U. S. Senator and ex-governor of Colorado. Earl is in the automobile business, and has a large garage in Santa Barbara.

Child:

965.   I. William Wheeler Hayward, b. Mar. 31, 1909.

772

CARRIE L. GAMBLE[9] (Mary [392] Eliza,[8] Martha,[7] Elizabeth,[6] David,[5] Simeon,[4] Cornelius,[3] Pieter Cornelisse,[2] Cornelis[1]), b. Dec. 9, 1878; m. July, 1908, HOYT PARTCH.

Children:

966.   I. Mary Partch, b. Oct. 28, 1909; d. Dec. 22, 1909.
967.   II. Robert Carleton Partch, b. Oct. 25, 1910.

787

WILLIAM STEWART POST[9] (Samuel[8] [401], Leonidas,[7] Elizabeth,[6] David,[5] Simeon,[4] Cornelius,[3] Pieter Cornelisse,[2] Cornelis[1]), b. Oct. 19, 1881, in Allen Co., Ohio; m. Feb. 23, 1900 CLARA ETTA CAREY of Shawnee Twp., Allen Co., Ohio.

Children:

968.   I. Helen Carey Post, b. Jan. 17, 1902.
969.   II. Alvin Donald Post, b. Aug. 31, 1908.

788

CORA ETHEL POST[9] (Samuel[8] [401], Leonidas,[7] Elizabeth,[6] David,[5] Simeon,[4] Cornelius,[3] Pieter Cornelisse,[2] Cornelis[1]), b. Nov. 22, 1882; m. ALVA BENEDUM of German Twp., Allen Co., Ohio.

Children:

970.   I. Ruth Evelyn Benedum, b. Dec. 2, 1903.
971.   II. Marguerite Post Benedum, b. July 28, 1911.

792

CLAIRE BRYANT POST[9] (Charles C.[8] [402], Leonidas H.,[7] Elizabeth,[6] David,[5] Simeon,[4] Cornelius,[3] Pieter Cornelisse,[2] Cornelis[1]), b. Aug. 18, 1885; m. Oct. 17, 1907, JESSIE CARR. Res., Alberta, Canada.

Children:

972.   I. John Post.
973.   II. Mary Post.

793

GERTRUDE POST[9] (Charles C.[8] [402], Leonidas H.,[7] Elizabeth,[6] David,[5] Simeon,[4] Cornelius,[3] Pieter Cornelisse,[2] Cornelis[1]), b. Mar. 8, 1889; m. June 19, 1912, EDWARD L. BAXTER. She was educated at the Lutheran College in Lima, Ohio, with the exception of the senior year, which was taken at Front Royal, Va.

827

RUBY SHELDON[9] (Lulu[8] [426], Edmund R.,[7] Jacob,[6] David,[5] Simeon,[4] Cornelius,[3] Pieter Cornelisse,[2] Cornelis[1]), b. Mar. 15, 1882; graduated from Hebron High School May 22, 1900; m. July 7, 1904, HAL O. BINYON, city salesman for Kimball Brick Co., Chicago. Res., 2535 Kimball Ave., Chicago.

Children:

974.   I.   John Sheldon Binyon, b. June 11, 1905; d. Nov. 2, 1906, in Chicago, Ill.
975.   II. Arline Binyon, b. Sept. 23, 1906.
976.   III. Hal O. Binyon, Jr., b. Aug. 2, 1909.

828

BERTA SHELDON[9] (Lulu[8] [426], Edmund Randolph,[7] Jacob,[6] David,[5] Simeon,[4] Cornelius,[3] Pieter Cornelisse,[2] Cornelis[1]), b. May 30, 1883; m. Jan. 8, 1902, JAY BALDWIN of Leroy, Ind., who was in the mercantile business. Res., Hebron, Ind.

Children:

977. I. Richard S. Baldwin, b. Sept. 3, 1905.
978. II. Mary Elizabeth Baldwin, b. July 16, 1911.

842

IDA BRYANT HOLLER[9] (Alice E.[8] [457], Bryant,[7] Jane,[6] David,[5] Simeon,[4] Cornelius,[3] Pieter Cornelisse,[2] Cornelis[1]), b. Sept. 3, 1879, in Peabody, Kan.; m. Aug. 14, 1901, at Colorado Springs, HALDINE ROLAND STEALY, who was b. Sept. 14, 1876, at Peabody, Kan., son of Amos Stealy and Katharine Seitz. Ida B. Holler graduated from the Peabody High School in 1898. Res., Peabody, Kan.

Children:

979. I. Kirk Holler Stealy, b. Oct. 18, 1902.
980. II. Elva Stealy, b. July 4, 1910.

843

EDNA E. HOLLER[9] (Alice E.[8] [457], Bryant,[7] Jane,[6] David,[5] Simeon,[4] Cornelius,[3] Pieter Cornelisse,[2] Cornelis[1]), b. June 18, 1882, Peabody, Kan.; m. ......, 1910, JOSEPH McLEAN. She graduated from the Peabody (Kan.) High School.

Child:

981. I. William Robert McLean.

NEW JERSEY BRYANTS

The following data was collected by W. B. Stout, of Newark, New Jersey, from New Jersey records of Bryants who from names and places of residences seem to have a common ancestry with David, 1756 (37). We publish this data hoping that the other branches will take up at once the collecting and preserving of much valuable data which will otherwise be lost.

BRYANT–BRIANT NOTES

TOMBSTONE INSCRIPTIONS, WESTFIELD CEMETERY

Andrew Briant, b. 1714; d. 1750, in 36th year of age.

John Briant, b. 1739; d. Oct. 26, 1801, in 62d year of age.

David Briant, b. 1756; d. Mar. 29, 1813, in 57th year of age.

Sarah Briant, b. Oct. 19, 1785; wife of Andrew; d. Feb. 2, 1856; age 70 years, 3 months, 13 days.

Andrew Briant, son of John and Abigail Briant, b. Jan. 25, 1770; d. Feb. 13, 1844; age 74 years and 19 days.

Mary, dau. of John and Abigail Briant, b. 1765; d. Oct. 8, 1775, in 10th year.

Mary, dau. of Andrew and Sarah Briant, b. Nov. 7, 1798; d. Apr. 19, 1828; age 29 years, 5 months and 12 days.

CONNECTICUT FARMS (N. J.) CEMETERY

Isaac H. Briant, b. 1798; d. Mar. 22, 1855, age 57.

[From the *Newark News* of Dec. 4, 1912.]

WILLIAM H. BRIANT

"Summit, N. J., Dec. 4.— William H. Briant, who was one of the early settlers of the city and had held several official positions, died late yesterday afternoon at his home, 84 Springfield Avenue, in the Huntly section. He had lived in that part of the city all his life.

"The cause of death was hardening of the arteries and the infirmities of age. Briant's Pond took its name from Mr. Briant.

"The funeral will be held at his home Friday afternoon at 2 o'clock. Rev. William S. Coeyman, pastor of the East Summit Chapel, will officiate. Interment will be in the Presbyterian Cemetery, Springfield.

"Mr. Briant was eighty-five years old. Fifteen years ago he was acting road master of the city and he held the position of freeholder sixteen years, retiring twelve years ago. For many years he was a justice of the peace.

"For many years, too, he had been superintendent of the Springfield Methodist Sunday school and was actively connected with the church of that denomination.

"Mr. Briant leaves a widow and two daughters, Mrs. Elizabeth Richardson, of Newark, and Mrs. Harriet A. Smith, of New York, as well as two stepsons, George F. Vreeland, a former mayor of the city, and Harry Vreeland, of the firm of Vreeland & Vought. He also leaves five grandchildren and four great-grandchildren. He was the last to survive of a family of eight."

SPRINGFIELD (N. J.) TOMBSTONE INSCRIPTIONS

Simeon Bryant, d. June 25, 1784, in 74th year.

Hannah Bryant, wife of Simeon, d. Apr. 7, 1785, in 67th year of age. (Evidently parents of following three children:)

Hannah, dau. of Simeon and Hannah Bryant, b. 1741; d. Feb. 20, 1803, in 62d year.

Rachel Ross, dau. of Simeon and Hannah Bryant, b. 1749; d. Sept. 14, 1810, in 61st year.

Simeon Bryant, b. 1760; d. Sept. 28, 1831, in 71st year.

Mary, wife of Simeon Bryant, b. Feb. 14, 1766; d. Aug. 22, 1856.

Cloe, dau. of Simeon and Mary Bryant, d. Dec. 12, 1786; age 4 weeks, 3 days.

Nancy, dau. of Simeon and Mary Bryant, d. Apr. 13, 1798; age 1 year, 2 months, 14 days.

Jacob, son of Simeon and Mary Bryant, d. Jan. 5, 1803; age 2 years, 9 months.

REPORT OF COMMISSION ON PUBLIC RECORDS OF NEW JERSEY FILED AT STATE HOUSE

PAGE 104

	£	s.
Hannah Briant, 1776–1780......................	16	..
Simeon Briant, 1776–1780......................	462	11

Inventory of losses by depredation of English troops, dated Springfield, N. J., May 11, 1789:

	SAME	£	s.
Benjamin Briant, 1780......................		11	5

Dated Connecticut Farms, N. J.

HISTORY OF MORRIS AND SUSSEX COUNTIES

Johannis Briant emigrated from Holland about 1690 and settled at Springfield, N. J. Had son Andrew, b. 1737 (seems improbable), in Essex County. Andrew had son John who was b. in Essex County; m. Mary Agnes of Long Island. John had son Lewis, b. Mt. Freedom, ...; m. Phoebe Hedden (who was b. 1810; d. Sept. 14, 1888), d. Oct. 14, 1879.

Children:
William O., b. Aug., 1828; d. Dec. 11, 1832.
Mary A., b. Feb., 1830; d. Dec. 1, 1832.
Sarah A., b. Nov. 20, 1832; m. Geo. Cummings.
Nancy T., b. June 13, 1837; m. Mahlon Stockman.
Thomas E., b. ......; d. young.
Phoebe E., b. Aug. 12, 1843; m. Geo. W. Skillborn.
Stephen F. Briant, m. Amelia Bailey; had children:
Mary E., m. Ernest Lawrence.
Henry A.
Matilda T., m. Jefferson Cooley.
Emma L., m. Frank Pool.

FIRST SETTLERS OF NEWTON TOWNSHIP, OLD GLOUCESTER, BY CLEMENT (N. Y. P. L.).

Thomas Briant, b. at Shippenwarden, Northampshire, England, in 1665; d. 1733; m. Rebecca Collins, who d. 1743. They owned an estate near Mt. Holly, Burlington Co. Children were:

Elizabeth, m. Daniel Harris.
Sarah, m. John Fennimore.
Ann.
Abraham.
Benjamin, m. Sarah Kay.

HEADSTONES IN CHURCHYARD OF PRESBYTERIAN CHURCH, MT. FREEDOM, N. Y.

Andrew Briant, b. 1737; d. July 4, 1821, in his 84th year.

Rachel, wife of Andrew, b. 1744; d. Mar. 28, 1829, in her 85th year.

Rev. Jacob, b. 1780; d. July 5, 1846, in his 66th year.

John, b. Mar. 10, 1764; d. Oct. 21, 1835; age 71 years and 21 days.

Mary, wife of John, d. May 30, 1835, 58 years, 7 months, 11 days.

Phebe Ann, wife of Samuel, d. May 6, 1844; age 26.

Isaac C., son of Elias and Electa, b. 1826; d. Apr. 12, 1842; age 18.

Orsemus O., son of Samuel and Elizabeth, d. Feb. 6, 1830; age 1 year, 6 months.

Mary Caroline, dau. of S. O. and E., d. Aug. 1, 1839; age 7 months.

Thomas E., son of Lewis and Phebe, d. Nov. 25, 1816; age 6 years and 7 months.

Mary A., dau. of Lewis and Phebe, d. Dec. 1, 1832, 2 years and 10 months.

William O., son of Lewis and Phebe; d. Dec. 11, 1832; 4 years and 9 months.

EARLY GERMANS OF NEW JERSEY

Peggy Bryant, m. Samuel Van Atta abt. 1815; p. 540.

Joseph Bryant, m. Naomi Beavers about 1830; p. 260.

Hannah Bryant, b. 1786; d. 1828; was 1st wife of Jonah Horton, p. 419.

Polly Bryant was 2nd wife of Robt. Skinner, who was b. 1777, Warren Co.; p. 497.

Elizabeth M. Bryant, dau. of Isaac, m. John Corwin, who was b. 1787; d. 1859; lived at Chester.

Sally Y. Briant, m. Lewis Nicholas, July 16, 1814; p. 454.

John Briant, m. Mary Ayers (b. Oct. 19, 1776); p. 244.

Elias Bryant, b. Aug. 30, 1770; m. Phebe Ann Dickerson, b. Nov. 10, 1772. Children were:

Rachel, m. Samuel Lawrence.

Sarah, m. . . . . . . Nicholas.

Elias.

Daniel C., m. Eliza Carroll.

Samuel C., m. (1st) Phebe Ann Garrison; m. (2nd) Mehitable Lewis.

Hannah, m. John Larison.

Samuel, died very young.

*Elizabeth C., m. Samuel Searing.

Nancy, m. Drake Cramer.

*Above information furnished by Alonzo Bryant Searing, son of Elizabeth Bryant Searing; letter Jan. 4, 1911.

MORRIS COUNTY, VOL. 2, P. 565

Samuel C. Bryant, son of Elias Bryant and Phebe Ann Dickenson, was b. 1808 at Ironia, N. J., on original Bryant tract. He m. Phebe Garrison; d. 1866. Children were:

Dorastus L., b. Apr. 1, 1840, at Succasunna; m. 1866 to Caroline Snelling.

Children:

Eliza M., m. M. B. Carrel.

Augustus S., m. Alice Coates.

Anna P., m. H. H. Jowett.

Dora L., m. Dolph De Hanne.

Robert B.

Freak C.

Irving G.

Alonzo.

VERBALLY BY ANNA A. PENNINGTON, JUNE 13, 1911.

Samuel O. Briant and wife Jane Cory Briant, lived at Mendham, N. J. He died about 1866–1867. Was a judge and frequently went to Morristown, N. J.

Children were, in order of age:

Sarah, m. . . . . . . Babbitt.

Adeline, m. Jos. Ballentine.
Letitia, m. Alva Day.
Helen, m. ...... Wood; went to Oakland, Calif.

TUTTLES, MORRIS COUNTY, ANNALS

Mrs. Rachel Briant (1797–1807) d. Feb. 6, 1858; was member, one of 35, of Presbyterian Ch., Rockaway, N. J.

BRIANT–BRYANT MARRIAGES

ESSEX COUNTY, N. J., MARRIAGE RECORDS. COURT HOUSE, NEWARK

Rev. Peter Bryant — Eliza Stites, both of Elizabeth⁸own, July 2, 1795.

Sarah Bryant — Joseph Halsey, 3rd, Feb. 4, 1796.

Betsy Briant — Stephen Townley, Jan. (or Feb.), 1806.

Sarah Briant — Uzal Crane, Aug. 3, 1806.

John Briant — Betsy Parson, May 2, 1806.

Aaron Briant — Betsy Sears, Jan. 5, 1807.

John Searin — Betsy Briant, Feb. 16, 1807.

Hannah Briant — John Parkhurst, Jan. (or Feb.), 1815.

Elizabeth Briant — Darling Beach (both of Newark), Mar. 15, 1814.

John Briant — Peggy Wade, Mar. 12, 1816.

Thos. Briant — Mary F. Ross, July 28, 1816.
          (Rev. Thos. Pierson, Westfield)

Gideon S. Briant of Chatham to Mary Garthwait of Connecticut Farms, N. J., Mar. 13, 1810.

Isaac H. Briant of Newark, to Mary Smith of Connecticut Farms, June 3, 1818.

Mary A. Briant of Springfield to Jonathan Cory of Westfield, Jan. 30, 1821.

Jane Briant of Springfield to Amos Keeler of New York, Nov. 23, 1822.

Betsy Bryant to Jerry Woodruff, Westfield, Jan. 20, 1822.

John Briant to Clarissa Tucker, New Providence, N. J., Oct. 3, 1824.

Mary Briant of Springfield to Apollos Stites of New Brunswick, N. J., Jan. 29, 1825.

Mary Briant of Springfield to David Kissam of Springfield, Dec. 18, 1825.

Mrs. Polly Briant of Westfield to Ithamar Bonnel of Springfield, June 4, 1825.

Hannah S. Briant to John H. Baker, both of Springfield, Nov. 13, 1826.

Samuel Briant to Sarah Marsh, both of Westfield, Apr. 20, 1828.

Nancy D. Briant to Ephriam D. Cramer, both of Randolph Twp., Morris Co., N. J., Feb. 12, 1834.

The will of William Bryant, Sr., Hopewell, Hunterdon Co., N. J., includes the following names:

> Son William.
> Son Benjamin.
> Son John.
> Daughter Sarah.
> Daughter Rebecca.
> Daughter May,
> Daughter Ann,   } unmarried at this date.
> Daughter Elizabeth.
> Grandson William Forster.
> Grandson Ralph Hunt, the son of my dau. Elizabeth.
> Granddaughter Mary, dau. of my son John.
> Granddaughter Charity, dau. of my dau. Elizabeth.
> April 7, 1786.
> Three Sons, Executors.

RACHEL BRYANT b. Aug. 15, 1758; m. Mar. 1, 1783, JAMES STOUT, lived at Chester, Morris Co., N. J.; died after 1815 (date uncertain—data concerning her and ancestry desired).

Children:

Mary, b. Sept. 28, 1783; d. Feb. 8, 1856; m. Robert Woodruff.

Thomas Bryant, Sr., b. Oct. 14, 1785; d. July 14, 1861; m. Deborah Terry.

Hannah, b. Sept. 18, 1787; d. 1828 or 1829; m. Luther Norris.

Eliza, b. Sept. 29, 1789; d. July 11, 1864; m. John Cooper.

Sarah, b. Dec. 5, 1791.

Charles T., b. Mar. 1, 1793; d. Aug. 17, 1849; m. Margaret McCord.

John, b. Jan. 26, 1795.

James, b. Feb. 2, 1796.

Rachel, b. Dec. 20, 1798; d. ......; m. Nicholas Quimby.

Jane, b. Feb. 1, 1801; d. Aug. 29, 1852; m. Jacob Emmons.

Warren Bryant Stout's ancestor is Thomas Bryant, Sr. Data of the above parentage of Rachel wanted. A dau. of Charles T. Stout, m. Geo. J. Warren Keifer, Springfield, Ohio, who was speaker of the house for many years. Still a member of Congress.

The above contributed by Warren B. Stout, South Orange, N. J.

William Bryant, Sr.

Hopewell, N. J. Feb. 10, 1742.

Wife Sarah.

Son Voluntino

Son William.

Daughters, Sarah, Ann, Elizabeth, Allies (Alice?). Above daughters must have been married at this date, for next mentioned is given as Mary, single.

William Bryant.

Dec. 20, 1732.

Daughter Joyce Terrill.

Granddaughter Johannah Terrill.

Granddaughter Hilyard Terrill.

THE WALING–VAN WINKLE ANCESTRY

The coat of arms of Pier Walichs appears on a document dated July 8, 1455, the original copy being on file in the manuscript division of the Konenklijke Bibliotheek at The Hague, a copy being in the Raabhuis at Winkel. Arms: Of gold, a chevron of red, accompanied with three leaves of holly sinister, with stems downward.

On June 3, 1621, the great Dutch West India Company was incorporated, subject to the States General of Holland. Trading posts were established on Manhattan Island and along the Hudson River for traffic with the Indians in furs and peltry. For the purpose of forming permanent settlements a charter was granted by the company, giving special privileges "to such as should within four years plant a colony of fifty adults in any part of New Netherland other than Manhattan Island." They were to be recognized and acknowledged as patroons and were to have absolute title in perpetuity to the lands within their grants. These grants might extend sixteen miles along one bank of a navigable stream, or half that distance on each side, reaching back indefinitely, "so far into the country as the situation of the occupiers will permit." Under this offer of patronage, Killian Van Rensalaer in 1629 secured a tract above and below Fort Orange (Albany) on both sides of the Hudson River called Rensalaerwyk. In 1630 ten settlers sailed for his colony. In 1634 Jacob Albertz Planck was made schout and he at once began the distribution of farms among the new colonisits. Of those who came early to Rensalaerwyk were Symon Walichs and Cornelius Maessen. Symon's farm was located on Papscanee Island which he occupied until May 1, 1647. On October 3, 1636, Van Rensalaer wrote: "These two farmers who have been very helpful to me, namely Cornelius Maessen and Symon Walichs, you will give a fair choice of the men who are coming." From the numerous allusions made in the Rensalaer papers to those who had been employed by Symon Walichs, we must esteem him to have been a personage of considerable importance in the new colony. On October 7, 1648, he agreed to buy Pieter Van Derlinden's plantation on Manhattan Island, but was killed by the Indians near Paulis Hook at Pavonia (now Jersey City), March, 1649.

JACOB WALIGH or WALINGEN (from whom the Van Winkle family is descended) made at least two voyages between Holland and this country before he settled permanently here, for the Dutch church at Hoorn, Holland, disclosed, that between September 25 and December 18, 1633, the following "have come over with certificate from other churches to our congregation: Symon Walingen of New Netherland, Jacob Walingen of New Netherland," proving that they must have resided in New Netherland long enough to have become established; to have united with the church and to be entitled to a certificate of dismissal, accorded only to members in good and regular standing. Jacob again sailed from Hoorn in 1634, arriving at New Amsterdam in June, 1635, in ship *King David*. The family of Jacob Waligh were residents of that part of North Holland, at or near the town of Winkle. This town is located one and a half miles southwest of Medenblick, eleven miles northeast of Alkmaar and about fifteen miles northwest of Hoorn.

Among the early inhabitants of this village of Winkle was the family of Walich. They were extensive land owners, as in 1326 one section of the dykes was designated as Walichsdyke, the custom being to give to the dykes the names of the owners of the lands they bounded. Records of 1610 show that the church of Winkle had acquired a tract of land of Peter Walig. The names Waligs, Walichs, Walinghs and Walighs appear interchangeably in the records at Winkle apparently as the transcriber chose to write it. The records show that the Walings were property owners in Winkle in the twelfth century and were residents there in the fourteenth and seventeenth centuries, which fact fully explains and verifies the origin of the name "Van Winkle" according to the system of nomenclature in vogue at that time. "Van" signifies "*from*" or "*of*" Winkle (place of residence); as, "Jacob Van Winkle," *Jacob from Winkel* (Holland). In early times a person might have, in addition to his given name, a name determined upon because of some physical or personal characteristic of the individual, or occupation, place of birth or residence. After a time an affix or suffix to the father's name became the custom and a generally adopted system in Holland. The terminations "s," "se," "sen," were added to the father's name and became the patronymic, thus indicating the line of descent. These different suffixes have the same meaning, signifying "*child of;*" thus *Symon Jacobse* would indicate *Symon* son of *Jacob, Cornelisse* son of *Cornelis*. This custom was not continued in America except in the early days, but the native place, or place from whence they came, gave the surname to many emigrants from Holland, as "Van Hoorn" *from Hoorn*, a town in Holland, "Van Ripen," *from Ripen*, "Van Winkle," etc. In the female line the given name of the daughters was that of a near relative with *je* added, meaning diminutive.

Jacob Waligh or Walingen (from whom the Bryants trace their descent) came to America prior to 1633; the exact date of his first arrival is not known; he, however, was among the first settlers of New Netherlands. He settled in 1636 on a farm at Rensalaerwyk. He returned to Manhattan October 1, 1650. He was elected one of "*The Twelve Men*," the first representative official body within the limits of New York and New Jersey. He led a movement to establish a settlement on the Connecticut River, but abandoned the project because of opposition of the English. On October 23, 1654, he secured a grant of land at Pavonia (now Jersey City, New Jersey). In 1664 Carteret issued a deed confirming all existing property rights. The deed in confirmation of the Walingen grant describes the property as follows: "Beginning at a stake on the edge of New York Bay and from said stake running north 27°, 27' west, 64 chains, 74 links to a stake between two cedar bushes at the edge of Newark Bay, thence south 46° 30' west, 10 chains and 30 links along said Bay to a stake, thence south 27° 30' east, 60 chains and 20 links to a stake standing by the edge of York Bay, on the easterly side of a small creek and thence northeasterly along said York Bay as it runs to the place of beginning."

In 1655 the inhabitants of Pavonia were driven from their homes and their property destroyed by the Indians. Through the efforts of Governor Stuyvesant peace was finally secured and some of the colonists returned to their ruined homes, among whom was Jacob Walingen. No record of date of marriage of Jacob Walingen has been found, although in the old Dutch church records of New Amsterdam of 1647 appear the names of Jacob Walingen and wife Trintje. Jacob Walingen died in the early part of the year 1657, leaving a widow, "Trintje Jacobs," and six minor children, three boys and three girls, as follows:

Maritje Jacobs, married Pieter Jansen Slot, Feburary 2, 1663.

Waling Jacobse, baptized October 10, 1650; married Catharina Michelse (Vreeland), March 15, 1671.

Grietje Jacobse, married Elias Michelse (Vreeland), August 30, 1665.

Jacob Jacobse, baptized October 10, 1650; married Adeltje Daniels, November 14, 1675; married (2nd) Grietje Hendrickse Hellingh, March 26, 1693.

SYMON JACOBSE, bap. July 24, 1653; married ANNATJE ARIANSE (SIP) Dec. 15, 1675.

Annatje Jacobse, bap. January 2, 1656; married Johannis Steymets, Nov. 30, 1676.

The name of Van Winkle had now become attached to the family (although some branches retained the name of Waling or Walling).

SYMON JACOBSE VAN WINKLE, son of Jacob Walingen and Trintje Jacobs, who was born 1653, and had wife Annatje Arianse Sip, had daughter MARGUERITE, born Nov. 4, 1676, who married (1st) Martin Winne, Oct. 30, 1697; (2nd) CORNELIUS BREYANT, Dec. 7, 1700. This Cornelius Breyant[3] was the son of

Pieter Cornelisse Breyant,[2] son of Cornelis.[1] He was the father of Simeon Bryant,[4] who was the father of David Bryant[5], born 1756 (No. 37). Although we have some knowledge of the Walings from the fourteenth century, we can give a connected line only from Jacob Walingen as follows: Jacob Walingen[1] and Trintje Jacobs, Symon Jacobse Van Winkle[2] and Annatje Arianse Sip, Marguerite Van Winkle[3] and Cornelius Breyant, Simeon Bryant[4] and Hannah Searing, David Bryant[5] and Catherine Woolley.

Bergen or Pavonia (now Jersey City and vicinity) as it was orig- inally called, where our ancestor Jacob Walingen lived, was the first permanent organized settlement in New Jersey. His sons Wal- ing and Symon settled upon the Acquackenonck grant (now Hackensack, Passaic, Paterson and vicinity). Jacob the second son remained at Bergen, where some of the descendants still reside.

We are indebted to Mr. Daniel Van Winkle of Jersey City, New Jersey, for this history of the Van Winkle family. Mr. Van Winkle was exceedingly generous in giving the correspondent information that he had spent many years in procuring and we extend to him our sincere gratitude.

The Bryant family probably were among those who sought refuge from religious persecution by emigrating to Holland and while sojourning there were united in marriage with the Wallinghs and Van Winkels, who became ancestors of the American family. We believe this infusion of Holland ancestry is shown in the char- acteristics of the descendants, for the American Bryant family has ever been ready to lead in the van of civilization; fearless in the face of danger, and exhibiting the sturdy qualities which led them to break the soil and till the broad acres which came into their possession. Holding the love of God pre-eminent, they estab- lished and maintained houses of worship wherever their lot was cast. The term Dutch, from the Anglo-Saxon "Theod," means people or "folks." They are described by John Fiske in his "The Dutch and Quaker Colonies in America," published in 1900, as "men of stalwart frame, indomitable in fight, at home upon the wave, venturesome, fond of good cheer, fierce sticklers for liberty, of strong individuality, and prone to do their own thinking."

Before the end of the eighth century the Hollanders were a Christian people. At the close of the Middle Ages the civilization of the Netherlands had assumed a more modern type than in any other part of Europe. The great Florentine historian, Guic-

ciardini, whose testimony is of the highest value, assures us that in
his day, or before 1540, even the peasants in Holland could com-
monly read and write their own language.   State archives of Holland show that free schools supported by public taxes were the subject of legislation at various times during the sixteenth century.
Erasmus, born in Rotterdam, 1467, through his translation of the
scriptures made The Netherlands a center of biblical scholarship.
During the sixteenth century the bible was nowhere else so generally
read by the common people.

STATE OF NEW JERSEY

OFFICE OF THE ADJUTANT GENERAL

Trenton, May 24, 1913.

It is Certified, That the records of this office show that JACOB
WOOLLEY served as a Private, in the Essex County, New Jersey,
Militia; enlisted March 1, 1777, for the war, as a Drummer in
Captain Silas Howell's Company, First Battalion, Second Estab-
lishment, New Jersey Continental Line; took part in an engagement
at Short Hills, New Jersey, June 26, 1777, in the battle of Brandy-
wine, Delaware, September 11, 1777, in the battle of White Horse
Tavern, Pennsylvania, September 27, 1777, and in the battle of
Germantown, Pennsylvania, October 4, 1777; reduced to Private,
November 1, 1777; transferred to Captain John Flahaven's Com-
pany, November 30, 1777; promoted Fifer March 1, 1778; Drummer, April 1, 1778; took part in the battle of Monmouth, New
Jersey, June 28, 1778; enlisted as Drummer, Captain Aaron Ogden's
Company, February 1, 1779; reduced to Private, September 30,
1779; served with the company and battalion in Brigadier General
William Maxwell's New Jersey Brigade, Major General John
Sullivan's Division, Continental Army, in the campaign against
the Six Nations in Western Pennsylvania and Western New York,
May 11 to November 5, 1779; took part in the battles of Newtown
and Chemung, New York, August 29, 1779; took part in the battle
of Connecticut Farms, New Jersey, June 7, 1780, and in the battle
of Springfield, New Jersey, June 23, 1780; transferred, as Private,
with Captain Aaron Ogden's Company, to First Regiment, New
Jersey Continental Line, January 1, 1781; transferred to Captain
Jonathan Forman's Company, same regiment, August 1, 1781;

served with the company and regiment in the Second Brigade (Colonel Elias Dayton commanding), Major General Benjamin Lincoln's Division, Continental Army, in the Virginia Campaign and siege of Yorktown, Virginia, April to October, 1781; took part in the battle of Yorktown, Virginia, October 6 to 19, 1781, and was present at the surrender of Lord Cornwallis, October 19, 1781; Private, Captain Alexander Mitchell's Company, New Jersey Regiment, March 1, 1783; served until the close of the Revolutionary War.

W. F. SADLER, JR.

[SEAL]   *The Adjutant General.*

WOOLLEY AND WOODRUFF ANCESTRY

CATHERINE WOOLLEY, the wife of DAVID BRYANT, number 37, page 31, was the daughter of

ABRAHAM WOOLLEY [5] of Springfield, N. J., and Catherine Woodruff, his wife, whose children, so far as known to us, were:

I. ABRAHAM WOOLLEY, born 1755, married Rhoda Mary Roll, parents of Maj. Abram Roll Woolley (Note 1) and grandparents of Mr. Charles Woodruff Woolley of Buffalo, New York, who has made extensive research on the Woolley family.

II. JACOB WOOLLEY, born 1757, married Hannah Thompson.

III. SARAH WOOLLEY, born 1759; died 1823; married Joseph Denman (who died 1819) as his fourth wife.

IV. CATHERINE WOOLLEY, born about 1761; married David Bryant.

ABRAHAM WOOLLEY, Sr.,[5] was the son of Jacob Woolley,[4] who served in the war of Revolution. (See record.) Grandson of Abraham,[3] great grandson of John,[2] and great great grandson of Robert Woolley[1] (Note 2), who married Anne Woodruff, a daughter of our emigrant ancestor John Woodruff [5] of Lynn, Massachusetts, and Southampton, Long Island. John Woodruff [6] "the elder," in September, 1665, recorded the sale of his house to Robert Woolley, husband of his sister Anne, page 30 (Note 3).

CATHERINE WOODRUFF, wife of Abraham Woolley, who was the mother of Catherine Woolley, wife of David Bryant, died at the home of her grandson Joseph Bryant at Owl Creek near Claysville, Washington County, Pennsylvania (probably buried at Claysville). She is said by descendants to have lived to be 106 years old. We have been unable to obtain the exact date of her birth or death. We leave it to be verified later. (See Foreword.) The David Bryant number 37 and Catherine Woolley Bryant descendants have the following Woodruff line of ancestry:

THOMAS WOODROVE,[1] whose name appears 1508 on the records of the town of Fordwich, Eng., was the "trusted envoy of the town" of Fordwich. In 1539 he was Jurat (Judge and Legislator or Magistrate and Municipal Councillor) and sat with his brother Magistrates in the Court at Fordwich to arrange for conveying to some favored friends of the king a portion of the possessions and estates captured in the wars. He died 1552. His son,

WILLIAM WOODROFFE,[2] is recorded as a Jurat of Fordwich in 1579 and was also a "Key Keeper of the Town Chest, a very honorable office conferred upon the two best men of the Liberty" (Borough). He died in 1587. The eldest son of William Woodroffe was

ROBERT WOODROFFE[3] of Fordwich who married in 1573 Alice Russell of Northgate. He is on record as a Jurat, and a Churchwarden in 1584; and died in 1611. His eldest son was

JOHN WOODROFFE,[4] born in 1574 at Fordwich, "On reaching Man's estate took up his residence at Northgate where his uncle William Russell was Churchwarden." In 1601 he married Elizabeth Cartwright. His will dated September, 1611, was proved in October, 1611, mentions his wife Elizabeth and his young and only son John. The will was witnessed by "John Gozmur," evidently a friend of the family and who, as the times were so stormy, very shortly became the legal protector of the widow and son, for on October 21, 1611, Elizabeth Woodruffe, and John Gosmore, both of the parish of St. Mary, Northgate, were married, page 9 (Note 3). In 1639

or 1640 they were among the settlers of Southampton, Long
Island, as was also the son,

JOHN WOODRUFF,[5] "The Emigrant," born in 1604 at Northgate, England, with his wife Anne whom he married in England,
and their baby John were living in the Gosmer household.
This John[6] (b. 1637), the first American ancestor of the New
Jersey Woodruffs, page 20 (Note 3), was the father of Anne
who married Robert Woolley as mentioned in Woolley record
page 235, Elizabeth, who married a Mr. Dayton, and what has
proved a most complicated genealogical problem, *two sons
named John*, both of whom lived to manhood and added to the
complication by giving to their children duplicate names.
John [5] "The Emigrant," being "weak in body," page 23 (see
Note 3), made his will May 4, 1670, which was proved on the
first day of the following month, in which he names his "wife
Anne Woodruff," "eldest son John of Elizabeth Town,"
daughters Anne, and Elizabeth, and "My youngest son John
Woodruff." The inventory of his estate shows that for the
times he was a man of wealth and refinement, and from the
requirements at that time of the important and difficult post
of Impounder to which he was elected, it may be inferred
that he was upright, of sound judgment, and, generally of a
character and standing that commanded the confidence and
respect of all in the community. The unusual proceeding of
giving a second son the name borne by an elder brother who
was still living seems to be accounted for by the fact that John
Gosmer having lost his only son Richard in 1649–50, page 31
(Note 3), legally adopted his stepson John Woodruff, born
1604, "who hath lived with me from a child," and the parents
in appreciation and love they bore for the adopted father,
John Gosmer, who was as well the stepfather, named the second
son John after John Gosmer. The Bryants derive their
descent from John "the elder," who was baptized in 1637, in
the Parish of Sturry, in Kent, England. He doubtless accompanied his parents from Fordwich to Southampton, Long Island, in 1639 or 1640. At twenty years of age he was on record
as one of the arms-bearing men. He is mentioned as a land-

owner in 1659–60; and about the same time he married Mary, a daughter of Mr. John Ogden of Southampton. In 1664 his father-in-law gave him the "house and home lot" on Main Street which Mr. Ogden had bought from his nephew (or cousin) John Ogden on the latter's departure from Southampton. Between August 29 and September 7, 1665, he recorded the sale of his house to Robert Woolley, the husband of his sister Anne, and his land to other fellow townsmen. He joined his father-in-law, Mr. Ogden, in the emigration to New Jersey. He owned a large tract of land in Essex County, New Jersey, near Elizabethtown, which is still known as Woodruff's Farms. He was a man of distinction in several important offices as Ensign, High Sheriff, Magistrate. He held the office of Chief Ranger by appointment of the General Assembly, December, 1683. He was styled "gent." At Elizabethtown, New Jersey, on April 27, 1691, when only fifty-four years old but "in hazard of life," he made his will and on May 25 it was proved. Following are the children of John Woodruff and Mary Ogden: John Woodruff, Jonathan Woodruff, Sarah Woodruff, born January 4, 1600, Hannah Woodruff, David Woodruff, JOSEPH WOODRUFF, Benjamin Woodruff, Elizabeth Woodruff, Daniel Woodruff. Mr. John M. Lindly of Winfield, Iowa, and Mr. Charles Woodruff Woolley of Buffalo, New York, both of whom have diligently searched the records, make the Catherine Woodruff Woolley line of descent through Joseph, son of John "the elder," and next Thomas, son of Joseph, and this Thomas as the father of Catherine Woodruff Woolley, who was the mother of Catherine Woolley who married David Bryant (No. 37). This Thomas, however, must not be mistaken for the Thomas who married first Mary Cory, and second Rebecca Merry, for he was the grandson of John "the younger."

Chamber's Encyclopedia states that a reeve in the Saxon period in England represents the lord of a district, at the folkmote (meeting or assembly) of the county; and within his district he levied his lord's dues, and performed some of his judicial functions. A "wood-reeve" was presumably reeve for his lord's woodlands. Woodruff has had various spellings: Woodreeve, Woodreefe, Woodrove, Woodroffe, Woodrow, Woodrufe, Woodruffe; Woodruff.

NOTE 1. Abram Roll Woolley, who was stationed at Fort Pitt, has the following record: "War Department, Washington, D. C. Abram R. Woolley of New Jersey was appointed Captain and Deputy Commissary of Ordinance, Dec. 24, 1812, and Major of Ordinance Department Feb. 9, 1815; transferred to the 7th U. S. Infantry June 1, 1821, and to the 6th U. S. Infantry March 11, 1823; that he was promoted to be Lieutenant Colonel December 16, 1825, and that he was dismissed the service May 1, 1829."

NOTE 2. Robert Woolley was the brother of Emanuel Woolley, whose descendants lived in East New Jersey. These brothers, Robert and Emanuel, probably came to Lynn, Massachusetts, in 1838 and to Connecticut in 1653; from there Robert went to South Hampton, Long Island, where he is mentioned on the list of 1657.

NOTE 3. Pages refer to a history of Woodruff family compiled by Francis E. Woodruff, entitled "A Branch of the Woodruff Stock."

INDEX